Praise for *Your Soul Is Required*

Most people know C. T. Vivian as a hero of the civil rights era, but he was so much more. *Your Soul Is Required*, a wonderful collection of his sermons, reveals him to be the man whom I was blessed to know in all his marvelous, uplifting complexity: joyful and loving, witty and down-to-earth, erudite and philosophical, intolerant of hypocrisy and disdainful of moral cowardice. Vivian's bold sermons provoke, question, contest. They are the sermonic orations of a deeply spiritual man who understood that, in the final analysis, true spirituality is not what we feel or profess, but what we do, how we live in community.

Are you willing to love, Vivian asks. Then you must be willing to stand up for love, he challenges. To fight for love, to call by name the enemies of love, to struggle for a world in which love and justice reign and evil holds no sway. Vivian was a man of consummate faith who dedicated his life to building a better world by treating the needs of the people as holy and inspiring others to do the same. The bold preachments in *Your Soul Is Required* give us a glimpse into the soul of this great man—great because he loved us so.

Obery M. Hendricks Jr., visiting scholar, departments of Religion and African American and African Diaspora Studies, Columbia University; professor emeritus, New York Theological Seminary; and author of *Christians Against Christianity: How Right-Wing Evangelicals Are Destroying Our Nation and Our Faith*

A generation of Black preachers led the United States to greater moral heights through their interpretations of Scripture by claiming simply—yet controversially—that God demands liberation over oppression. In *Your Soul Is Required*, we experience the transformative words of one of the greatest preachers among them—C. T. Vivian. Through his preaching, Vivian (and ministers like him) tended to the mind, body, and spirit of those subjugated by racism. Ultimately, this work defined Christianity anew and, in the process, saved both a nation and a faith tradition from the worst versions of themselves. *Your Soul Is Required* offers a salient reminder from the civil rights movement that hope in the face of adversity is one of humanity's greatest stories.

Marla F. Frederick, dean, Harvard Divinity School

Civil rights icon C. T. Vivian preached in the streets to racist law enforcement officers and in the pulpit to congregants whom he inspired to work for racial justice. *Your Soul Is Required* is a treasure trove of sermonic samplings from Vivian and includes reflections from an esteemed assortment of today's expositors and scholars of preaching. This collection is a must-read for racial justice preachers, activists, and academics.

Curtiss Paul DeYoung, racial justice academic, activist, and author of *Living Faith: How Faith Inspires Social Justice*

I have long admired the fierce, faith-inspired activism of C. T. Vivian. *Your Soul Is Required* is essential and urgent reading for anyone committed to advancing the long-overdue project of redeeming the soul of America, particularly in our current age, in which a resurgent Christian nationalism threatens our democracy and civil rights. In a similar spirit as Martin Luther King Jr.'s compilation of sermons in *Strength to Love*, this collection of Vivian's brilliant sermons brings theological and spiritual clarity to the ongoing struggle for human dignity and social justice.

Adam Russell Taylor, president of Sojourners and author of *A More Perfect Union: A New Vision for Building the Beloved Community*

YOUR SOUL IS REQUIRED

YOUR SOUL IS REQUIRED

The Theology & Sermons of C. T. VIVIAN

Jo Anna Walker
Mark E. Vivian
Al Vivian
Anita Charisse Thornton
Kira E. Vivian
Denise Vivian Morse
editors

FORTRESS PRESS
Minneapolis

YOUR SOUL IS REQUIRED
The Theology and Sermons of C. T. Vivian

30 29 28 27 26 25 1 2 3 4 5 6 7 8 9

Library of Congress Control Number: 2025938609 (print)

Cover image: Photo of C. T. Vivian by Jason Getz/The Atlanta Journal-Constitution
Cover design: Kris E. Miller

Print ISBN: 979-8-8898-3711-4
eBook ISBN: 979-8-8898-3712-1

Printed in China.

Dedicated to the end
of hypocrisy in the Christian religion

CONTENTS

ACKNOWLEDGMENTS

With one exception, the fifteen sermons in this book were transcribed from audiotapes and were preached by Rev. Dr. C. T. Vivian numerous times throughout the United States. We consider them to be his favorites. Many of the sermons are not dated because Dr. Vivian rarely put dates on anything, but we believe that most of them were written during the 1970s, 1980s and 1990s. His favorite, "America's Joseph," was originally preached in the late 1960s or early 1970s.

Special thanks go to Rev. John K. Stoner, who saved the audiotapes of Dr. Vivian's sermons and returned them to our family after Vivian's death in July 2020. Without those recordings, this book might not exist. The two men intended to publish these sermons long ago, but time and age got the better of them both. We are hopeful that Rev. Stoner will take special pleasure in receiving the first printed copy.

We are also indebted to the following professionals who aided our efforts to bring these sermons of Dr. Vivian to the public:

Transcriber Francesca Miroballi of Chicago, Illinois, spent many hours moving Dr. Vivian's words from decades-old audiotape to text. We trust that she was as blessed by her work as we hope our readers will be.

Kate Sloan Fiffer of Sun Prairie, Wisconsin, completed much of the preliminary editing that gave us the push we needed early in the project. We are extremely grateful for her answer to our request for help.

Our loving appreciation goes to Edward Austin Hall of Atlanta, Georgia, who brought Dr. Vivian's work full circle by completing the copy editing of the sermons and theological commentaries. Because of his expertise and dedication, we were able to move to the project's finality. Thank you, Ed.

Both Dr. Walter Fluker Sr. and Dr. Clinton Fluker of Emory University in Atlanta, Georgia, were instrumental in guiding us with suggestions, critical thinking, and contacts.

To Ambassador Andrew Young, who listened to our plans and then, with humor, noted that Dr. Vivian's words would become a "cheat sheet" for pastors across the county: We sure hope so!

And a loving thanks to Rev. Bernard Lafayette and the late Rev. James Lawson, whose encouragement and viewpoints paid off. May their legacy of love continue until it is finally achieved.

To Bill King of Nashville, Tennessee, thank you. Your support of the Vivian family has been immeasurable.

Finally, we are grateful to all the theologians across many denominations who analyzed Dr. Vivian's sermons and provided their perspective on his theology of justice and love.

In Faith,

Jo Anna Walker,
Mark E. Vivian,
Al Vivian,
Anita Charisse Thornton,
Kira E. Vivian,
and Denise Vivian Morse

PREFACE

Our father, C. T. Vivian, was a different kind of preacher. He wasn't necessarily focused on addressing every perceived human sin or explaining every scripture. Rather, he was focused on how the Scriptures lead people to love others, love God, ask forgiveness, and reconcile. To him, a person's primary sin was a lack of love. That was C. T.'s main concern. He believed that no human being can intentionally and systematically mistreat others and love God at the same time. He was concerned about opposing hatred. He was concerned about fostering love. And he was concerned about how love can conquer hate.

C. T. didn't always design his sermons around one particular scripture either. For instance, the sermons "God Is with You," "The Evil of Racism," "America: A Christian Nation," and even "America's Joseph," which is his most well-known sermon, are not centered on a specific text. In other sermons, such as "Creating the Promised Land" and "Using What You Have," C. T. used broad Bible stories to shine a light on the current state of the world and the human condition.

C. T. was also an extemporaneous speaker. In fact, he never preached from a fully written or typed manuscript. He would take a few pieces of 8 ½ × 11-inch white paper, fold them in half, and begin writing an outline. His sermon notes were always handwritten, and he never read a sermon directly from them. Because he didn't read his sermons word for word, he was able to keep constant eye contact with his listeners and only occasionally checked his notes to ensure he wasn't forgetting anything relevant. We struggled to date each of his sermons because C. T. rarely recorded dates on his work. Please grant us grace in that area.

It's important to know that C. T. struggled to remember the proper names of people, places, and events. As a result, he would often speak in generalities rather than specifics. His struggle was so frequent that it was often a point of family teasing. He would laugh about it, too. You will notice in some of his sermons that he discusses specific occurrences but doesn't give the exact name of the event. In the sermon "God Is with You" he said, "When you ask who produced what bill, who produced the changes in America, they tell me about some other people."[1] We suspect he had specific legislation in mind but couldn't remember its name. Later he says, "I'm thinking about one of 'em, and he stayed in Harlem, too. I'm thinking about another who went to Africa as soon as he could. He didn't stay here."[2] He probably had specific people in mind, but our guess is that he couldn't name them in the moment. However, C. T.'s greater point was that while many Black people in the struggle came and went, the ministers of the faith stayed for the long haul. These are examples of how C. T. used generalities to elevate his arguments without being able to recall specific details.

C. T. was a forward thinker. In "America: A Christian Nation," he addresses the question "Are we Christian enough to save democracy?"[3] The quest to answer that question remains front and center in our nation today. In addition, C. T. always spoke truth to power, no matter the consequences. Truth always mattered. This conviction is displayed clearly when he accuses America of murder in his sermon "America: A Christian Nation." Regarding the country's response to the 9/11 terrorist attacks, he says,

> Our response was to kill, and under this response, we not only went in to kill but we also went in to rob. And we have not yet, out of our Christian faith, counted the dead on both sides. We were concerned about every American that died; they didn't even have to be Christian. But we weren't concerned about those we murdered.[4]

He not only had no fear of any person but had no fear of words. This is clearly exhibited when he addresses the disciple Peter as "nigger" in his sermon "Peter: The Profound Nigger." Although many people, both Black and white, experience offense or are uncomfortable with the use of the term, C. T. ensured that the origin and reason for the negative term are dealt with.

As theologians, pastors, and students study Dad's sermons, we hope you will use his thoughts to help others also understand the value of his theology of love, justice, and reconciliation. Dad knew that God is a God of love and a God of justice. Because of that, he believed that there is no justice without love and that the converse is also true: There is no love without justice. These are the beliefs C. T. preached. And Dad had a clarity of thought about the matter. Love, justice, and reconciliation—all of these must work together. This is what the theology and sermons of C. T. Vivian are all about.

FOREWORD

From lying in the middle of the street in protest for not being allowed to go to church at the age of four; to his first demonstration, which successfully integrated Barton Cafeteria in Peoria, Illinois, in 1947; to his protesting against Sheriff Jim Clark in Selma, Alabama for the right to register to vote: The legacy of one of God's warriors among us has been entrusted in us to preserve.

Our paths crossed in my early days while working for the National Council of Churches during my youth work there. C. T. Vivian was professor at American Baptist Seminary in Nashville. I would come to know him later, during the height of the civil rights movement. He was a tall, nut-brown, angular man full of nervous energy and perpetually optimistic, well-suited for the task at hand. A soldier for the movement. The thing that struck me about C. T. was that he was raised in the North and grew up around white people, and he had no fear of them. Although he may have experienced racism, it was very different from what we experienced in the Deep South.

He was a veteran of the Nashville sit-ins movement, where he worked with Jim Lawson, Diane Nash, James Farmer, Bernard Lafayette, and John Lewis (who was fifteen years younger than he). They integrated the city of Nashville in 1960. When my wife and I saw this on television, we were living in New York City. It inspired us to move back to the South. After Nashville, he tackled public transportation (the freedom rides). His actions were rooted in personal faith and conviction. There was a testing that he experienced through the marches, the prison cells, and near-death experiences.

Influenced by Jim Lawson and Martin Luther King Jr., Vivian chose the path of nonviolence to facilitate his direct action of confrontation, speaking truth to power.

If Dr. King was the face of the movement, C. T. Vivian was the feet of the movement. So Dr. King asked him to come on board as national director of affiliates for the Southern Christian Leadership Conference. This is when he and I started to share the vision of SCLC's theme: To Redeem the Soul of America.

One leg of the freedom ride trip was to test the Interstate Commerce Commission Ruling of the land. C. T. and crew were arrested in Jackson, Mississippi, beaten, and taken to Parchman Farm (Mississippi State Penitentiary).

Here, he would spend two weeks in that prison, being beaten and almost murdered.

He continued his efforts by staging an integration of the Atlantic Ocean: a "wade-in" on the beach of St. Augustine, Florida, 1964. For a man who at that time didn't know how to swim, he surely had the courage to confront an angry mob of men who threw him down to the ocean floor. A police officer pulled him out of the water as he regained his bearings.

After this, he had another direct action/confrontation, again with Sheriff Jim Clark. In this instance, C. T. Vivian was trying to register the citizen of Selma, Alabama to vote. He and the sheriff exchanged a heated discussion, and Clark punched C. T. Vivian in the jaw, which sent him tumbling down the courthouse steps.

In the pages that follow, you will be pulled into his well-versed theology of biblical Scripture and the idea of social gospel playing out in our modern-day lives; along with ancient parables juxtaposed to the twentieth-century dilemma of race in America. C. T. Vivian was steeped with the clarity and courage to impart the messages we needed to hear. Inspired through his baptism and social gospel theology, along with his constant mantra of "trust and obey God," he is a twentieth-century man of mark as defined by William J. Simmons in his influential book, *Men of Mark*.

We are indebted to him and his wife, Octavia, because their fear of God has made our world a better place.

November 2023
Ambassador Andrew J. Young

INTRODUCTION

Eddie S. Glaude Jr.

I FIRST SAW C. T. Vivian on a television screen in grainy, black-and-white footage. I was watching the *Eyes on the Prize* documentary for the first time. Elegant. Brazen. Wildly courageous. Vivian stood on the steps of the Dallas County courthouse in Selma, Alabama, in 1965, confronting Sheriff Jim Clark and his deputies. I remember the rhythm of his speech as he warned the stone-faced deputies of the costs of their loyalty to Sheriff Clark. Prophetic and pastoral. He stood tall, pointed his finger at the officers and then at the hulk of a man who loomed in the shadows, glaring down at him with absolute disdain. On that day, Vivian lectured. He questioned. He preached. The confidence in his witness was mesmerizing. He understood the dramatic tension in the moment as the cameras captured it all and as Clark lost his temper. I jumped in my seat when I heard the punch. I saw Vivian fall and cover his head. "If you are going to arrest us, arrest us," he said. "You don't have to beat us."[1]

I will never forget the image of this courageous man, with blood dripping from his mouth, who got up and continued to challenge the white policemen whose faces contorted with hate as he demanded our right to vote. In the interview for the film, with his eyes as intense as they were in 1965, Vivian put it this way:

> With Jim Clark, it was a clear engagement between the forces of movement and the forces of the structure that would destroy movement. It was a clear engagement between those who wished the fullness of their personalities to be met and those who would destroy us physically and psychologically. You do not walk away from that. This is what movement meant. Movement meant that finally we were encountering, on a mass scale, the evil that had been destroying us on a mass scale. You do not walk away from that. You continue to answer it.[2]

As a young man, I heard these words and only thought about the mettle necessary to stand by them. How does one confront peacefully those hell-bent on destroying you? I focused on the ways in which he (and the ordinary people alongside him) dared to face the evil of Sheriff Clark and segregation, and how they served as examples for me and generations to come. The virtue of courage stood out, but I have come to understand that much more is at work here.

Vivian's emphasis on the fullness of personality and on the necessity to confront evil revealed a faith and political theology that shaped and guided his actions. His activism was grounded in an understanding of the Gospel and of the power of God in history, an old theology that guided the hearts of those enslaved Africans who accepted Christianity in the antebellum South and bequeath to generations a powerful faith to resist the evil of white supremacy. For them and for Vivian, God was sovereign and would remain so, no matter what white America thought or did. "I don't care if the clock has turned or not; God hasn't turned," he declared. "God is the general."[3] To remember that fact grounded one's actions in the world. In the end, his was a righteous radicalism rooted in his Christian faith—the deep well of his courage.

To truly understand the scope and breath of Vivian's contributions to the civil rights movement and to us, I believe, one must encounter the full weight of that faith in the form of his preaching. *Your Soul Is Required* makes available for the first time a collection of sermons and prayers that offer a glimpse into the power of faith that motivated Dr. Vivian's witness over the course of his life. What one immediately sees is that his faith is textured, theologically complex, and readily accessible by ordinary folk. Perhaps more importantly, one feels, after reading these sermons and prayers, fortified to muster the courage to continue the fight for the kingdom in a world that has lost its way.

All too often we tend to read the men and women around Martin Luther King Jr. as only faithful disciples of nonviolence and followers of a prophet called to lead America during its second reconstruction. But that tendency reflects a historiographical prejudice that focuses on the exceptional personality, the world-historical figure, or the great person who changes the course of history. King emerges in these accounts as a singular personality without whom the civil rights movement would have faltered. Of course, one cannot minimize the importance of his role and presence in the mid-twentieth century. Vivian is right to describe King as a prophet. And the men and women around him were indeed faithful disciples.

But we must also remember the power of ordinary people—in Montgomery, for example—who called King to serve as their spokesperson, or the extraordinary courage of students in Nashville, with Vivian among them, who dared to sit in and engaged in a direct assault on Jim Crow. Many of these individuals were more than "shock troops" answering the call of history. They were thinkers and people of faith who understood their actions within a broader framework worthy of serious exploration. We should not only tell their stories—biographies of individuals who participated in the movement abound. We should also, when possible, examine and explore their thoughts. Here can be found a trove of sophisticated ideas about democracy and faith. *Your Soul Is Required* works in this register as a compilation of practical wisdom, with commentaries by noted preachers and scholars, that not only calls the nation to account but passionately implores the Christian to live up to the demands of her faith.

The beauty and power of Vivian's preaching can be found in his ability to render complex ideas in ways that are digestible by ordinary folk. His sermons aren't peppered with references to Saint Augustine or Saint Thomas Aquinas or Reinhold Niebuhr or James Cone. Common sense wisdom seeps from these pages. His invocation of the sovereignty of God, for example, does not come with an explicit riff on the Reformed tradition by someone trained at American Baptist Seminary. He refuses to perform his theological bona fides. Instead, Vivian enacts what the prophet Habakkuk recommended. As Vivian puts it in his sermon "Law of the Spiritual Life,"

> He said that God told him to write it so that it's plain. Put it so that the people can't miss it. Don't put it in jargon that people can manipulate. So plain, one little sentence, [so] that they can't get around it. So that the oppressed will know that the just—those that stand before me and desire to be on my side—live by faith. That there's no other thing worth only living by but . . . faith.[4]

This plain, truthful speech *(parrhesia)* characterizes these sermons with simple (not simplistic) sentences conveying complex and powerful ideas.

Vivian could easily cite H. Richard Niebuhr's *Christ and Culture* in the sermon "What Does It Mean to Be a Christian?" when he asks, "Are we so much a part of this culture that we can't hear Jesus plainly? Are we so much a part of what has happened around us that we can't separate ourselves?"[5] He makes the point even more explicit in the sermon "God of History: Five Stones": "The difference between us was that we believed that the church was to serve Christ, not culture. Central issue always is—do you serve culture or [do you serve] Christ?"[6] Here, the point is not to billboard his erudition but to call Christians to live into the truth of their convictions and to understand that life as it is lived in this society, with its assault on human personality and its idolatry with regard to material possessions, can distort and disfigure what it means to live in Christ.

Vivian doesn't make this point to convince his listeners to give up on the world and to retreat into some isolated community of the faithful but rather to reorient them to their faith so that they might work to transform the world in the name of God. I was struck by this moment in his sermon "This God of History and Racism":

> So, we have to ask ourselves, what was the central issue of the civil rights movement? Was the central issue my right to vote? I fought for it, bled for it, all that kind of stuff. That wasn't the central issue. Was the central

> issue the fact that I can have a better a job? I do have a better job, more security, my children are better off than they would be, but is that the central issue? The central issue of the civil rights movement, if we look at the mind of God, was, Whose god is God?[7]

The politics matter, of course. But at the heart of his righteous radicalism rests the question of who actually sits on the throne. This is what Gary Percesepe perceptively describes as "the art of the prophetic interrogative in preaching,"[8] where Vivian uses "finely honed questions to interrogate a nation, an ideology, a system of domination, and ultimately a faith."[9] "They thought they were God," Vivian said, "and we thought we were unworthy. How sinful can you get?"[10] In another sermon, "America: A Christian Nation," he asks the question in a different way, and here we see the powerful arc of his preaching and what he is asking of us: "Are we worthy of our faith in a world that needs us?"[11]

That question hits hard in our current moment, when some who claim Christianity as their own passionately embrace Trumpism and declare themselves white Christian nationalists. Whose god is God? Vivian challenges directly the Christian to live her faith in an effort to make our world more just and loving. He understood the stakes.

> The confrontation between the church and the secular world comes only when we are serious. Because the secular world is as serious as murder. The secular world is as serious as repression and isolation. The secular world is as serious as death. But we can only meet it when we are as serious as life.[12]

He said this in 1973. And here we are, more than fifty years later, still fighting those who would have us believe that the color of your skin determines your value in this world and in the eyes of God. The seriousness of death still holds. One wonders what Vivian felt in his heart during his last days, as he saw the rise of white grievance and hatred in the form of Donald Trump, as he witnessed state legislatures pass a spate of voter suppression laws throughout the country, saw the horrific violence in Charlottesville, at the Tree of Life Synagogue, and in El Paso, and heard the clamor of those spouting the nonsense of the Great Replacement and bitter debates about American history. I wonder if his heart was broken, but then I read these sermons, and I know that, until the day he took his last breath, Vivian believed that God sat on the throne. He remained thankful for victory in the face of darkness.

The question for the Christian today, the prophetic interrogative, is, Will you walk with God? In 1994, Vivian declared that "a nation is being decided today. We're in the dark night of our soul."[13] We are still there. In our moment of storm and stress, we find ourselves living among men and women mad with the fever of a distorted view of liberty, willing to throw away this entire experiment in democracy as they cling to their fantasies. The old ghosts continue to haunt. As James Baldwin suggests, the horror is that America changes all the time without ever changing at all.[14] How will Christians respond?

It seems to me, if we are sincere (and the question of sincerity is always a vexing one in this country), that the time has come for us to examine ourselves for who we really are and in the full light of what we have done. We have to confront the madness that sits at the heart of American life and take the full measure of the seriousness of life. As Vivian preached in "America: A Christian Nation," "There comes a time when we have to face reality in order to remain sane. We have to face reality and the responsibilities that come with it."[15] That time is now.

The future of this nation is our responsibility. And if we are going to fight for it or, better still, fight for the love of God in the world, our souls are required.

I had a chance to have lunch with Vivian a few years before he died. Before the bombast of Trump. Before the devastation of Covid. It was a beautiful day. I can't remember if we were in Atlanta or Nashville. I just remember the sun competing with the smile and joy of C. T. Vivian. He laughed. He asked questions. He taught. His eyes danced with each word, like he knew the secret, and it was in the marrow of his bones. What I know for sure is, you don't walk away from that!

Part One

A Theology of Love

1

It Does Not Yet Appear

Romans 8:18–26

It's a little embarrassing, but it's great fun. I don't think this church can get much better, but I said that a year or two ago. It's getting better all the time, and the music is phenomenal, and the worship is phenomenal. All of our ministers, we are so fortunate. I come and I sit anywhere available. If I come in late, I sit closer to the back. But it doesn't matter where you sit when you're in the presence of the Lord. And if you can't reflect on your life here, I don't know where you're going to go. And it doesn't matter what Sunday you show up. It's great material, and it's always something different that fits your soul, and your background, and who you are. So, with this subject in mind and with the understanding that we come at a time when our pastor has set aside an entire year for us to deal with that central issue of identity and its meaning for us as we think about our story—who tells it, how it's told, what is its meaning. And as I come to this normally, thinking of the speeches I give, but never in the normal situation being able to talk about the background, the undergirding, the stuff that made it all possible. It's easy to lift those great personalities. And we so seldom talk about what was behind them and the people that made the difference, and the spirit that was behind that.

And it's with that that I wanted to start this morning with a short Scripture. It's in your book. You don't have to follow me unless you're already placed. I just want you to start at the 26th verse of Romans 8. When you go home, you can start at the 18th, but I just want to start with the 26th. Here it says, in certain ways, that "the spirit is here to help us." For example, when we don't know what to pray for, the spirit prays for us in ways that cannot be put into words. All of our thoughts are known to God, and He can understand what is in the mind of the spirit as the spirit prays for God's people. Listen to that, the mystery of it all. And we know that God is always at work for the good of everyone that loves Him. They are the ones that God has chosen for His purpose, and he has always known who His chosen ones would be.

In this month, Black History Month, we come to that great understanding, and what I want to share today is something that we seldom get to talk about, and that's God in history. That this almighty not only made life but continues to work in it. He is a god of history that never lets history alone, that wherever

His people are, He will be with them. He didn't just create the world and fly off somewhere. And He didn't create people and leave us here. And then I want you to see that God works with it. He has to work in the midst of this great conflict between good and evil. And that we are in the midst of this, working as we see it, and we have to see it now, and we have to see it very, very clearly. During this month in our history, it should be made clear that when you think of who we are and where we've been and where we've come from and how we made it over—that this God has been with us in the midst of good and evil, and the forces that would destroy us, and the forces that would enslave us, and though we were weak, we are still here.

We came here as twenty of us, and now there are twenty million of us. God has kept us quite well. God's been working in history for His people and for His purposes. And that sometime the thing that we miss is that God is not just with us, He is with us for a purpose higher than we can see and understand. That it's for His purpose that we are. How do we answer the question of why we're here, and we have to answer it with the understanding that God has us here for a special reason, and that God works with us in the midst of it all. God is not only God of the individual, but God is the God of peoples and races. God is the God of those who seek freedom, wherever they are, whether they're in a time in Egypt, in another land in the greatest country of that time, or whether they're in America, the greatest country of this time. God works with whole peoples. God doesn't only work with individuals. God, to change this world, doesn't have time to save us one at a time. He has to make a witness to all of us in great groups. And we are the witness to America and to the world that God can take you from slavery to freedom in a short time. We are that witness.

Our Scripture speaks of the people—of the people who pray, and the people who've grown to be, and of the people—how does it say it? It says it so well—whose sigh is "too deep for words." That's how I can understand Frederick Douglass and our history. That's how I can understand how we got out of slavery. You see, the Black mother couldn't write, and she couldn't read, and neither could her sons and her daughters and husband, but there were sighs so deep that God himself interpreted them. That, the Spirit was with us in the midst of it all. That's the thing that has to be seen—we don't get to talk about this very much. The spirit that interpreted our cries and our sighs: That's what made Frederick Douglass possible.

One Scripture passage says that the saints think for you and interpret for you, that the Holy Spirit thinks for you. Do you understand? How much do we see the spiritual power we brought here in the first place? You have to understand that to understand us—we did not come here without an understanding of what was sacred and godly. We did not come here with some understanding of what low life was, without an understanding of the greatness of God's spirit. We came here having created all the great religions of the world. We came here exuding a spirituality. We came here, from the beginning, with a God relationship. This is what's most important. We may not have known who Jesus was, but we'd known who God was.

And I tell you what, in Egypt, we'd already learned about a mother and a child. The very symbols that were to come later, we already had. Before Moses ever received the Ten Commandments, we had the negative code from which the Ten Commandments were made. And before there was a declaration about love being the ultimate, and that you should not in fact destroy your fellow man, we had kings that refused to fight and let their people go—not into battle, but go into prayer to bring a spirit about. We kept our souls in the midst of life, always. We didn't come here "without"; we came here with! We came here more spiritually aware than the people that were around us. If we had not have been, there would not have had slavery in the first place.

Now, I know what you're going to say. Didn't Africa have slavery? Yes, but you see, there was a higher calling. We had slavery, but it never meant that a man was never a man and a woman was never a woman. It was not slavery based on race; it was not lifetime slavery. You see, those slaves were still human beings and their owners married into the same families of the slaves that served them because they understood that God was in charge of the universe, and that no man could be strong enough, powerful enough, to make others servants with masters for life, with no way out. In fact, whites were never our masters. Why don't we tell the truth—they were our murderers!

You have to understand, before we can even begin to think, to look at the Scriptures straight on. You see, we were groaning, we were sighing, and we had these deep desires, and we knew what we wanted when we came out of slavery. That's what has to be understood, and that I believe that God will not let it rest until He's satisfied! The prayers, and sighs, and groaning, and the interpretations of the Spirit to the Almighty. We knew what we wanted when we came out of slavery. We wanted land first. We wanted money second. Now, you think that's shortsighted? No, you see, when you got land, you can get money. When you got money, you might never get land. [laughter] And then, the next thing they wanted was political power—they knew what it was. The fourth thing they wanted was education, and finally we wanted a little fun. And when you look at it, you see, I believe we will not stop until it is there, that God's in charge of the universe. And He heard my great-great grandfather, hm? God will not let it rest until He knows that His children are on par with all other men and women in the world. Believe that.

Now I want us this morning to think in terms of Black history, in terms not of great men but of great strategies. And that those great strategies did not necessarily come from those great men. But that underneath it all, something was happening that just lifted them into place. That they were used as vessels, but that they were not the ultimate piece of the action. Douglass was great. Douglass was a great speaker, a great orator, talked Lincoln into the Emancipation Proclamation, guided Black men into the final battle for freedom. He demanded the vote based on all that—great man! But what you see have to understand is that before he demanded the Emancipation Proclamation, Black men and women who had been praying got out and were escaping every day from that system because they believed that there was a better place. Had they just been standing around, Douglass would not have been believable. But because they'd been praying and escaping and knowing about the North Star, and going on and taking their chances with God, even though they knew they could be slaughtered because they believed there could be a better life somewhere. They kept moving, and it gave Douglass the chance to be believable. Think about it. Out of those prayers, and out of that understanding they were praying for—I remember, something just came to me—Douglass had a time when he got despondent, and he was down, and he was preaching at one of the great churches, and he wasn't for certain, and you know who bolstered him up? Sojourner Truth. Sojourner Truth asked him, "Is God dead, Frederick?"[1] That's what it's all about. When you get despondent, just know that God's not dead. The sister knew that God was not dead, and knew that God would take us on regardless, no matter how despondent it seems, no matter how backward it seems to go, that God's in the midst of it all.

That battle for righteousness, that battle to overcome the evil in this society, and we're pivotal to it because America can never be what it was meant to be. Democracy can never be real until Black people are free, and until Black people are free then there is no freedom in America. Until a tenth of your population is allowed to be full and free, you're just talking back about something that really doesn't make any difference. Black men will be free—so that America can be. But America can't be until Black men and women are free. Gods in the midst of it all, huh?

God is trying to use us to educate them. Isn't it interesting that this church that we stand in—Southern Baptist Convention—took 138 years before they came to understand that this was our church, not their church. [applause] Oh, I'm saying it like it is. But you see there's an economy in God's word. In the final analysis, God is using us to deliver them. And 138 years later they apologized to Black people. Southern Baptist Convention—do you know what it means? For a white Southerner reared to think he's superior, interprets God as white, believes that he was meant to control the world, to have to come to people and apologize because what he was saying (and we need to understand what he was saying)—is that when the Emancipation Proclamation was signed, how Lincoln saw it and how we saw it were two different things. One was coming from a legalistic understanding; the other was coming from a spiritual understanding—and that makes a difference. You can be reading the same piece of paper but what you're hearing it's different. And what Lincoln was saying is, Now the law says you're free.

My wife has an 1864 newspaper, and it tells us about who we are and what our story really is. When the Emancipation Proclamation was signed, that newspaper article says that at the great Abyssinia Baptist Church, that Friday night, people praised God. At Cooper Institute the next night, they praised God. And the great HHR Garnett[2] stood and said, "My friends, we must remember that it is God that has brought us to this great evening." And then he said, "First let us stand on our feet and stand in solemn reverence and thankfulness before Him." In Chicago, they started praising God before they got the reading of the document. They knew it was going to happen. In Washington, DC, and in Virginia—everybody wasn't free in Virginia under the Emancipation Proclamation, but as they called off the counties, someone would say "That's me." Someone would say, "Thank you, Lord," and someone would say, "You've done it for me, Lord." And you know what they sang in the great churches? It's the year of Jubilee. We understood it from a scriptural standpoint, so that when we heard the Emancipation Proclamation, we rejoiced for one thing, but "they" rejoiced for another. What we heard them saying was, "My daddy was wrong, my granddaddy was wrong, and your granddaddy was right, and we shouldn't have done it in the first place!" Oh, that's a different story! A different story! It was based on right and wrong; it was based upon what is evil and what is good. The war that goes on between us has never been simply a legal matter; it's been a war of moral and spiritual understanding, and to understand the spirit underneath and the *crying and the groaning* and God fulfilling the people who come to him.

You cannot understand who we are, how our story needs to be told, and what it means in the end, and all those that have suffered to bring it about. Douglass and all the rest were front men. I want to thank God for them. But if you see them as more than symbols for the rest of us, then you've missed the understanding of who we are. Love them, but understand the place at which he must be placed, alright?

Now, you have to see the history, because no sooner had we won that battle, then seven or eight years later, about ten years later, they started using every evil force to destroy us. The struggle between good and evil was ongoing. The Ku Klux Klan destroyed us with violence—burned down our houses, burned down our churches, burned down our schools. We had 146 Black colleges—well, at least we named them colleges, but at least when you started you may have started in grade school but when you ended you could end with college. They burned them down because we knew more than they did. My grandfather—they fired him from a job because he was teaching algebra, but the school board—white of course—didn't know algebra. So, they fired him, right? [pause] But it didn't stop him because he was one of God's people. We don't get stopped and we have to understand that. [applause]

So, when we get into it—the Reconstruction comes, but it doesn't last too long because of the lynchings. Several people every week were lynched in the United States, and nothing was done about it. And then, finally, President Hayes makes a compromise with the South in order to be elected. We must see the nature of the evil; the political evils, as well as the physical violence that is visited against us. So many forms of evil have been used to stop us, but everything that has been used to destroy us has become a means of developing us. That's what we've got to see. That's why there's twenty million of us now.

And the Republicans are doing the same thing right now, coming into the South with the idea of the Southern strategy. What they really mean is, they're going to bring racism back, and on the back of it, they're going to ride into power. That's what they've been doing. It's the same thing that Hayes did, they're doing now. Evil is evil, and it keeps on repeating itself, but God's good stands in the middle and will defeat it every time. That's got to be our faith this morning, as we come.

What I'm trying to say to you is—don't worry, God's working this out. There's no one man standing in the midst of any time and period of our history. Too many people are praying, too many people are sighing, too many people are hoping. There is too deep a religious—not just religious—spiritual thing going on in who we are and what we're about. And God's responding to that spiritual nature and that spiritual desire, and that spiritual desire is to be free. I think God needs us as a witness in the modern world. God is a god of history. I think He needs us as a witness in a world that thinks that it's God. And thinks that God is somewhere off in space and doesn't do anything. But I think that after the politicians have finished, and they can't bring freedom and get rid of racism, after money can't do it, God steps on the scene, and says, "With My spirit, not by thy power," says the Lord. That's what makes the difference now. God's always working, and we were involved in a little fight then.

Got in a little argument about—who's greatest, Booker T. [Washington] or W. E. B. [Du Bois]. Oh, you know the poems—we know the writings, and we love to stand around and talk the talk. You see, God had both of them because he had people north and people south delivering his people. He had leadership for who would be our leadership—the Talented Ten. But you see, God worked more with Booker T., with common folk who just needed a skill to be able to live—putting food in their mouth, rearing their children, being able to make it through a horrible time of Black history, from 1877 to 1910. Booker T. stepped in. Booker T. was put in place. God's people were trained to improve the skills they already had. Everything was built on what was already there.

And when, as the Ku Klux Klan continued to move in, we went north, but we didn't go north dumb, we didn't go north without. We went north with skills, and what you have to see is that God had prepared us—for what? To live with the new age. Because we moved in that very period. We moved from an agricultural age to an industrial age. Booker T. had prepared us for it. And if it hadn't been for that great change in American history, the rich bankers in New York would have never given him the money to train our people, and we would not have had that training.

God's working in the midst of it. And even those that don't know that they're being used are being used. And those that are using us for one purpose don't realize that God's using us for another purpose. You have to understand that God is there—God is there. Look for Him. He is your invisible means of support, but He's always there. Look for Him. Because when you pray, realize that your prayers are being answered. Pray, and realize that your granddaddy and your great granddaddy and those before him, that you're in line with a whole history that can't be understood without understanding God. We were arguing over who was the greatest—we were petty and didn't know it. But God was liberating us all, and He knew it. God's always working, and that's the important thing.

The great legal strategy then came into view. W. E. B. Du Bois was building, and it was interesting to me that, as he came into his greatest achievement—the founding of the NAACP—Booker T. was dying. Booker T. died [in] 1915, but those who study his papers question his Age of Compromise. He knew that an Age of Compromise would allow us to survive. Always understand! Compromise? But he wasn't compromising on the side of evil. He had to compromise with evil so we could survive. Understand that. It is easy to be self-righteous after it's over and talk about what should have been done. [applause]

You have to understand, he was doing the best he could under the circumstances in which he found himself—delivering a people. God's liberating us! The issue wasn't Booker T.; the issue was God's work in our life, and those who studied the paper said even he knew that the compromise was over, because the struggle has never been one that you could compromise with ultimately. It is a struggle between radical evil and radical good. And to the extent you can be radically good, to that extent, you can overcome radical evil. Otherwise, evil wins the day. You got to understand it; that's who we are. That's why we believe in the Scriptures as they're written. We might compromise with white people some, but we don't compromise with the Scriptures. And what he did—as one passed off, the other one came on.

The NAACP came on, the greatest achievement of W. E. B. Du Bois. Then, another great achievement—Howard University began to be the school that turned out the lawyers to do the work that changed the laws, and it took the next great leader to fulfill it. The NAACP was to desegregate things, and we did. The NAACP desegregated the schools—they did all of that. But you know, it's an interesting thing that God always wants to let us know, that change on a piece of paper doesn't set you free. Woo! Yes, you see, it's understandable that a Martin King had to come on the scene to fulfill what had already been done legally. When a man of God comes on the scene, it will be delivered.

Desegregation of schools was the law, but nothing changed. They still claimed state's rights; nothing changed. They still had the same evil ways; nothing changed. White senators still controlled the Senate, and you couldn't get anything through. I remember—oh, I'm just throwing it in—I remember, after we'd started the nonviolent movement, we brought Thurgood Marshall into Nashville to speak for us. We were in the back room, waiting around the table until everybody arrived, and we were just talking small talk. And suddenly Marshall pointed his finger at me across the table and said, "You are a dangerous man!" [laughter] I looked at the brother, and I honored the brother, but I didn't understand it. He said, "You are a dangerous man"—he didn't understand. He thought it was somehow in law, he thought it was somehow in the Supreme Court. He did not know that a supreme being was working, not the Supreme Court. [applause] He didn't understand that it's not by your power, *but by My Spirit*, said the Lord. He didn't understand, it's not what we shall be—but that's it. It could not be done in a corner. The freedom of man—wherever we are in the world—can't be achieved in a corner. It has to be done in some way that makes it clear that only God finally delivers, that the spirit of man delivers, that the masses of people working together changed the world in which we live.

I want you to see God as this kind of person who has been delivering us faster than we know. Let me give it to you this way. I've lived half as long as we've been out of slavery. Oh, sometimes we think it's been a long, long time, but it hasn't been that long. Nobody has ever been free in a shorter length of time than we have. And that everything moved on everything else. That is, that every one of these strategies followed each other almost immediately. Do you know what, Martin King had no desire to go to Montgomery to lead "movement"? Martin King went to Montgomery to finish his doctorate. It was just a nice pulpit to hang out at until he got his work done and then decide what he was going to do. But you see, God was there. Martin thought he was going down to preach. But when you start preaching for God, you better watch it, baby! God has an agenda, whether you've got one or not.

It is the mystery of it all that I want to share with you because you have to understand that, at that moment Lerone Bennett had authored *The Negro Mood*. Last time it was called *The Black Mood*. Next time it'll be called the *African American Mood*, but in *The Black Mood*. I had it in my pocket one time when I was going to jail somewhere—Jackson, Mississippi, I believe, I don't know where it was—because you see, you always put something to read in your pocket because there's nothing but comic books in those jails. [laughter] So, I put Lerone Bennett in my pocket to read, and I was reading him, and it said, at the time Martin King came on the scene, that the African American dilemma was this: That we would be so destroyed that, if we fought back physically, they would destroy us physically and if we did not fight back, we would be destroyed spiritually and morally. That's why Martin King comes on the scene—now God is ready to finish the work in the sense that it had never been finished before.

The great conflict between good and evil—we were ready for it because we'd learned to turn the other cheek, we'd learned to love those despite how they used us, we'd learned to have the courage to stand up. We'd learned that this life wasn't the only thing that's important, and that if this is all there is, it's not worth it anyway, so let's get it on! [applause] I love the mystery of it all, and I know that God works in history and that His hand is there, and we will never be without it. And that, one day, we will fulfill everything that our great-grandparents dreamed and prayed and sighed and hoped for that would happen.

When Martin goes to Montgomery, you know the street he lived on? At the end of it was a cemetery. I came to Atlanta one day, and I followed Martin Luther King Jr. Drive, and you know where it ends? It ends in a cemetery. God has a way of delivering people. At the day that we were at the March on Washington when Martin King ascended to his high point, we got the message that morning as we assembled around the Washington Monument, getting ready to go down to the Lincoln Memorial, we got the message that W. E. B. Du Bois had died. No sooner had one great past, than another came on. And the great intellectual genius of his time passed on, and the great spiritual genius of our time came on!

Egypt went down, all the great ones have gone down. America is not so great; she can also go down. You see, America is not too great to die. Because God doesn't care. God is about saving people; He's not about nations. He doesn't care what our names are and how many guns we've got. God is concerned that, spiritually, we will live like His children.

They laid Martin out finally after they shot him on that balcony in Memphis. They brought him down, and when they stretched him on a hospital table and ripped open his shirt, there was a cross on his chest. God continued to reach out to mankind after it was over. It is the mystery!

God's working with us, and it does not yet appear what we shall be. But one day our children and our grandchildren and our great grandchildren will live like everyone else in this world! [applause] It does not yet appear, but one day, those who hate us today will love us tomorrow! It does not yet appear, but for those that enslaved us today, we will take slavery away from them tomorrow. From our physical, their spiritual. We're here to free humankind.

It does not yet appear what we shall be, either in this world or in the world to come, but one day, oh yes! We will be bright, shining like the sun. One day! [applause]

Delivered: February 22, 1998
Providence Missionary Baptist Church
Atlanta, Georgia

COMMENTARY

Emilie M. Townes

Romans 8:18–25, the passage that Vivian encourages us to read for ourselves, introduces the last section of the eighth chapter that ends with the soaring words "For I am convinced that neither death, nor life, nor angels, nor ruler, nor things present, nor things to come, nor powers, nor height, nor depth, nor anything else in all creation will be able to separate us from the love of God in Christ Jesus our Lord" (NRSV 8:38–39). However, this is not Vivian's aim or message in this sermon, although he knew that those who are biblically literate would know the sweep of the whole chapter and would have a greater appreciation for both his focus on 8:26 and the message of his sermon in relation to it.

The Scripture passages before 8:26, describe the difficulties or sufferings that Christians will likely face from day to day. Further, the freedom that we experience in our new life in Christ require a transition period in verses 21–23 "that the creation itself will be set free from its enslavement to decay and will obtain the freedom of the glory of the children of God. We know that the whole creation has been groaning together as it suffers together the pains of labor, and not only the creation, but we ourselves, who have the first fruits of the Spirit, groan inwardly while we wait for adoption, the redemption of our bodies." Suffering and freedom become natural dance partners as we must endure and expect however God's grace is enduring and liberating and will sustain us despite the trials we face.

It is in this context that Vivian focuses on verse 26: "Likewise the Spirit helps us in our weakness, for we do not know how to pray as we ought, but that very Spirit intercedes with groanings too deep for words." Here, Paul describes the difference between our future (new life in God's realm) and our present (waiting, enduring, and living in hope in the midst of suffering) as Christians. We take heart and carry on because God's Spirit never leaves us or abandons us as we make our way with and through faith and deep belief, into the holy realm of God.

Vivian, the lover of history—personal and communal—is evident in this sermon. The hearer (and now reader) is struck by the depth of his knowledge of not only Black history but also the Black freedom struggle that is an integral part of that history. In this sermon, originally preached during Black History Month, he takes us from slavery to the present moment of 1998, when this sermon was preached. As we read his words today, we experience how Vivian underscores his aim to talk about God's abiding presence in history and in the lives of Black people. For Vivian, you must know your history to know who you are and what mission God may be setting before you, as well as the resources at your disposal to meet the challenges that are sure to be found in answering God's call into a deep partnership grounded in justice and freedom. Further, one must also understand and be able to address the challenges themselves—not as inchoate structures or attitudes—but as concrete realities that effect peoples' lives, be it guiding the choices they make or helping to develop constructive strategies to combat the sinful acts that we do both consciously and unconsciously that can echo from our past into our current times and into our future hopes and dreams.

As the sermon unfolds, Vivian reminds us of the power of God's presence and how this is both balm and resource for Black folks as we come to know what is at stake in the conflict between good and evil that we face. Despite all that has been destructive and life-denying in this struggle, we have survived because "God has us here for a special reason and that God works with us in the midst of it all."[3] He goes on to stress that the relationship God forges with us is not only on the individual level but also that "God is the god of peoples and races."[4] This is a God of freedom, who is here for us in the midst of our groans—from Egyptian captivity to enslavement in the West to the present moment—not as individuals but as whole peoples. Vivian says that "God works with whole peoples. God doesn't only work with individuals."[5] He then makes the pithy observation that "God, to change this world, doesn't have time to save us one at a time. He has to make a witness to all of us in great groups."[6] And further: "And we are the witness to America and to the world that God can take you from slavery to freedom in a short time. We are that witness."[7]

Leaning into the prophetic and freeing power of lament, Vivian brings us back to the Scripture passage and reminds us that the "Spirit intercedes with groanings too deep for words." He shares this powerful reminder before he challenges his listeners (and readers) with the assertion that Black folk were brought to this country with a fully formed spirituality or, as he puts it, with "spiritual power"[8] that we must remember and draw on as a resource that sustains over centuries. Indeed, for Vivian, Black folks were brought here with a rich spiritual life in which we had a relationship with God and then learned about Jesus.

Using a recounting of Black history through the lens of "great strategies" rather than "great men," Vivian compellingly emphasizes the communal nature of God's presence and salvation in the battle for righteousness in the face of evil from the first arrival of enslaved Blacks to the present. He emphasizes again and again that we must recognize and feel the importance of the way that God delivers us and uses us as agents of deliverance—for the Southern Baptist Church in the particular setting for this sermon, although one can also draw a much broader implication for society at large. We cannot do this without knowing the history that helps shape their identity, which informs us of how we must respond faithfully in a new age.

In somewhat of an excursus, he underscores his message that we should not focus on individuals but whole peoples. He uses the debate of whether Booker T. Washington's accommodationist position or W. E. B. Du Bois's protest tradition were the greatest in the late 1800s and early 1900s to remind us that both approaches were needed when combating systemic, structural, centuries-long radical evil. He continues to draw the historic line of the power of God's presence in the journey of Black folks to Martin Luther King, Jr. who did not go to Montgomery, Alabama, to lead a movement but found himself called to lead one, or—as Vivian so vividly puts it—"Martin thought he was going down to preach, but when you start preaching for God, you better watch it, baby! God has an agenda, whether you've got one or not."[9]

In Vivian's eyes, those who oppress—Egypt of old and America of the contemporary era—cannot sustain their systemic evil. Driving the point home, Vivian tells us "America is not so great. . . . Is it that America is not too great to die? Because God doesn't care. God is about saving people; he's not about nations. He doesn't care what our names are and how many guns we've got. God is concerned that, spiritually, we will live like his children."[10]

God's deep, wordless groaning is God's way of breaking into time and space, and to walk with us when we do not know what to pray for, or perhaps, when we know that we need to pray for salvation, but all we can do to name our pain is groan. Vivian assures us, like the apostle Paul encouraged believers in the early church, that we must hold on to hope and the assurance that the Spirit, the living God, will deliver us as we become agents of God's radical goodness moving in creation, sustaining over time, and settling into our lives.

2

God Is with You

I HAVE TO start with something that's a little different. The subject was "God is with us." But I was up in Michigan State University, and they didn't get my luggage back to me, and the sermon was in there. But as they say, the Lord works in mysterious ways!

So, I think He was having something to say about it. But I knew He was when my wife told me—when I got home she told me a story. My youngest grandson—that's the way we say it when we get older—my youngest grandson, we like to talk about how many we got. My grandson says, "I like granddaddy because granddaddy talks to me about trains and Martin Luther King." And I knew then what I was gonna preach about, and to say God is with us as well. Now, this is really for him. I'm gonna give him a copy of the tape, from granddaddy to grandson.

Now, we are in February, nearly the end of Black History Month. We have just finished January, which is what I call Martin Luther King Jr. Month. It's putting these two together that causes us to be able to celebrate these two months. Martin was martyred on the fourth of April. We're gonna figure out how to make March—we're gonna have a whole quarter of Black History Month. Right? Just give us a little time.

And this is much of what I want to talk about—I haven't picked a given Scripture for today [as] I don't think it's necessary. We're talking about what it means to have God in your midst, what it means to know, to be able to witness God in our midst. Not just as individuals but as a people. Too much of our religion has been so personal that we forget that God put us together in community. God works with us in community, and that we may have these individual churches, but God sees us as a total people working, all right? He is about saving us all, and He is about sending from the parish leadership for all of us if we are God's people. That is the meaning of it to me, and as I come in to see the leadership of the new age in January. I see this great force of people that [backs] that leadership, that made it possible that we would change this great nation. But God uses His people far beyond anything that is personal, far beyond anything that is their group, but God is about saving this entire world.

And so, what has happened to us in America gives us an understanding, and a meaning, and an ultimate reason for everything that has happened to us here. Because God was in our midst in all of it. God was in our midst in the suffering that our sister talked about. God was in our midst as we were trying to find ways out of all of that, so that we could go toward a freedom. We were thinking about a personal freedom, but I have to think that God was thinking about a freedom for all of us. And when I say all of us, I mean every living person within this nation. We may be concerned about Black/white, but God is concerned about all of us regardless.

And so, as we see, as we see ourselves, we have to see ourselves in relationship, too, and understand that all that we do saves other people, as well as ourselves, all right? And we see this great leader inspired by God in January, and we are very clear now that this nation was in the process of being saved when it happened. We should have been understanding, but could not in the earlier days, that we were a part of saving this nation.

Now, this is not in my notes, but let me go here—any people who had to have slaves were not worthy of God. And any people that had to dehumanize a whole race of people brought [into] their midst in order to be able to say that they were somebody were not worthy of being somebody in God's eyes. And that we find ourselves being told that we were less than, but [in] every decade, it was being proved that we were more than, that we were here for greater purposes than what was immediately observed, and that we saw ourselves as not having things, but at the same time as our brother told us last week, everybody [who] talks about heaven ain't going there.

And so, when we really look at this stage upon which we're placed, and this breadth of history which we have created, it becomes clear that, together with God, we became a prophetic people with the prophetic movement that was, in fact, looking so far ahead that it would make a difference in the history of mankind. That is what has to be seen. A movement that helped us free ourselves and all others who had the eyes to see and the ears to hear but, more important, had the desire to be and become and satisfy God, and together we made demands on the most powerful nation in the world without a gun, without hate, and won when they didn't want us to win. We made them say yes when they wanted to say no. It is amazing: We changed America. Almost everything about America has been changed by us. In every century, we drug them into the new century by their thumbs, hollering and shouting and crying, and then like little children getting up and saying, *That's pretty good after all.* We did that. And we did it in spite of all the forces against us, but we did it. We changed everything. Almost everything about America has been changed. America was reformed in our own time. We saw it.

We're witnesses. That's what God talks about. When God's in your midst, you've got to have something to [bear] witness to. This is what I mean by my little grandson. I want him to understand that we are telling him what really happened. We know that it happened because we lived it. And that he's got a God that will deliver you. He has to know that! This generation has to know that. And they talk about—we know that we did not do it without God. And the higher you were up in the whole thing, you know you didn't. And in fact, a Martin King was the product of our seminaries, our churches, our thinking. He was called by God . . . not just happened to be on the corner standing around. You understand what I'm talking about, right?

Almost everything about us has been changed. Our thoughts were polished, our central years given meaning, and for the first time, we were able to have a life worthy of our humanity and the faith of God that was within us. A good deal of what we are—Black or white—was directed by that movement. It moved for us, and it moved with us, and it made possible for openings to come that we couldn't even dream of. And while Martin and the church people of Montgomery moved out of their churches to face the world with the faith that God and the church had given them, we were at the bottom of American thought and concern. It was at the bottom that we became a world people. We became the strugglers for justice that everybody in the world looks up to. At a luncheon meeting yesterday, a Nobel Prize winner from Ireland wanted to sit and meet with us. Why? Because he said if it hadn't been for the civil rights movement, we wouldn't be free in Ireland. That's what I'm talking about.

And we become real believers in the ultimate worth of humankind. We found that love will deliver us from evil. We found that our radical love can overcome radical evil. We had a chance to believe because it happened. We lived it. It wasn't just something we read. Whatever we are is the result of our action, reaction to that movement led by a Christian minister and Christian people that came up, out of a Christian church, hit the streets, took a chance on life and death for the life of all of us.

We made this nation, America, as Moses did for Egypt, cry out for new human priorities. Before us, they thought they were good. Before us, they went to church every Sunday morning, thinking, *Well, God has so blessed us, and we are so good, and we've lived up to it.* I think of the Southern Baptist Convention—leaving [behind people] that they were mistreating; leaving maids and so forth behind, [so] that they were not paid; going to church and lifting their eyes to God, thinking that they were good, but when we moved out, no man in America could talk about being good if he was [in] any way a part of this situation. And I tell you what, it wasn't only down south; it was up south [where] they had to do a lot of thinking. What happened—they were faced with godly methods of nonviolence and superior spiritual leadership, both in terms of the names we know and in terms of the names we will all never know. That's spiritual leadership, and it made America admit that it was a sick society. It was sick racially, it was sick with greed, it was sick with hate, it was sick with violence. Made [the nation] admit it—they wouldn't say it before, but we made them admit it. With violence to both body and spirit, and the masses of America had to come forward and see themselves, but they got to see themselves because of us—we became the mirror for America. We countered their hate and their violence and their greed with our faith. And that's all we had. But we didn't need nothin' else! That's what has to be learned, that a people who love God don't need anything but the love of God.

Now, it's not that you don't need anything, so you just sit on your knees and wait—that's not what I mean, you see. That passage, by the way, is all wrong. Waiting on the Lord didn't mean waiting on the Lord. It meant that you act as God has told you, and you wait for God to deliver you, that's what it meant. That you just keep fighting, you just keep working, you just keep going, you just keep believing, and God will deliver you, and this is the way God works, because in the final analysis, He must have the glory. And if we're willing to obey God, God will ultimately have the glory, we'll have good, and we will know that He's our God—that's what this has been all about. And we were religious before we came here—we were spiritual people before we came here, but every step of the way, you have to know that God is your God because of what He does for you, and what you do for Him.

What did we do for this nation? We created an organized consensus that allowed good men and women, for the first time, regardless of their color, to speak out on war, on racism, on poverty, and on peace. If you had done that before the movement, you were called a communist, and that was a word meant to put you down. It was said that if you talked about those kinds of things—peace—well, the Russians talked about those kinds of things, so you must be a communist. And if you see anything against American wars, then you must be unpatriotic. And that you can't talk about race—remember? We didn't talk much about race if there were any white people around. It was the thing that was killing us! We didn't talk about it, and anybody who talked about it was radical.

And the higher up we were in the order, the less we talked outside. And even among ourselves, we said it in ways that didn't express what we felt emotionally. But what happened when we began to obey God, a new consciousness came, and we made these concepts the core of democratic thought in America. And when you look at war, Martin King's speech was the greatest thing that the whole peace movement had. When you talk about racism, it was [our] coming together that changed all that. When you talk about poverty, we knew what it was. The poverty program was created by us as a result of our movement. It helped all poor people, and there were plenty of 'em in America besides Black people. And together, we became the conscience of America. *We* who? The Christian church. There are those that say, *It wasn't just you Christians.* But you see, the point being [that] they came in on the edges, they weren't at the center. The center thinking came out of our churches. The masses of people that stayed with it came out of our churches. It was led by ministers, all the way up and down the line, in the heart of it.

When you ask who produced what bill, who produced the changes in America, they tell me about some other people.[1] And yeah, I'm thinking about some other people. And yeah, I'm thinking about one of 'em, and he stayed in Harlem, too. I'm thinking about another who went to Africa as soon as he could. He didn't stay here.[2] You understand what I'm talking about? But who stayed here, right up until their death? And who is still fighting the battle until their death? It was they who knew that God was involved. It was they who knew that who delivered them was out of their spiritual understanding of life. And together, as the conscience of America, we created the strategy. We acted out a strategy to free a nation, and that strategy was based on the Sermon on the Mount. Read it! The whole strategy that made us free was based on the Sermon on the Mount.

When we began to believe it enough to carry it out, it all came together. All you have to do is trust and obey, trust and obey. There's no other way. But when you trust and obey, things happen that you [don't] understand. The problem is the problem of faith—is that, because we use God's strategy, we acted out a strategy that changed this nation. We created the Civil Rights Bill, and the Voting Rights Bill, and the Fair Housing Bill, and the Equal Pay Bill, and Title VII, and we can keep on going. Now, I know those that say, *You people are talking about nonviolence, but what they really were scared of was that violent fringe, and if they didn't listen to you, they were going to have to deal with us, right*? Well, let me tell you what there [were] "bad negroes" long before there was a civil rights movement. And there were white people, like the Weathermen, who they killed outright and sent out of the country.[3] So, you know if they kill white boys that, in fact, were the sons and daughters of some of the richest in the nation, they killed any Black boy that thought that he was big enough. So, don't get the idea that there was some violent fringe that they were afraid of. In fact, the truth is, they wanted to kill all of us. The method we used so reached the conscience of the nation that they couldn't get by with [killing]. That's what it was about. And that every time they killed anybody in the South, it only helped our cause all over the nation. That's what nonviolence does for you. When you obey, you become a martyr. But nobody cares what happens in a dogfight. You just let 'em fight and see who's gonna win. But you see, if you know that you're obeying God in the midst of what you're doing, it makes a difference for everybody that comes on.

Let me put it succinctly. Nobody has been so influential for so many people on so many critical issues as Martin Luther King Jr. Called by God, trained in Christian seminaries, pastored in his churches, [he] preached everywhere that they asked him, spoke with Jesus's principles even in the speeches across the world. And he did it all to free people. And where did he learn it? He learned it in the Christian church. That's where you learn to free everybody.

Our movement, church as its base, freed so many people, freed white people from false assumptions and taking racist hate for granted as a way of life. Before this movement, racist hate was taken for granted as a way of life. Is there any other way of life? That's the way it was! And you knew you were at the bottom, and you knew you were gonna be mistreated, and you took being mistreated as common for life. Not today! Not today. It's because we trusted and obeyed, and because there is a God in this world, and because we let those who thought that they believe in God understand that they didn't believe in God. If you're not willing to speak up, then you'll be put down. But when you get willing to speak up, when God is obeyed, when God is acted upon, radical changes are made in every part of life.

We're witnesses. That's not just talk. When we acted out, when we went into the streets and we took a chance on being shot down for what was right, law changed. Religion changed. Oh, you can go through a whole list of legal change, whole list of denominations that changed their policies. Just name it, it changed. Politics changed. We got a Southern president. Weren't any Southern presidents before that?

Now, I want to rethink that part. I just have to trust in God on that part because these boys that become presidents from Texas worry me, except for [Lyndon B.] Johnson. It balances [things] off. But you know what Johnson said? Johnson did what was right, but he said that *I just delivered the South to the Republican Party*. He knew it! But he said, race has to be changed in the nation. And he did it. [Jimmy] Carter—a Christian, the only one that had taught Christian school for forty years. And yet they wanted to put him down as less than, and he was the only Christian there, but he delivered. And every movement followed our movement because when we [obeyed] God, we found ways to solve social problems without violence. And as a result, the youth movement; as a result, the women's movement; as a result, the labor [movement] came back together; as a result, the old people came back in; as a result, those who, one way or the other, who had physical problems, were treated differently in this country.

When you obey God, it may take a little time. See, we think it just has to happen all of a sudden. But you see, I had my first nonviolent direct-action movement in Peoria, Illinois, nine years before my government. But Martin knew how to move it. He moved it from fifteen years up the hill. And finally, we got the good out of it. If you're not willing to obey, don't expect goodness just to drop on you! If you're not willing to love God, don't expect it just to fall on you. Don't love people, don't expect to be loved!

Every movement followed our movement, and it should have. We turned the world upside down to turn it right side up so that God could have the glory. I know where that line came from—came from the early Christian church. They turned the world upside down to turn it right side up. We can say it now, which proves that what God was then, God is now! That's what's important. And the glory goes to God for it all. We even freed our enemies, and nobody but Christians ever even wrote it down.

Think about that. When Christ said that we are to love our enemies, I mean, all religions backed up. They said, either he's crazy or he's God, and he proved it, right? Because that's the only people that talked that way. But we even loved our enemies. The proof of it is the new South. Before the civil rights movement, this was the stupid, stumbling South. Now it's called the sunshine states. You understand what I'm talking about? [Before] the civil rights movement, there wasn't anyone well educated in the South. I don't mean any one group. There were a few individuals here and there. Remember, Martin Luther King Jr. was probably the only minister in a pulpit that had a PhD. In a pulpit. There were some in seminaries but in a pulpit. In the South. But in the East and the West and the North, they took that all for granted. They didn't even let you in, they didn't let you teach unless you had a doctorate. But you couldn't [do] it here. Why? Because this was the poorest area, and we had three—sometimes three—school systems.

Now, if you don't have any money, how are you gonna educate well? And you've got to split it up between two and three school systems. Sister looks up at me and wonders. The point is, in North Carolina they had three. But nobody got a good education. In fact, the public universities of this nation were not good. The five in the South that were of value were all private schools. Emory was one of them. It's not a state school. But you see, now, because we changed that old system, the schools of the South get better and better and better. You gotta realize what we have done. But we didn't do it just . . . it's because God was involved. It's because we obeyed.

We did it because we were willing to sacrifice, we did it because we had the faith—that if you believe God would deliver you, that's what made it all possible. But not only there—money, more money in the South than there ever was before. Why? Because who was gonna bring billion-dollar companies into an area, in an era, where in fact if people got in a racial struggle, they would destroy the equipment? Who's gonna bring a million dollars into a nation where you can't use the best human resources within it? But when we change things, now you see the big companies coming. They came to Atlanta first—they didn't come to

Birmingham—they came to Atlanta, that was [the] testing ground, and they sent people out to see if the South was really gonna change or not. And then they started to move into the other cities of the South. You understand what I'm saying? [We] did that—the process wouldn't have been there had it not been for us.

What I'm saying is, the movement that we created prepared this nation for the twenty-first century. With the world three-quarters dark to Black, who's gonna believe in America? In fact, we not only prepared it for the nation, our leadership was also going to extend to the world. Remember, we started at the bottom. God does that. But when you end up, the whole world sees. Isn't it interesting that the secretary of state—how we're viewed in the world became General [Colin] Powell—Black man, followed by Condoleezza Rice—father was a minister?[4] And Carter, a Christian, chose Andy Young before that—who was also a minister. You understand what I'm saying? [When] you look at it, we're on our way to world leadership, and after pulling this nation into each century, and when I heard the fellow yesterday who was a Nobel Prize winner talk about what we've done in Ireland,[5] and when I go to South Africa and I hear them say that had we not created a situation here to boycott South Africa, they wouldn't be free there.[6] And wherever I go, I understand that what Black people do will change the world that we live in. That the need for the world today is spiritual leadership. Politicians aren't good enough. They don't have the answers. Who has to put the world on [a] real and even keel? It has to be spiritual leadership—don't think all of it is gonna be Christian right quick. God is a god of us all. And God will use all of us toward His end. And in the end, we'll find out who came out. But it won't matter, because we'll be with Him.

What you have to see is, this movement under Martin King had a deeper understanding of ideas and issues and concerns, and it had a greater goal that could see the problem. See, Martin wrote on the window of SCLC, not civil rights. He went deeper than that; he understood that; he wrote on the window—and I've said this before, I just want to repeat it, every year we need to repeat it—he said to redeem the soul of America. Martin understood that America's sins were too deep to simply pass a law. Laws don't change anything until you change more than the law. The law is based on custom and tradition and mores. Until you can change those, you cannot change the law. You may change the words, but you will not change the laws in their hearts. Martin understood you had to redeem the soul of America. You see, you have to understand that Martin had a deeper understanding growing out of his Christian faith. In fact, the world was talking about peace —as what? As if nobody shooting nobody must be peace. If nobody is beating me today, it's a peaceful world. It's nonsense. That's a definition of peace we desired, because that's all we could get to. I don't mean we, Black—I mean we, people in the world.

So, we defined it, but Martin comes along as a representative of God and says, no. Peace is not the absence of things, peace is the presence of things. And if you don't have truth, if you don't have love, if you don't have justice, you don't have peace. You see, Martin loved us, and he didn't have to love nobody. There's a difference between loving people when you have to and when you love people when you don't have to. That's what God's all about. God doesn't have to love us. This is why we should be so thankful that he even cares to look this way! And Martin was well-off. Family had been professional for two generations. There weren't many of us could say that, right? His father was on a bank board. Now my point being, see, there is a tendency in yesterday. Now I want to watch it because I'm on a bank board now. But what I mean by that is, yesterday when you were on a bank board, Black or white, the bank went out of its way to do things for you so you could own things that other people couldn't because the money could come quicker to you than it could come to others. You understand what I'm saying? But you see, the federal government stepped in, and we can't do that today. And that's the way it should be. If you don't come up with the stuff, you shouldn't get the money. That's the way it is. I got off, so I just had to say it.

But you see, Martin loved us. He didn't have to love us; he didn't have to love white people. That he didn't have to love white people is obvious. But he didn't have to love us. Because we didn't even love ourselves. When this movement started, we didn't even love ourselves. In fact, the good deal of all the hollering and stomping at church had to do with getting all the negative emotions out of us. You hear what I'm saying? And this is one thing the church was doing for us—allowing us to have it happen, so that we could find some solace until we found a solution. The church has always been there for us. Martin loved us enough to die for us. And that's the thing that stands out for me that came to me a little late. Martin taught us how to live, and he taught us how to die, and all he was doing was imitating Jesus.

But he taught us that it didn't stop in the Holy Lands; it's wherever people who love God stand, all right? If you obey Him, if you live like He said live, you'll die like He said live, and others will remember you because you died like Jesus. You'll carry the marks on your body. Martin King was the greatest social strategist of our time. He delivered us. But he delivered a people in the process. Just one thing—I know, time. I work in time, but I live beyond time. [Martin] was deeper. Martin was giving a talk one afternoon, and he said—because he didn't know any other way to say it—he said, "If you will allow me to preach for just a moment," and the crowd allowed him because they [knew] that something good was coming. And the crowd praised and said, "Right on, Rev" and "Amen," and Martin says that a man came to Jesus by night and asked him the question, *What must I do to be saved*? That great and most profound question, either for man or for nation. And Martin was talking about the nation at the time that he broke in with this, and he said, this man came and asked the question, and Jesus looked at him, and Jesus could have said, "If you're lying, you may just stop your lying." Could have said to him, "If you're threatening people's lives, you need to stop your wanting to kill." He could have said, "If you're drinking excessively"—and I remember that because I wondered why he added it, but he did—"then you better stop drinking." Now, he could have, but you see, he was Jesus's man. And he wasn't talking about stopping the negative; he was talking about doing the good. What my brother was talking about last week was the negative code of Egypt.[7] What Moses did was pick out the ten best ones. It was still the negative code.

The point being that Jesus went beyond it. Jesus said it's not just the negative code; it's not that you have to stop this and stop that. Jesus understood that a man who will lie will steal. And a man who will steal will kill in order to keep the oil he just stole. Martin understood, so Martin said, "Jesus said to him, you must be born again!" That's [what] we as a Christian nation, as a Christian people, are saying to this nation that has never been Christian. Is that you must be born again, America. You will not accept Black people until you are born again. You will not accept poor people until you are born again. You will not stop your killing until you are born again. You will not stop until you're born again. And you will not satisfy God, no matter how many crosses you put on the wall. Until you're born again!

Delivered: February 20, 2005
Providence Missionary Baptist Church
Atlanta, Georgia

COMMENTARY

Gerald L. Durley

C. T. Vivian once again draws upon his wise and insightful gifts to exhort the reader to the understanding and appreciation for the truth that God is always with us. We live in a world with many complexities that systematically separate who we are from whose we are. Life moves so swiftly that we seldom take the time to realize that God is still in control, which can result in our falling into the trap of depending on our finite human capabilities.

In his revealing sermon "God Is with You," Vivian succinctly shares what he learned and applied as a top lieutenant to Martin L. King Jr. during the civil and human rights movement of the sixties. This sermon talks about "what it means to have God in your midst, what it means to know, to be able to witness God in our midst."[8] Vivian asserts that God is about redeeming all of humanity, but there are two primary actions that must be adhered to if humanity is to be saved. Vivian, a very devout and spiritual Christian prophet, deeply believes in and lives the life of one who will trust and obey God. In this sermon, he outlines a definitive lifestyle from lessons that resulted in the successful accomplishments of the civil and human rights movement.

King and others realized they, in and of themselves, could not have envisioned or sustained their ordained calling. Vivian said "it becomes clear that, together with God, we became a prophetic people with the prophetic movement that was, in fact, looking so far ahead that it would make a difference in the history of mankind."[9] He contends that the success of their purpose and mission came because God was not merely recognized, honored, and respected in the midst of their challenges but was their strength and guidance as they continued to trust and obey.

This profound sermon provides specific agenda for changing a nation. It teaches, first of all, that one must believe in God and never doubt that God is in the midst of the highest and lowest moments of one's life. Vivian teaches that reaction is action.

Regardless of the institutionalized racism, violence, ignorance, hate, and misplaced prejudices, love will always prevail. Vivian writes "a people who love God don't need anything but the love of God."[10] He is saying that God is with you, but do not merely get on your knees, pray, and wait for God to resolve your circumstances. This sermon suggests that once someone realizes that God is with them, they should internalize that truth and must "keep fighting, . . . just keep working, . . . just keep going, . . . just keep believing, and God will deliver you"[11] because God has the final word.

This sermon is even more relevant today than when it was first preached because America has become a nation that depends on anything and everything except God. This myopic and seductive mentality encourages many people to believe that they are achieving success on their own and that God is merely rubber-stamping their behavior. Vivian's message is challenging the nation to recognize, realize, and not rationalize that, without God's divine intervention, failure is inevitable.

3

This God of History and Racism

1 Corinthians 2:16

You know, it's wonderful to have a church that, when you are here, you can have the worship that we have here. I go to churches all over the world, and I would rather have worship here than any other place. [applause] And it's really the character of the pastor and what he's created, and what's in his mind, and what's in his history, that makes the difference. It gives us additional hope for the future. Why don't we move down here, closer to the center? Let's share here, together, as a family. We're sort of stretched out right now. You don't want to be reaching out too far when you don't have to. I prefer it to be close, so, as we talk, we really talk together, we share together, and we feel each other together.

Your pastor mentioned South Africa, and I want you to know I've been there twice in the last sixty to seventy days. But now the point of being [in that nation] is that I was there with a group of academics from Brazil and the United States, and I thought I had a good grasp of what was going on when I left there. But the last time, I was in four cities, and I talked to average South Africans who came in for a conference. We then went from town to town, and I realized that I didn't learn during the first trip what was really happening. And I want you to know that things are not what you might have thought. And that, in spite of the fact that [Black Africans in the post-apartheid era] have the presidential office and some political offices, they run very little. All the money is in the hands of the people who hated them before and are waiting for the chance to take over again.

And I tell you that not because I want to put something down. I tell you that because I want you to know how hard they are struggling to be truly free. And that they need our help. It's a strange thing. And [their struggle] is central to something I'm going to say, but you won't realize it until the end. That, in fact, the world of African peoples, wherever we've been spread in the world, are looking to us, and we may think of ourselves as not being able to even handle our own drive for freedom. But regardless of what we may think about ourselves, the world is looking to us—the Black world that I believe will be the first world. Well, we'll get to that, the African world looking to us for leadership. And I do not believe that we can fail them.

It is not an accident that [President Bill] Clinton is in Nigeria this week. It's not an accident. We must begin to see that the African world is the world of activity, where things can really happen. And that no matter what nation we discuss that is part of the industrial world, that nation has to depend on the African in one form or [another]. And I want you to know that, everywhere I went in Africa, what really moved me was the young people, and how bright they are, and how much they desire learning and try every way they can to learn. I walked into a high school with 1,800 students, and the library shelves, only about a third of them were filled. And they had about sixteen computers, and only half of them worked. And the principal said that they need paper and pencils—stuff that we don't even think about. And if we think that we're at the bottom, we don't know what the bottom is. All right? What I'm saying is that we can help in more ways than we can think, in elementary ways.

I was at a church with a group in Soweto, and before it was halfway over, we were crying. And it wasn't because of the greatness of the preaching—one of our fellows did the preaching, that wasn't the point—it was the people. Their sharing, their attempts to be, and their young people moved us. They didn't have any instruments, but they had a thing like a book with a string on the back of it, and they made music, baby! I am talking about what comes out of the soul and the spirit of who we are. When we left, we were crying, and there were guys gambling across the street, just like we used to do. I don't want you to get the idea that everybody there is spiritually wonderful, but everybody is trying to be. That's what I want you to see—that people are working against poverty and problems and disillusionment [at a time] when they thought they were going to be in charge of their lives, and they really aren't now. But the first steps have been taken, and I think that's a thing we have to see.

Now, let's get down to it. I think we have to see it, and see ourselves, in a way that we seldom do. That we call on God for our personal needs, and we see Him paying our rent, and we sing our songs about that. And that's quite all right. Because God is more than one kind of God. But God is a god of history, and I think, before we can understand who we are and what we should be and who we are to become, we have to see this God of history because if we don't, we'll begin to think that we're just here in some cycle as some of the historians have described. Or see ourselves as a civilization that comes on and then turns into something else.

God's in charge of His word, and that's what has to be seen. And God has been guiding us from the very beginning. That He who created us also guides us. Or He wouldn't be a God of love. How could you be a mother and give birth to children and act like that child don't exist? It's impossible to do so. And one of the worst things we know in human existence is for a mother to deny her children. Father, maybe, but not mother. There is something about it. God is leading us and guiding us, not [as] individuals but as [a] people—His people and His work. Now, God has always stepped in when He sees that the sins of the world are too much for our moment. You see, when we look at Israel, it's a history of a people. When we look at the Old Testament, we have to understand that God is a god of all of history. But He's letting us see how it works by letting us see the people and how He works with them. And whenever their evil became too much, God intervened in one way or another.

God stepped in with the prophets, time and time again. When we see those prophets step in, that's a time when the sins were so integrated into government. And I'm not talking about in normal ways, but when government itself is in struggle and fighting with God. He stepped in when whole tribes of Israel were at odds; He stepped in with a prophet. When we see whatever the sins are and however they come, structured at one level or another that couldn't be handled by a normal kind of prayer life or beyond our individuality, [that] is what I'm talking about. God stepped in. And to see that picture is to see what forms our history.

There is no history without God. Now, you see, that sounds good, and I know what it sounds like—that I'm trying to move you, but what I'm trying to say is that we have to see it. In fact, that God is working in our history. And that He didn't just work in history *then*. God is working in history *now*. It's the thing that I see that is almost forgotten. Let's look at it for a moment because we can hardly understand God working in history now. When we begin to look, I think we have to see it in quite another way for us. It is not an accident that the South, of which we're a part, has been the most sinful place, even in the United States. I'm not saying that the North is good; it's just up south. I'm talking about [the fact] that we then became the vortex at the center of evil that was so deep that people thought it was their culture.

See, if you look at the Old Testament, it's a struggle between the prophets and the kings. If you look at the New Testament and what's happened since the New Testament, it's a struggle between a culture and Christ. Understand: What I'm saying is that men have tried to make culture into God, or they have tried to take Christ, and tried to show that their culture is edifying Him when in fact they're using Him for their cultural ends. That's exactly what the South has been. If you ask any Southerner, they'll tell you that God ordained them to have slavery. God ordained prejudice; God ordained it all—and they won't use this language, but they don't have to love people because, after all, God chose them to be greater than. If you don't believe that, why do you think there's white superiority, right? And how do you believe that the people who believe in white superiority go to church every Sunday? It's because they believe that, for no other reason than they are white, that they're superior, and that God has made it so. That is sin so horrible that you have to step in, as God did in the Old Testament and as God did with Jesus, when the whole world was so sinful that there was no way to get over it without sending Jesus. And it's not an accident that He's been sending prophets as His way of acting through history.

Now, as we look at who we are, we have to understand who we are in the way those South Africans see us, as the hope of their world. But I want you to see that I believe that God has chosen us as the hope of this nation right now. Let me give it to you this way. It is not an accident that a Martin King is the prophet of this nation. It is not an accident that he was a minister. It is not an accident that [all the men who] worked with him were ministers. It was not an accident that the church was the base of bringing the new freedom. It is not an accident that the only man that stands on a stamp today is Martin Luther King Jr. It is not an accident that the only minister to have gotten a Nobel Peace Prize was Martin Luther King Jr. It is not an accident that he was Black and comes out of the United States. It is not an accident that our parents and fore-parents and fore-parents before them prayed for generations for deliverance, and it came in the name of Jesus Christ and one [other] name, Martin Luther King, who raised the Lord Jesus as his God.

Now, when I look at that, I think that sometimes we don't understand who we are. Let me put it another way for you: *White people don't really believe that they have to obey the Scriptures.* They don't really believe that if they don't love their fellow man, then they're going to hell. And I don't believe that many of us believe that white people are going to hell because they don't love us. I don't think you really believe that.

I don't believe we consider ourselves [people worthy of] going to heaven because they don't care about us. And if we don't, it says we don't know who we are and how God sees us, and what our role is in the world. Because if you don't think you're worthy [but] God thinks you're worthy, I know God's not wrong. It says there's something wrong with our concept and our attitude. But you see, it's difficult to know who you are if you don't know what God thinks of you. *See, our greatness depends upon what God thinks, not what we think.* But if God can love you, then why can't you love you?

The other thing that's so important is that you don't know what to do until you know what your God wants to do. Now, we know that we're supposed to praise Him, so we come to church and we praise Him. But what is God's agenda in the world? Because if you're God's people, you want to do what God's doing. In fact, if you are not doing what God's involved in doing, it's doubtful how good a people you are. And if God chooses out of us the people to answer the prayers of us, isn't it interesting that we've been praying for freedom, when white people were in charge of it, but Black people delivered? But it is not an accident, you see. Egyptians did not free Jews. God sent a Jew to deliver Jews. If we understand how God works in history, then we can begin to understand who we are. And that the slaves of Egypt became the deliverers of their own freedom. We, who are the slaves of America, can deliver our own freedom because we've got the same God! And that this God of history is the same God that delivered slaves from Egypt, same God that delivered in America, and the same God that has made certain that in Christian countries, slavery no longer exists.

So, we have to ask ourselves, what was the central issue of the civil rights movement? Was the central issue my right to vote? I fought for it, bled for it, all that kind of stuff. That wasn't the central issue. Was the central issue the fact that I can have a better job? I do have a better job, more security, my children are better off than they would be, but is that the central issue? The central issue of the civil rights movement, if we look at the mind of God, was *Whose god is God*? Is God the god of First Baptist Church Southern Baptist, who believed in a God of slavery and segregation and separation? Is that God? That can't be my God! Because my God is a god of truth and love and justice! And open the Old Testament, and anywhere in the New Testament, and God is a god of love and truth and justice. He's not a God of slavery, segregation, and separation. The central issue of the civil rights movement is, Whose god is God? And they lost it, and we won it. They lost the Civil War and couldn't get it straight. And one hundred years later, our prophet arrives, and they lose the nonviolent war as well. But what does that say to you and I? Who did we pray to [to] deliver us?

He's a god of history, but he can't deliver us overnight because the sins of the world keep him from doing so. See, we asked the wrong questions. *Why doesn't God do this or why doesn't God do that?* Because He's already made us, all [of us, and each] of us, a free person. And He has to work within the concept of the freedom He's given us, and if our sins keep getting in the way, it takes Him longer to get there. But God's always working to help us get there. I don't mean as individuals now. I'm talking about as the human community! He sends a prophet because we were so far off, and our sins were so deep in America that this nation could never be saved. And we had low esteem of ourselves, and they had such exaggerated opinions of who they were. You see, they thought they were God, and we thought we were unworthy. How sinful can you get? God had to step in and send a prophet to begin the deliverance. But we have been so off into our secular understanding of our own experience that we can't even capture who we are, and what God is doing with us, and [how He] used us and sees us.

See, if you believe that the major issues of the civil rights movement are not religious or spiritual, you've missed the story! God came to save us all. We're so tied up in Black/white, we don't understand that God's not concerned about Black or white, he's concerned about saving his people. And those who will obey will be saved. Those that will love, those that will seek for truth and justice, will be saved.

Most of us get in the way. I don't care whether we're Black or white or yellow or pink. But it is not an accident that God has a way of reaching down to the bottom—woo!—and taking that which many others thought could not be, and using it as a way [of] proving that God's in charge. And that those who think they should be [in charge] are not, and the low places will become high, and the high places will become low. Because that's the only way we can see the glory of God. Otherwise, we'll think we did it. A good deal of us think that way now because we don't have a spiritual understanding of history, of what God's doing in our midst, and what it means for us. Remember, it's thinking from the mind of God. That's why the disciple says: Have that mind in you that was also in Christ Jesus.[1]

Think about the mind of God. Do you think God went through all of that just so that we could get a better job? God's a god of history! God's a god who brings salvation. God's a god of redemption. Those were His issues. And without seeing that issue in light, you're not watching God work. If you're not watching God work, why come worship Him? And if you're not working with Him, why say, "Oh, Lord, what you want is what I want"? Oh, that conversation is nonsense. The point is, at what point do we understand what God asks for us to do? God is concerned about the saving, about the redemption. And you see, isn't it interesting [that] white people can't save themselves because they think so much of themselves? "The stiff neck," they called them in the Old Testament. The high and the haughty. You are better than God when you think that you can dictate the terms of your own salvation, when you think that you don't have to love [anyone] but those you want to.

See, I think that God is saying to us something like this: I think he's saying to white people that if you're not willing to equally share the goods of this world, you will lose your soul in the process. And I think he's saying to Black Americans, if you're not willing to save their souls, you will never have the goods you want for you and your generation. There's a tradeoff. God has gingerbread for both of [our peoples]! But this time we got to cut the wood first. [applause] It's that He's saying to us, *I'm not concerned about your color, I'm concerned about all of you, and I'm tired of seeing Black folk over there and white folk over here, and both praising me and neither one of them understanding what's going on*. And you know what I have found [by] doing workshops with white folks? That it gets extremely quiet when I tell them the Scriptures say that, if you can't love your fellow man as you love yourself—woooo—it gets quiet. It gets real quiet. But it's profound quietness, you see. Because they begin to understand that everything they thought they were, is not. Everything they thought they were going to have, they will not. Everything they thought was going to be good for their children, can't be. That's why they can have the riches they have in the suburbs, but the worst cases of dope and sex abuse in young people have been found out there; it's not in here.

That's why, even the advertisers can say, if one-fourth of dope is in the inner city, where's the other three-fourths? They're dying spiritually. But now, once you know it, you know what I've found—that the best of white people is at their worst. When we tried to integrate the churches, we weren't trying to integrate them. We were just trying to come in and join worship. But deacons were standing in front with clubs in some cases. At the house of the Lord! The very presence of Black people is a declaration of the depth of sin of America. We've got to say it. And instead, we do this little dance of accommodation. We do this dance of laughing and talking, and we can't wait to get away from each other. Now, you know how it is when we do it. Think what it means when God watches it. And we're both going to be going to different churches in three or four days, talking about how much we love Him. It's in the mind of God that things are real. I believe that God has said to us, "Save *white people*." And white people will save other white people because God's concerned just as much about white people as He is concerned about Black folk.

Remember, Black folk don't hate. We are mad! [applause] And we're mad because of how we're treated. But you see, when they stop mistreating us, we won't be mad anymore. And so, God doesn't like to see us mad, and He doesn't like to see them hating. And we can solve it if we do what God has already set up. Remember what Martin King wrote on the window, remember [that] the prophet is what I'm talking about. See, because the press is giving us a civil rights leader, we don't understand that God is giving us a spiritual leader. And that what Martin was about was not just getting something for Black people; it was for this nation. But in the beginning of that ministry, he wrote on the window of the SCLC, "TO SAVE THE SOUL OF AMERICA." To save the jobs for Black people? No, to save the soul of America. To save the vote for Black people? No, to save the soul of America. Because Martin the prophet knew what God knew: That until the soul of the South is changed, and the soul of America is changed, nothing else will really change. But the sin of America is so deep, that the very soul has got be saved before the nation can be saved. And God knows that this nation is the premier, number-one nation in the world—that we have a better chance of saving the rest of the world than anyone else.

This is a God of history. He's working in historic proportions, not one by one. I'm talking about a God that sees His world and stands atop it, and sees the suffering and knows that those who He created he's going to have to condemn to death unless they come around. God's about saving the world, and He knows that through us, who He picks from the bottom, that the message will be clear. As we save first his church—the Christian church in America can't be saved right now. Cut it any way you want it. The Christian church in America can't be saved by itself. We've got to save it. It's got to be brought together, and we're the ones to bring it together. Number one, we're right. Number two, we can out preach them. Number three, we need their stuff. Most important of all. God sent the prophet to us. This God of history.

Martin could out preach them all, too. They thought because Billy Graham had 'em coming on down . . . but Billy Graham can't preach. [laughter] We got at least a hundred brothers, and as many sisters, that can out preach Billy Graham. But you see, why is that so? Because we have come out of this history of racism. It's not an accident that Jesus picked fishermen. That was the common work. Because He knew they had in their souls the stuff God was concerned about. It doesn't matter what's up here [pointing to his head] if you haven't got something here [pointing to his heart]. But when you can put the two together, then you can be a prophet that speaks for the King. That's why Moses, that's why Martin King, that's why Isaiah. We can go through the list. Call them! None of them were backward in either soul or mind. And God used them to awaken a people for the good of the whole people. There weren't just Jews to be awakened there. But when Jesus came, He said you must go out to all parts of the world.

Delivered: August 27, 2000
Christians For Change
Baptist Convention

COMMENTARY

Kevin R. Murriel

In 2016, I journeyed with a group of clergy and laity to Meru County, Kenya, to explore a new ministry opportunity. This effort would open the door for our congregation to support a group of orphans for three years to help them escape the devastation of extreme poverty and emerge as entrepreneurs. As we traveled throughout the countryside, I was captivated by the pristine imagery painted on the canvas of creation by God, who made the first earthly creation in Africa—the garden of Eden. As we were driving to our first location, we stopped to visit a school where the children were clearing a field that had grown too high for them to enjoy their recess. These children were remarkable. I immediately felt God's urging toward a probing question: What are we called to do to impact in the lives of our children?

Wonderful things can happen when we are inspired by children to ask questions we might otherwise ignore. This is at the heart of C. T. Vivian's sermon titled "The God of History and Racism." Vivian uses 1 Corinthians 2:16 as a scriptural backdrop and argues that God is a god of history. He draws our attention to the creative work of God in Genesis and to God's deliverance of God's people from Egyptian slavery. Vivian creates a bridge from the past to the present, highlighting God's divine agency in our human condition. He makes the case that there is no history without God and that God is always working in our history.

Drawing the parallel with God's activity, Vivian uses the metaphor of a mother and her child. He contends that there is a love uniquely woven into the fabric of that relationship and, therefore, it is impossible for the mother to act as if the child doesn't exist. In the same way, Dr. Vivian says God is connected to God's people in the past, present, and future.

This sermon raises relevant issues that are timeless in our struggle for freedom in America. Vivian first turns to that which is personal. That is, to consider our individual moral center and our personal response to the cycle of poverty and injustice that we witness in our own social location daily. He mentions this interpersonal quality in the context of evil corrupting government. Yet, for Vivian, God is not detached from this reality. The qualities of God make God the active agent in human deliverance. That God always intervenes through human participation when government systems are saturated with the sin of injustice.

He says, "God stepped in with the prophets time and time again. When we see those prophets step in, that's a time when the sins were so integrated into government."[2] We have seen this condition manifested historically through the Exodus narrative into the period of the Judges, into the post-exilic period, through the New Testament, and even into more modern movements, such as the civil rights and Black Lives Matter movements. Vivian suggests that, because of God's love for humanity, God always raises up prophets in times when systemic injustice is pervasive in the culture. For Vivian, God is not relegated to the past but, instead, is active in the affairs of humanity as an interconnected deity, identifying with the suffering and oppression of God's people.

Geography is also important to Vivian's argument for God's agency in history. The South, he argues, is a prominent place where the idea of white superiority was spread through a misinterpretation of Scripture and in connection with a portrayal of Christ that is antithetical to the historical Jesus that we find in the Gospels. And, inasmuch as Dr. Vivian highlights the problems of the nation, he is clear that human involvement must accompany God's agency. He says,

> But I want you to see that I believe that God has chosen us as the hope of this nation right now. Let me give it to you this way. It is not an accident that a Martin King is the prophet of this nation. It is not an accident

> that he was a minister. It is not an accident that everybody that worked with him were ministers. It was not an accident that the church was the base of bringing the new freedom. It is not an accident that the only man that stands on a stamp today is Martin Luther King, Jr. It is not an accident that the only minister to have gotten a Nobel Peace Prize was Martin Luther King, Jr. It is not an accident that he was Black and comes out of the United States. It is not an accident that our parents and fore-parents and fore-parents before them prayed for generations for deliverance and it came in the name of Jesus Christ and one [other] name, Martin Luther King, who raised the Lord Jesus as his God.[3]

Vivian lifts Dr. King as a prime example of God's call upon our lives to stand against injustice and work to create the beloved community that God intended. Dr. King, for Vivian, is the modern prophetic prototype. He considers the Kingian call as one of many—an example of how God chooses us to do God's justice work on earth.

At the climactic turn in this sermon, Dr. Vivian asks the question, "What is God's agenda for the world?" He raises it to disprove any notion of a planless God who produces a directionless people. Dr. Vivian's deep Christology centers on God's ultimate plan for humanity, and that God is calling us to participate in our own deliverance. Dr. Vivian asserts that God's people should want to do what God is doing. This connects us to the God of history and to the God who raises up deliverers from among the oppressed. For Vivian, God is concerned with the salvation of all of God's people. He describes this as a tradeoff. White people who aren't willing to share equally will lose their souls, and Black people must be willing to do the work to help save the souls of white people from the sin of racism.

For Dr. Vivian, this key component of Christ's love ethic comes through love of God, love of neighbor, and love of self (Matthew 22:37). The mistreatment of Black people, Vivian argues, bothers God; and the salvation work that must be done isn't just for Black people or white people, but it is to save the soul of America. Until that happens, the struggle continues from generation to generation. This work must be done in both the head and the heart, and it is possible only with the help of the God of history.

Part Two

A Theology of Social Justice

4

Your Soul Is Required

A Modern Parable for Ancient Times Luke 12:13

SEE, I MADE the mistake of getting up too soon! If I had been in a Baptist church, I would have known not to get up until the pianist stopped. I didn't expect it here, but isn't it good to know that the Spirit is everywhere? [applause]

When I think of this church, I visited you. I live right around the corner. This is our neighborhood, and we were so glad to have you come into our neighborhood and to do such a beautiful job. And you know how neighbors get. [laughter] So we were very grateful to know that you have such a great church, and that you brought it here, and it's a testimony to God, and it's a witness to disciples.

You know, when I think of a church, I think it is an answering back to the love of God. It's a way of saying, *God, you've been good to us. We're going to let the world know how good you've been in ways that can be as permanent as we can make [them].* You have a wonderful pastor, and we always say that, as visiting preachers. It's a part of what you learn. [laughter] But there's something deeper than that when coming to this church. You do have a marvelous pastor. This is the second time around [that I have visited], and you still fill the church. It's a witness in itself. And you start so early on a Sunday. You [might] think that most wouldn't be there, and more men than women in a prayer meeting? Who would've "thunk" it? It's that kind of understanding that is so marvelous as we come.

I want to introduce you to my family because I want you to know my family. Right now, there's just one row of them. [laughter] Give me a little time. See, our children, all six of them, have just begun to learn the purpose of children is to have grandchildren. [laughter] My wife—please stand up, baby. That's my wife, Octavia. [applause] And then my children and grandchildren. Why don't you stand together? [applause]

Let's pray together. Oh, mystic God, and yet our Father. Alpha of our preexistence, Omega of our unknown futures. We come, in this place, we come, in our visibility we stand before thee, but in our invisibility, we yearn for thee, for thy understanding, for thy wisdom, for thy love. And finally, one day for thy full presence before us. Help us in our struggle to be, help us to speak thy language in ways acceptable to thee. In this hour, Lord, help us strengthen our will. In this hour, help us maintain our hope in the core of our being, show us thy holy light, and reveal to us, Lord, what must we do to be whole and share thy wholesomeness. We ask that thy will be done here and now in this spot. Amen.

I would like for us to think about Luke the twelfth chapter, thirteenth verse, for those who'd like to turn [to it]. Let's start with the sixteenth verse. The ground of a certain rich man yielded an abundant harvest. He thought to himself, "What shall I do? I have no place to store my crops." Then he said, "This is what I'll do. I will tear down my barns and build bigger ones, and there I will store my surplus grain. And I'll say to myself, 'You have plenty of grain laid up for many years. Take life easy; eat, drink and be merry.'" But God said to him, "You fool! This very night your soul will be demanded from you. Then who will get what you have prepared for yourself?"

This is one of the shortest parables, and I want us to think about this short parable, but mainly about there's only about one hundred eight words here, about four full sentences. They're complex sentences, but only about four full sentences, one hundred eight words. And yet, when we look at it, almost twenty centuries of Christian people have thought about it, have examined it, have found direction in it, and it is still here for us.

I remember when I first became a Christian and began to really, truly read the bible. One of the mysteries of the Bible was this little parable, and I passed it over because I was young in the faith, and it didn't matter that much. But I find that, over the years, more and more, I returned to this short little parable and [began] to think in terms of its meaning and [realized] that, through all those centuries, men have been thinking about [it], gaining thought, and have been able to get some sort of meaning [from it], and [yet], when I went to look in the normal kinds of sources to find some sort of understanding, I never really found it. I think it's a kind of verse that grows on you and through your own experiences. You begin to accumulate ideas and understandings that relate to it in some positive way until, finally, you, even as preacher, feel free to preach it out of yourself. And it is that kind of parable and that kind of understanding that I bring, because you see, I keep thinking about this man, and I begin to think that he's not a dumb man, and yet Jesus calls him a fool. He must be a thinking man, and was probably a man of the church—a good man for his time. Yet Jesus calls him a fool. [He] was a man not without substance, yet a fool. Not a man without wit and culture, yet Jesus calls him a fool.

Puzzlement—for you see, there's something about the word *fool* that I do not like. I grew up in Sunday school, thinking you never called a man a fool. We were told we couldn't even call the children [whom] we played with fools. But you see, Jesus calls him a fool—there's something quite different about that. I dislike it, but you see, I had to explore why I disliked the term *fool.*

And I found that, for me personally, the reason is that I more easily associate myself with the fool than with the Lord of light. And that as I looked back at my life, I think back to the foolish times. Someone said that we can forgive ourselves for many of the sins that we produce, but twenty years later we can think of the times we'd been stupid and cringe, and in a very real way, that's true. I can tell by the nodding of heads, right?

When we think of it, here is this man that Jesus calls a fool, and I suppose that the worst thing that could be said of a man is that Jesus would consider his lifestyle that of a fool. This man has no name; a name is unnecessary. Jesus gives him one, and one that no one would want. In these four lines, this simple passage from Jesus. Then Jesus links life and abundance. Life itself, direction, is here, and judgment is here. Judgment stands out of what I would call a parable of the present, for it is not something of yesterday. It is a parable of the present. And when we think of the judgment, judgment is in relationship to his soul, judgment is in relationship to his abundance. There is something about the wisdom of Jesus here, that he links [these things] together. They are only separate as we conceive philosophically and theologically, but always together in real living situations, and that's why Jesus told parables, because they were of life itself. These four lines are linked together, and this is really the way we live.

Judgment is so often decided by our abundance. So often, the levels of our spiritual life end up being decided by our abundance or our lack of it. And the most important thing is to have a relationship to our abundance, and what is [in] that relationship decides a good deal of all of the rest. Now, for most of us, our abundance is not in money; our abundance comes in other forms—brains, talents, leadership, skills. But always, in the final analysis, soul is required. Now, so often as this parable has been read and talked about, it has been talked about in terms of death, that we're talking about death. But it's necessary here that Jesus is talking about a quality of life that goes beyond death. And it is necessary to see not in one form but in its various forms to really understand the mind of God. For these four lines—and always the message of Jesus—must be seen in its larger context and its spiritual context before we're really able to comprehend where he's coming from. I think that's why it says that the Scriptures are such that fools can wade but wise men must swim. It is as deep as life itself.

Well, let's think of another. If you don't know, please read Saint John of the Cross. He's one of the great spiritual devotionals, and it's called "The Dark Night of the Soul." And each of us has a dark night. Each of us [goes] through some dark nights of the soul before we really die. [God] is not really concerned about death in its normal form because death is not a demand of God; it's the outcome of our decision, of how we live in relationship to all of life. And you see, when you think about it, it's this dark night that we go through that is so important, and this man was going through the dark night of his soul, and the tragedy here is not that he was going through the dark night of his soul, it's that he didn't even know he was in darkness—that's the tragedy. He was still going about the normal things of life without even knowing that he was on the verge of death itself. Not physical death but spiritual death—a deeper kind of understanding of life. It doesn't say that it will bury him. He will be walking around. But he is already dead to everything important in life.

Let us look at this man. Let's look in the car. Oh, it could have been a town car, could have been a Mercedes, [its owner] rich enough that it could have been a Rolls. But you see, what's important is when we look not at his car but in his eyes, through the window on the other side. As we look in his eyes, we see his thought, and his thought is about money and fame and ego. There was the arrogance of materialism about him, but something deeper was required of him as God looked through the window at him. Something deeper was required, but he just rolled on down the road, thinking about his goods and his properties and his lands, thinking about his stocks and his bonds and his Rolex. [He] had no idea where he was rolling to, but God did. The tragedy was right there. You see, in these four lines, life really is here. This is the very stuff of life that Jesus is talking about. The dark night comes on before death itself. The darkest night of a relationship, the dark night of a deep desire, the dark night of a dream, the dark night to be and to do and to become. These dark nights are determined. You see, much more is needed to come out of the dark night.

I work with students in this town and talk to them. And I see men and women with plenty of brains, fine brains. But there is something deep beneath, a commitment to learning, soul. You can have a fine mind, but if you don't have a commitment to learning, it's just a bit of flesh. It has no real meaning beyond [itself]. Soul is required in order to keep the brain from being just another organ, like an arm and a leg. Something deep is always required. It's this issue of soul that's required.

Husband and wife—probably we see the fur coats as they come along, the fine house, what most of us want to give, whether we can or not. But you see, men know it almost instinctively as we come to this Men's Day. That, [because] we can only do so much, [we are] always afraid that, [one day] down the line [in spite of all we have given] there comes [a] time that we've given that love [will be] required. Soul, and ultimately everything, will be decided not by what we gave along the way, but by how much soul we bring to the situation. It's this kind of something deeper [that] is required. A professional may begin your profession so often to make money. And you are successful, and you're making the money, and you've got the things, you feel good. But you see, there's something else that happens. You can never be at the top of your profession simply by looking for money.

There comes a time when soul is demanded of you. That's what it takes to break through and become fine in your profession, no matter what it is. The desire for money can only take you so far. The man didn't know it; that was the tragedy. The tragedy was that he couldn't break through because he thought money was what it was all about. When something deeper was demanded, he didn't even know it was demanded. It wasn't that his preacher hadn't preached it—oh, he'd been to the synagogue, he'd sat at the tabernacle—probably owned a special seat. But because he was there, [that] doesn't mean he understood what was going on. For it is not what the preacher says; it is how much soul you bring. See, when we really look at it, soul really finally decides the issues of life and death. And at this dark night, the issue is, do we have enough soul to save ourselves or will we hear God say, "Fool, this night"?

This America, this America is this parable. Our nation is the personification of this parable. For are we not they who store into barns? Do we not have a 7.5 trillion dollar gross national product? We have the abundance but not enough soul to feed the hungry. We have the abundance, but it's so disproportionate in relationship to our soul that we don't have the concern for those who are in the streets [and] need to be housed. We're the richest nation in the world, but we don't have enough soul to share our abundance. You know we have just enough soul to cut the aid to women and children, just enough soul to not support a health system in the richest country in the world. Not enough soul to stop death from dope or to really get serious about it. We have the money, we have the technology, we have the talent—our problem in America is not any of those. It is the fact that we do not have the soul. This night, this dark night of the American experience, the sun shines outside, but this is a dark night through which we go in the American experience. [applause] And the issue is not whether we have the money. The issue is, Do we have the soul? We have churches on every corner, but do we have the soul to go with it? We've built the buildings, we have the books, we have the knowledge, we line libraries with information. But do we have the soul to go with it?

In this dark night of the American experience, we do not know if democracy as we're supposed to know it will ever become a reality. We are now living through a period where we're deciding the permanent rich and the permanent poor. We're going through a period of American life where we're not for certain if we'll really be on top. We like to think that there's no one greater than we, but when we look at the statistics, we are down. We're being outcompeted by smaller nations than we. We used to take things for granted that we can't take for granted anymore. This is a dark night of the American experience. And the point is, can we in fact live up to it? If you don't have soul, you fall. That's what happened to twenty great civilizations. Because judgment is always linked to abundance, and abundance to the nature of soul.

When we really begin to look at it, I remember a line that sticks out for me; many of you will not remember, but Fred Gray was the first lawyer of Martin Luther King Jr. And his father was an outstanding minister, a fine spiritual man. Oh, he did not shout and holler, but he was a great minister. A depth of thought and understanding. And I remember a conversation where he said, "What this nation must remember, America is not too young to die." Judgment, judgment!

Let us think about this man, this fool, on [this] Men's Day. Why was Jesus so unrelenting on this man? Why did Jesus treat him the way he did? Why did Jesus almost designate him to the dark? Why was Jesus so hard on this man? Well, if we think about it, was he doing what others had done before him? Wasn't he a frugal man, wasn't he a hard worker? Didn't he have conscientious business practices? Didn't he plan for the future like you and I do? Didn't he have dreams like you and I?

Jesus seems to be clear. Some qualities of an experience are infinitely more important than all the rest. And we can see him as a hardworking man, as a saver, as a man with hopes and dreams and desires, but you see that was not enough to save him. There was the most important quality in the experience [that] he had left out. [For you to] miss certain things, God calls you a fool. His soul and his abundance had a relationship that he didn't honor because he didn't honor his relationship between his soul and his abundance, so Jesus writes him off as a fool.

I remember talking to an executive who used to be in this city. As a young man, he founded a company. and he put it this way: "When I came here, I had the same attitudes and principles as you [who] sit here talking to me. But I put them in a drawer when I came to the company, thinking that when I go up in the company, when I'm a top executive and I have the money and they can't hurt me anymore, that then I will go back to the drawer and get my principles." And then the judgment! He said, "And when I went back to get them, they were not there."

That's the way life is, isn't it? You see, it doesn't happen all at once. They slowly seep out. This man didn't start out as a fool. He became a fool. Most of us don't start out to be less than. We start out to be more than. In the process of the living experience, we find that something seeps out, and we are no longer what we wanted to be, don't have the direction that'll take us where we want to go.

It's like America. It didn't happen all at once. Listen, when we first started in America, we used to say, "In God we trust." We were intending to serve God. Then, in a few generations, we got a lot more money, and we began to say God was on our side. And then a little later, "My country, right or wrong." We assumed that just because we said we were Christian, we were Christian and didn't have to worry. We knew we were right and God was on our side. Not necessarily so. And when we look at it, we assumed it. And then came Vietnam. Too late. What was needed was a little bit of soul, and we didn't have it in time.

And so, as we come to this Men's Day as Christian men, we have to ask, What is our task now? I believe God is depending on us, not simply to save persons only. For this would be the normal thing if we were talking in normal times. If the kingdom were at hand, we could say go forth and save those around you. But it is deeper than that. This time, a greater degree of soul is required of us. That we're here to save the institutions that save whole countries and whole peoples.

The greatest challenge in our Christian life now is to save the Christian church. Can the Christian church be used to steal the resources of the world for a few people, and we stand by silently and say that it is doing the work of God? Can we allow the Christian church to be a racist church in a world that is three quarters dark to Black? Can we allow conservative Christians—a conflict in terms, if you listen—to support cheap politics in the name of Jesus, and we keep quiet about it? Can we do that when we know that the very people they're teaching to hate are Christians like them? And when we know that the code words that are used to get around their pretense of being good is an evil endeavor?

The politics of America is being decided right now by so-called Christians who are closet racists, who do not care for poor people, in fact, whether they be Black or white. And who cover false patriotisms with false Christianity. The politics of this nation [are] being decided right now. They are paying for the church in an inordinate way, and they even got some Black ministers they pay off to talk that talk. See, what we have to ask is, Who raises the issues? Who will, in fact, fight the good fight? Who will speak out? Not simply from the pulpit, but who will speak out in the workplace? Who will be there in the office to make a witness? Who will say to them that this is not of God? Who will be there to be a pure witness for Christ in the midst of it all?

A nation is being decided today. We're in the dark night of our soul. The witness that is necessary is not simply the old witness of our yesterday but a new witness that begins the process of saving the only institution we have that can save us all. That takes a depth of soul to separate ourselves from Western ways and save our church so it can save the world. See, if God was to say to me right now, Vivian, ask what you would, and it will be given. Of course, I would say, yes, Lord. I know you're right. And if He would make that promise, I would say, convert the Christian church. I would say, covert the white Christian church in particular. This is the great issue of our time; the darkness that pervades our nation can only be broken through by the Christian church. Not only by the Christian church but by the religion of Christ himself. And we cannot have that until we know the conversion of itself.

Somebody needs to save the church from its fame-mess because we're a fame-centered church. We're a money-centered church, and the main issue is, Who will convert it? From racism, to sexism, to materialism, I believe this is our role as Christian men. Now, because we're in the church we are, and because we have the history we have, and the heritage from which we come, it's not enough to say, What is the task of Christian men today? You have to also ask, What is the task of Black Christian men today? For those two things are one on one hand and separate on another. Because, you see, that's another issue. An issue when we use our talent, time, and resources—a man's soul is ultimately related to that abundance, and this is the dark night of a people. This is a dark night.

We've had the greatest years we've ever had as Black people in this nation in the last forty-five years. Since World War II, the greatest years we've ever had. As bad as they are, they are the greatest years we've had. But you see, they've started going backwards with the end of Martin King, a spiritual voice in the midst of this nation. Think about it. This nation has not had a spiritual voice—Black or white or polka dot or pink—since Martin King. Think about it. [applause] I did not think that it was an accident that he was a minister. I did not think it was an accident that he was a Black minister, and I don't think it was an accident that he had a PhD.

Let's look at the statistics. Forty-eight percent of Black children are born and live under the poverty level. Fifty percent of Black children are born out of wedlock, and it's going up, not down. Thirty-six percent of Black families live below the poverty level, and the poverty level, as it's politically constrained, was used by the Reagans to make certain they didn't have to spend money. So, when we talk about the poverty level, we're talking about below what it takes to really live at all in this society.

One-third of our Black families are set to disintegrate, and the horror of that is that the makers of the study say that it was the highest percentage since they have been keeping figures. This is a dark night of the experience. Seventeen to 26 percent of young Black men, the stats [say], may never find a steady job. I wake up with it on my mind, because I know what it means in terms of dope. I know what it means in terms of children born out of wedlock. I know what it means in terms of families that should be here that will never be here. What it means for women who yearn for a real life but could never have it. We're not talking about statistics. We're talking about life. This is the dark night of our soul.

There's a tendency to want to blame the victim. Well, I'll tell you, we don't know what to do about it. So let's blame them. Well, you see, 5 percent of people will do anything. But when you think about 5 percent, something's wrong with the culture, not just with the common folk. And it doesn't matter what color you are, when you've got 5 percent, there's something wrong with a culture that allows it, especially when they can store it into bonds. See, no Black child is born deciding that he wants to live in the gutter. No Black girl wants to ruin her life with too-early pregnancy. No Black woman wants to give her life to prostitution.

Black men don't want to be in a food line. Black men don't want to be killing each other. Can't blame the victim because this society does not have the soul that is necessary. That is the issue. And this night, the issue is up to us.

One reason we have so many drive-by shootings is because we have so many drive-by Christians. [applause] See, we have to ask ourselves, who fights for the left-out, who will, who should? Only those who have the soul. And I believe it is we, I believe it is church. You are a microcosm of that which can save this nation. For when soul is demanded, I think that God is coming to us. And looking at a soul that has matured in four hundred years of struggle and survival, four hundred years of fight and faith. The bottom line is this: that Black [Christians] cannot keep their soul if the Black Christian church can't keep its soul. For that's who we are, and that's who we were meant to be.

Our task is then clear. It is to keep the pure spiritual life of Black church and Black Christianity as it was given to us. I believe God is really saying to the white church, "Thou fool, you store into barns without concern for others. You who quote Scripture and tote Bibles on a Sunday morning and build great temples but compromise your religion through racism." I think He's saying, "You're a fool," but [what] I think He's [also] saying is that "I'm going to show you what it means to be a fool. If you're not willing to save their Black bodies, I will not save your white soul."

But you see, as we look at it, God's not speaking to them only. I believe God's saying to you and I—Black Christian men and women, the Black Christian church—saying to us, you who have toiled in the heat of the day, you who have been isolated and left lonely by this society, you who have so little to store into barns, and yet have made a great deal of it. You, when this great nation. Let's put it another way. When this nation set you aside, rejected you, you became the cornerstone for the possibilities of democracy and Christianity. That you—the Black Christian men—I think God is speaking to us in particular. He's saying to us that if you're not willing to save their soul, you will lose your body. The issue is not one or the other. God doesn't care about Black or white. God is concerned about justice and injustice, about right and wrong, about decency and indecency, about righteousness and unrighteousness. And, in the final analysis, God's judgment comes as we use our abundance, and all our abundance of soul. We've got a chance to save this nation and take it through the dark night. Out of their abundance, we can save a third to a half of Black people in this nation. We're not separate; we're one. It is the links of our souls.

Delivered: September 25, 1994
Cascade United Methodist Church
Men's Day

COMMENTARY

Forrest E. Harris

The sermon "Your Soul Is Required (A Modern Parable for Ancient Times)" illustrates the Black preaching tradition at its best. The homiletic design, scriptural exegesis, and hermeneutical genius of the sermon remarkably model the prophetic oratory, Black storytelling art form, and biblically based proclamation distinctive and known in Black preaching. Vivian digs deep into the theological reasoning of the Gospel's portrayal of liberation, spirituality, and the justice of God. For Vivian, Jesus portrays or models God's compassion and justice on every level of life. What matters to God is explicit—compassion, love, and justice in human relationships. Through this lens, these cardinal principles of the kingdom of God, Vivian exegetes the parable of the rich fool, applying and using it as a theological template for moral decisions.

Hermeneutically and theologically, Vivian grasps the inseparableness of abundance and judgment. Thus, when it comes to the ultimacy of the Rich Man's "soul," there is a void that his material abundance could neither account for nor fulfill. The Rich Fool misses applying a theology of compassion, love, and justice for his life's goal, building surplus barns with no attention to God's ultimate concern.

For Reverend Vivian, the soul bears the divine imprint or the deepest essence of being, the purpose of being. Vivian calls it *beingness*, the depths of the self. Jesus calls the Rich Man a fool because he fails to understand or see his beingness in relationship to his accumulated abundance. Building barns for surplus and material security to the neglect of life's communal and numinous qualities of compassion and justice, in Vivian's estimation, is why Jesus calls the man a fool. Vivian references sixteenth-century mystic Saint John of the Cross—specifically his poem "Dark Night of the Soul"—to make the point of ultimacy.[1] The Rich Man wastes his intelligence, energies, and time to build surplus, with no concern for the soul's journey from its bodily home to its union with God. "Night" represents the hardship and difficulties the soul meets, detachment from the world, and reaching the creator's light. The Rich Man's dark night of the soul came when death made the announcement of judgment and moral accountability. The idolatry of abundance could not save his soul. According to Vivian's theology, the darkest reality is when one's soul or authenticity of beingness is lost in the fallacies of materialism.

Reverend Vivian preaches this sermon on the occasion of a Black church's Men's Day celebration. The parable of the Rich Fool is a theological challenge to—and prophetic judgment of—America's centuries of building abundance for self-centered democracy to the neglect of the suffering masses. Why would Vivian choose the parable of the Rich Fool to speak to Black Christian men, mostly ones of low-and middle-class income? Whose existential history in America has been that of victims of economic exploitation for the benefit of white comfort, privilege, power, and economic advantage?

Vivian sees the parable of the Rich Fool as a parable of modern America. The American culture started with colonization, the genocide of Indigenous people through taking their land and forcibly removing and exterminating their populace. Soon after that, chattel slavery became a pillar of American economic life, using slave labor to grow abundant surplus—two hundred and fifty years of placing material profit as more important than the bodies of Black people. Like the Rich Fool, America's abundance of hedge fund securities, building sanctuaries of capitalism, militarism, and racism, apart from the world's more extensive communal needs for justice, is a moral judgment upon the nation. With all of America's abundance, the soul of America is empty of compassion and justice to confront and change systems of oppression.

In Vivian's eyes, who should lead the way? Whose history and human experience best positions them, spiritually and socially, to redeem the soul of America: the Black Christian Church. The greatest challenge in Black Christian life today is to save Christianity. The soul-force of Black faith's life-affirming strength and moral resilience is in holding on to Jesus's truth. Holding on to Jesus's truth requires soul. Black men and women surviving American oppression are prime agents for leading the way of justice and compassion. They can be modern parables of God's compassion and justice, as Jesus was the parable of God for the ancient world. Vivian encourages us to be the best of humanity to have enough soul to do justice, love mercy, feed the hungry, tackle systems that unjustly imprison, and still have enough soul to be a parable of God's love in the world.

5

They Don't Know How to Do Right

Amos 2:6–8 and 3:10

YOU HAVE HEARD the Scriptures this morning, and I want you to think about this man, this prophet. I love the eighth-century prophets. In fact, I think of them as part of the New Testament, not part of the Old Testament. I have problems with people just wanting to preach the Old Testament when we're really a New Testament church. A good deal of the problems we face right now, as we are on our way to being pushed into a war, is the fact that we keep talking about God Jehovah, and we don't talk about God that is Christ, a man of love and truth and justice.

I love these eighth-century prophets because they put ethics and content into the whole idea. It's that they call them minor prophets, but giants are never minor. They call them minor prophets because they didn't write as much as Isaiah, Ezekiel, and Daniel. But you see, these prophets cut to the very core of things, and what they did was to make it clear in one sentence what others take a chapter to explain. Reading Micah and Hosea and Amos is like reading whole books of religious tomes because they cut to the core of where it really is. They're able to take a few words because they had the experiences that allowed them to speak.

When we think of this man, Amos, we have to ask: Who was he really? Amos was a shepherd. And we have to say: What does a shepherd know of international affairs? What does a shepherd know about running a country? What does a shepherd know that all men should listen to? Hasn't he just been fooling around with the animals up in the hills somewhere? That's exactly right, and that's why God called him. Because he understood animals so well that he understood men when they become animals.

And somehow, you see, all the prophets in the end say the same great things, whether they're prophets from Amos or whether they're prophets to Martin King. They're speaking the same message over and over again because men don't change, and the Word is really from God and not from the prophet himself. So we always have to be disciplined and brought in. In fact, we are like the sheep and the animals that have to be shepherded, because when we look at the shepherd, he understood animals, and he saw them.

Now we think of sheep, for instance, as cuddly little creatures that just follow along, and all you have to do is take them up in your arms like in the stain glass windows with Jesus. But the real truth is those are the little sheep. What happens when they grow up is another thing. What happens when they get fat is another thing. What happens when they get bigger than the other sheep is another thing. In fact, if you read this whole book [of Amos], don't just read two or three verses. That's why I asked the sister to skip all over, to pick out some verses, [it's] because you have to read the whole message of a prophet to understand what's going on. You have to see a prophet in relationship to his time. When you hear Reverend [Gerald] Durley speak, you're hearing a man speaking in relationship to his time. He's applying what God is talking about to the life you've got to live. He's not talking about heaven after a while; he's talking about right here, right now.

You see, this is what Amos was doing, and he was doing it so well that we are still repeating it today and find that it fits perfectly. [You] see, he saw these animals that would push others off the pasture. He saw these animals as those who broke down the barriers between where they're supposed to be and go, and as eating the food of others as well as their own. He saw these animals as people that believe that size determines their ethics, and that if they were big enough they could do whatever they wanted to do. And that if they could get by the shepherd when he wasn't looking, they could do whatever else they wanted to do. He understood the animal, and it seems we can say the same thing today. He likened the rich of his time to those animals. They seemed as if they could change everything; they thought about size, they thought if they were big enough and bad enough, they could do anything they wanted to do. They pushed others off of the pastures.

You see, we're looking at a nation now where billionaires have destroyed the lives of hundreds of thousands of average people just because they could. We see that they told their employees, "Put your money into stock, and we got a 401(c)(3), or whatever it is, and we'll add fifty cents to the dollar." And then, after you put your fifty cents in for five years, they come and rob the whole trade from you. And so, it became bait. And what happens is that the thousands of families lost everything they hoped for and dreamed for. Their hopes went down the drain, years of work went back to those at the top, and the billionaires don't mind because they can take.

This is what Amos was talking about when he described those who bring and garner violence and robbery into their strongholds. He wasn't wrong; he got it right. And it doesn't matter what century you're in. We see it happening right now. Those families that were cheated, children that would no longer go to college, husbands that were left out thinking where did their manhood go because they're made helpless.

Amos had it right. He said, "They do not know how to do right." That's their problem. They don't know how to do right. One of the Scriptures said the trumpet blows in the city and the people are afraid, and you can't help but be afraid in today's world. You don't know when it's coming down on you, or your children, or everything you've worked for. You don't know when it's coming down; that's how we live today. Amos wasn't wrong. The middle class that thought they were well off, and [thought] nothing would happen to them, no longer feel like the middle class. They feel like the poor. And maybe that's good because they really are, and some of us that have been acting like middle class are afraid that that second or third week's check won't be there, and we will be out there again.

But there's a tension in the land because the animals break down the barriers. When I talk about breaking down the barriers, [that's] the rich [who] change a law here and a law there. Breaking down the barriers that wisdom has put up between those who have and those who have not, so that those who have can steal the little bit that the have-nots have.

Remember, we see the Enron scandal. We already had been warned. We had the mutual savings and loan scandal before that. Do you remember? You ought to remember because you're still paying for it. Because those that stole it don't have to pay for it. 'Cause we're paying for it out of our taxes, but nobody talks about it. But the president comes before us the other night, and he talks about everything except the Enron scandal because his friends are involved and those who drink with him. Do you understand what I mean? [For] whom do they really work? The law was changed in banking and finance. The difference was so that they could loan themselves money and loan their board members money and loan their friend's money with no collateral needed. And when the game is over, we pay for it, and they live—just like Amos said—they live in multimillion-dollar homes overlooking the cities containing the poor and those that they've made destitute. But nobody touches them or calls their name, and their lawyers who help them are also super rich. They laugh and wait for the time that they can do it again because nothing happened to them, and memory of the folk [is] wiped out. God gives us opportunities, but read Amos. God won't do it forever. God won't do it forever.

Let's look at it any way you want. How did Amos say it? They were so rich they had ivory ceilings. And ivory houses. They didn't know what to do with the money. They don't know what to do with a billion dollars now! In fact, one of the decent billionaires who happens to live in this town is now moving to Florida. You know who I mean. When the economy went down, how many billions did the paper say he lost? He was laughing about it. He has many billions more. That was no problem, all right? The problem is just with you and I. That is the problem. They steal the money, destroy the people. Their greed is beyond their need, and generations of people will go cheated. Do you think this is over because the day changed? Think about your children. Amos says it. He says, they put a hook in you, but they can take your children with just a little fishhook because they will be helpless in the deep water. Nothing that they can do will [let them] save themselves.

Listen to Amos reinterpret violence. So, when he talks about violence, I can hear those at the top saying, *I didn't shoot anybody! Well, I didn't draw a gun. I don't even own a gun. I don't even like guns. I don't like violence. I'm too brilliant for that.* Oh, you can hear them, can't you? *That's just for people in the street! Those who are so dumb, they have to use a gun.* You understand? *But up here we don't like violence. We don't agree with violence.* But you see, robbery can be a piece of paper that, once it's signed, robbery can be fine print. We call it predatory lending, [which] takes away a lifetime of work and stores it in someone else's storehouse. They don't want to call it robbery. They call it uses of the law. But you see, Amos cuts where it really is. He calls it robbery. He calls it violence. He calls it the misuse of people. Amos said, *They don't know how to do right. And the bigger they come, the less they know how to do right.* They remake the language so it fits their vocabulary of violence and robbery. They create the law so that that law reflects their vocabulary, and then they can sleep at night. Can you imagine that? They can sleep at night?!

It's violence anytime people are destroyed. In fact, Amos talks about Andersons. He didn't call him by name. He said it's violence when you sell grain that won't reproduce. That's what's happening all over Africa today. American companies are trying to sell people grain that won't reproduce, and then they have to come back to those [companies] and pay their price so that [the people] can eat. They won't do that in the United States yet. Why? Because we got a market over there. [Who] do you destroy? You destroy those that you force into a situation [where] they can't do anything else. When I say *force*, please believe me [when I say] that they don't know how to do right.

An example: The United States government says to the people with the big smiling face in front of them, coming out of a laughing and grinning Texas: Let's open our markets to each other. And not only that—we will give you four hundred billion dollars if you will accept our grain. We know you're hungry, and people are starving. If you would just open up your market. How do we know they're starving? Because the laws of ours and our friends have made them starve. And then, when they say no to it—because if they did buy on those terms, then there would be no farming, and those are agricultural countries where most of the people live off the farming and have to eat by putting in a new crop—the desire is not to do right.

Who is Amos's *they*? 'Cause until you know who they are, you can't get to the root of the problem. Isn't it interesting that we know the names of just a few people who've robbed us? And that only a very few will go to jail? Who is Amos's *they*? Is it they who walk the streets today? No, it can't be them. They don't have any power, much less money. Is it the hungry, who we have provided food banks for? It's not they. Is it the people without clothing that have to go to clothing banks? No, it's not they. Is it just the people that are trying to educate their children? Is it the people that are paying too much taxes and hope to be able to buy a house? Is it those that just want a wife and a roof over their heads and [to] have children and hope for something better? It's not they.

Amos tells us [that] it is the masters of the poor. The masters—he calls them the masters. But what are they mastering? They are mastering the poor, so they can rob them—that is the game. How many more can you make poor so you can rob them more? We see it with predatory lenders; they are masters of the poor. They got the billions of dollars to do it. They can throw the rock and hide their hands—you don't know their name. And if you find out what companies it is, they change the name of the companies. How is the game played? They make the rules that decide how the rest of us will live. I mean us, right here, on these seats! I mean us that may think we're getting by but [we're] not. I mean us, who are at the bottom of the ladder, but we want to at least act like we're middle class. But [whoever] makes the rules decides who works and who doesn't work; who will get paid what and who's not gonna get paid what. It doesn't matter what you know or who you are or where you are—they will decide for you. If you think you decide salaries, ask the chamber of commerce about it—and they're just little fish in the game.

We have to ask ourselves, *How do we understand that we are being mastered by those who don't know how to do right*? They collect robbery and violence into their stronghold, and they have insatiable diets—it's never enough. Because they have a game among themselves—we've gone from millionaires to billionaires—and they call them the elite class now, [ones] that are trying to make a trillion dollars. And they don't count money like you and I count money. If we have assets of a million dollars, we think we're millionaires. You know how they count money? If you don't make a million dollars a year, you're not even in the game. And if you make less than ten million dollars per year, you may not be able to belong to certain country clubs or live in certain apartments. They play the game because they want to play it with each other. Someone might tell the truth that's in the group by what they hear: We have to understand *they should have known better* becomes the excuse to those that are robbed.

You know how the game is played? First, you create a victim, if you're the masters of the poor. Then you blame the victim for being a victim, and then you make him blame himself until he runs around trying to find his own tail, running in a circle, until he goes mad in the streets. Until we have a whole class, like Black people are a class, but they're telling us everything is race neutral now. They create a language! Race neutral? How can you have a race neutral thing in a racist country?

You see, those that want to break the barriers and bomb other nations don't need to prove anything. You see, this is where we are: The poor have to join the military to study war. Even when their grandmothers prayed and sang, *I'm not gonna study war no more.* Those who keep telling us that we are a nation, or a group of nations, that are the only good people on earth, those who define human rights as "only certain humans have rights," those who live by a different ethic than the prophets of God. They believe in the signs, the big animal, the bombs, make 'em big. Size, power, is their ethic, and the F-16 bomb is their logo. And nobody else is supposed to have it but them and the ones they want to have it. And even when they're forced to sell an F-15, they already know that person's enemy has an F-16, because he's a better friend than those you gave the F-15 to.

They don't know how to do right.

But they will tell you that they're against war. In fact, we no longer have a Department of War. I can give you right now the only person that talked about a department of peace—in the 1700s, not now—or the Black man that wrote an almanac, you know the name, I got the almanac where he asked for a department of peace,[1] and he gave God as the reason for it. But you don't find anybody talking about God in war and peace because if you do, you are unpatriotic—something's wrong with you.

The masters of the poor control the media so that you don't hear that there are a whole lot of ex-generals who are against this war. They control the school systems, so that you're supposed to run out and die for your country, and the expression is, "Right or wrong, my country, right or wrong." You drill it in! The masters of the poor control not only the medium in the schools but—listen to Amos—they also control the churches of the nation. Listen to Amos. And this is why a pastor like our pastor is dangerous to this country, if you hear them speak. But he's not dangerous to God. That's why a church like this one shouldn't exist, according to the masters of the poor, 'cause all our churches are supposed to do [is] be the garbage collectors. So, you can't destroy that many people without having some agency to pick [up their bodies].

They mess over so many people that [if] they turn on you, they're too hungry to do anything but destroy you. And you may make them so hungry they discover the truth. And when they discover the truth and find out who you are, they may come get you. See, listen very clearly, because if you look through Amos, what you're really hearing is that the problem is not the poor; the problem is not even the miseducated; the problem isn't even those that are left out. The problem is where we're told never to look for it. The central issue is, how do we humanize not the poor, [but] the central problem is how do we humanize—save the mind and the manner and the thought—of the rich and powerful of this country? That's the real issue. Until we can do that, we're just playing games; we're picking up their garbage.

This is why Jesus was a threat and had to be destroyed—because he was a revolutionary! Because he had new ideas for the nation. He was saying, *Yeah, bring your poor unto me, but I know who made them poor. Bring them unto me, because I know who keeps them that way.* And when we started talking about a poverty program like Martin King did, that's when they killed him. He became dangerous because people were listening to him.

What I'm talking about is that you have to be ready. Because they beat the drums so loud that the idiots on the edge—they don't have to make them idiots—they already out there. But you see, instead of controlling them, you let them loose, so that they know. Because the one thing everybody in this country wants to do and be is like the masters of the poor. Oh, do you hear me? We all want to be rich. And what does that mean? That means you're gonna go along. That means you're gonna quit the program. That's right. You know who designed and made the program? The masters of the poor, that's who did it.

The issue is, How do you humanize those who you don't even think about? They must be already good people. They go to church, like us. Now, you go to church after you've been elected president because, after all, they may talk about you. Is that how you humanize them? How do we save their souls? That is the central issue of American society. How do we, with all these churches, save the soul of those who control the nation? Not: How do we save the soul of the person that's down in the gutter? Yes, with our left hand and with our right hand we must be trying to save those on the top of the nation. We see [that] those [people] are Christ. We must learn how to spiritually feed those Christians. They oppress the poor, but how do we get to them and let them know, in their souls, that they're wrong?

When I talk about education, I remember I grew up in the Depression, when you could be a lot more honest because, you see, the masters of the poor were poor too. And I remember a painting. It was done by a French painter, and it hung in my third grade room, and they asked a question. They asked, "Who made this man who does not understand? He is bereft of knowledge and power to control his destiny. Who made this man?" But you can't ask those questions today because, you see, the masters of the poor are so rich, they don't want you to ask. Who makes the poor? Who makes those that are not eligible? And Amos gave us the answer.

You see, I have another painting in my house today. And it's a lynching on an open road, and three Black women are watching and looking at this body that was lynched right out in the open, and one of them is looking and is so horrified by what she sees [that] she can't think, she can't do anything but look at the object that the rich and powerful have destroyed.

Now, there's another woman, but she's older and she's looking up, and she's just, *Oh Lord, Oh Lord, Oh Lord, Oh Lord.* She doesn't want to blame God, 'cause He may strike her, too, so she says, *Oh Lord, why don't you do something?* What she means is, *If it wasn't for You, it wouldn't happen.* How many of us are afraid to tell God what we really think? How many of us will let truth come to the surface in our own souls? How many of us will face the fact that God's not the problem?

Now, the third woman is not looking at the body. She's seen that, she understands violence, she understands robbery, she understands that. She's looking to where they went, who did it! I keep it in the house because I want to remind myself—it could be three Black women; it could be three Black men. Doesn't matter; the painter just happened to make them women. But you see, we all have the tendency to do exactly those three things. Those are the strategies that are before us; that's why I love the painting. The strategy is [for you] to be so horrified that you will do nothing. Or that you will say, *God, you do it all. I'm done with this; you do it all.* Or be like the third woman and say, *I'm gonna get 'em.* See, Amos had it right. They do not know how to do right. They who bring fire and robbery into their stronghold.

And I have to ask you another question: How do they get by, from Amos to Martin King? How do they get by from century to century? Now, I had it wrong in my notes, but at the beginning of one of the chapters, he talks about—how does he put it? *Come, let us drink together.* When you get home, read all nine chapters. It's not very long, and if you aren't getting it straight because there're some ancient words and ideas, get you some good commentary. Because you shouldn't be reading the Bible anyway without some commentary. Because none of us are smart enough to get it all by ourselves. [Because] then you can see what's really going on in the situation, what they really mean when they're talking.

And it's not mild when you deal with the prophets. They tell it like it is. Because you see, how do the rich and powerful get by with it? They don't have to call anybody; people come to them saying *let us sit and drink together. 'Cause I got skills, and I think I can help you. And all I want is a piece, and I'll help you rob them.* Read it. It's there! It says, *I'll defend you against them. Not only that, I'll step in between them. They won't know who you are or what you really did; I will change the language so that they'll be so mixed up and will wonder what is going on.*

But Amos understood because he went to the truth. He said, *They are robbing you! They don't know how to do right.* Amos speaks of the warriors, Amos speaks of the courts, calls them by name. He speaks of the courts who do their bidding until the people are punished instead of those that should be punished. It's gotten worse! 'Cause now the Supreme Court elects presidents that preside over budgets that feed the rich and destroy the poor. They break down the barriers, push aside the weak, and power becomes the only effort—are you rich enough, are you powerful enough? If you're not powerful enough to make them president, then you don't count.

One thing we got going is that we still supposedly have a democratic country. Believe that? The point being is that we can get together if we got the nerve, the guts, the understanding—if we got the leadership. Then we can stop it if we want to. There are enough votes in the Black community to change any law or stop any law that is in this country. But you see, Amos understood that. We have to see it as that, when the animals break down the barriers and the people are trampled on, Amos has the answer. [That] the people must come together, all right?

Why is it so important that God called a prophet up out of a pasture? Because the nation had lost its conscience. Listen to me. See, that's the real top gun. That's where America is headed; we have no conscience. And when you really come to the point to understand that evil builds, a man has power without conscience, a few men have money, then a greater number of people will have power without conscience because they came to sup together. And then a class loses its conscience because it simply wants to be rich. And then, pretty soon, it filters down until we begin to tell each other that the only thing that matters is money. And if you don't have green, then there's something wrong with you. Until, even from the pulpit, they begin to talk about a gospel of success.

A nation loses its conscience—or when a nation loses its conscience, it doesn't know right from wrong, or good and evil become the same thing. The words are changed. The nation and its people find excuses. We look for rationalizations that allow us to feel good; right and wrong no longer even enter the equation. Because it's money neutral. It becomes morally neutral. Why, what I do with money has nothing to do with right and wrong, so I can come to church and it doesn't matter. It's because the preacher isn't going to say anything to hurt my feelings anyway, if I'm rich enough.

In fact, another of us good ol' boys, who are neither, will get together, and we'll control a denomination. And we will use the funds from common people to work against their interests, but [we'll] use words they won't understand. Through media we rationalize, to education we beat the drums for war, through poverty we will have no jobs if we don't go along with government and the corporation and the rich.

And what am I gonna do if I don't have a job? Until we all enter into destroying ourselves and the nation that we're afraid to say we don't love? They do not know how to do right, those who steward violence—mighty armies, in other words. And [drag] robbery, oil, and jewels, and another's land into their struggle. When a nation has lost its conscience, when it no longer acts on right and wrong, when it no longer sees its own evil, when you can break down all the barriers, you can go bomb anybody you want. Because they may bomb you—anybody may bomb you. Liberia may bomb you, and they don't even have any bombs. It all gets down to "maybe," but as my grandmother told me, she said, "This is June. May bees aren't flying right now."

There's this little conversation between God and Amos, and God says, *You abuse the poor and demand heavy taxes from the poor.* Oh, you never heard of it. And He says, *You hate honest judges and honest witnesses.* You cheat poor people, you rob the poor of justice, but not the rich. It's the context and it's the truth.

The nation has lost its conscience so that even the church is quiet. But God doesn't stop there. He speaks of His people and what is expected of us. He hates the nation for silencing His creatures. In fact, He says, *I gave you prophets*, and then He says, *I gave you Nazarenes*, and what He meant was, *Those who are pure, and you forced them to drink wine.* He said, *You made alcoholics out of the best you had. You made the best you had less than, so you could have an excuse for your own evil, so you can say, "Well, we're all human, aren't we?"* God has something for us to do. It's not just all those bad people out there, it's those people that are not good enough inside. Listen to Amos: They don't know how to do right.

They dilute and destroy a nation. That was the issue for Amos. That the whole nation was being destroyed, the very conscience was being taken out. Then God says judgment is coming. I don't care whether you're in the first century BC or the twenty-first century AD. Judgment is in the House of the Lord. Judgment is coming. So, God says, *If you really want to live, whether you're a nation or a neighbor, you must stop doing wrong.* God puts the burden on his people, not just on us individuals. But on us as the people of God. Change the conscience of the nation, so talk, so witness. They hate honest witnesses, but you're the witness anyway.

And do it before it's too late. What happened to Jews in Germany, they waited too long. Being at the bottom of that German ladder, even though they had produced the three greatest geniuses of Germany, they were the first to be taken out. It's not an accident. You and I are who God speaks to stronger, we are the people who've got nothing to really lose. We are the people that have more to say. Given our history, we're the most definite voice in Christianity. Considering how God has lifted us from nothing to something, we owe God. The issue is not what God can do for us, but what we can do for God.

Finally, the prophets in every age see the connection. The prophets of any age connect the dots. They see the reason for power is wealth; that's the only reason for it. And the reason for wealth is to oppress. And the reason for oppression is to make millions instead of just dollars. And to make millions of people go to work for you. If you can rob more people and store up more wealth, you can pay the lawyers and the scientists that sup with you. And the more [wealth] they get, the harder their conscience becomes and the greater their full words that don't use things like right and wrong, justice and injustice; they don't use things like that. So it goes on that you silence the churches with faith initiatives from the wealth that you already robbed. Martin King, another prophet, called it directive crime. One crime comes out of another; the crime that you allow today causes another crime to happen tomorrow. The people you let off the hook today are hooking more people tomorrow. The class [of people] you don't want to talk about, [all that] filters down to destroy you, and you are sick and don't even know it. That's the point. How do we stop it?

Amos saw the connect between war and poverty and the misuse of people. Martin King saw the connect between war and poverty and the misuse not only of certain people but also [of what] would lead all the rest of the people into a poverty. Isn't it interesting that even Eisenhower understood King, but he wouldn't say anything until he was out of office? Because the power up above wouldn't let him talk when he was in office. But he said it so well. He said every tank, every gun we buy, every airplane we put in the air, every army we keep, is a robbery of the poor. Because where'd all the money go? Why was this man so willing and quick and ready to go to war without reason? When you declare war, the rich get richer, and the poor get poorer, so they have to go fight the war that you want to fight.

And what does that do? [You] garner into your strongholds the wealth of other nations. That's what war's about anyway, taking the wealth from other nations. But who's gonna get it? You gonna get a dropout and think you feel good. So the taxes are rigged, so that the people who elected him at the top that gave him the multimillions of dollars, so he didn't have to take public funds, so he did not have to be concerned about [himself]. They are the ones that are making money off [war].

Look at the tax break. At best, you're gonna get four hundred dollars. They're breaking the nation. That's the tax break. They're leaving you poor; that's the tax break. They're leaving you dependent upon those that have it, and you don't have it. That's the tax break that's involved.

But we have to see for ourselves that the prophets have told them, in every age, *God will bring your kingdom down*. My grandma, I heard her sing in church. I didn't quite understand what she was talking about. I'm not for certain she understood at all, but I know one thing she understood is that man's kingdom comes down when he defies God. Through God, we have the power to change the nation for good. Through God, we have the power to speak out and protest for all to hear. Through God, we have the power to influence the rich and the powerful; we may not change their hearts, but we can limit their actions. We may not change them, but we can let them know that we know. Oh, there's a power in that. It's hard for a man to sleep at night when he knows that you know that he's misusing you. Every woman knows that, and will not let him sleep until he learns to do right. And if he doesn't hear, she may put some water on the stove. But he won't put it in his mouth!

God has given us the power, more than [what He has given to] any other people. In our lifetime, we stopped the last war. We can stop this one. It has been foreseen that there were white people all over the country that were against the Vietnam War, but they didn't come together until Martin King stood in a church in New York City. And when he preached, the world came together and [was] saying no. And three weeks after he said no, the pope said no, and from that time on, things changed. But it took Black people to change the conscious [people] and stop the silence of the pope, with all that power over the world. You know what I'm saying? We know we can do it because it's been done in our lifetime. We stopped the excesses of racism. I didn't say "racism, I said the excesses of it. And all we have to do is follow up, and we can stop it.

Isn't it interesting that when a CEO gets one thousand times more than his average [worker's salary], one thousand times more—we know there's enough money! But we got to civilize, we got to save the soul of the people that are on the rocks and hiding their head. When I was in Mali, just a few weeks ago, I saw fabulous things that our people did in the tenth, eleventh, and twelfth [centuries]. I'll talk about that some other time. But the thing that stood out to me was a bridge in Mali. It was like our bridge in Selma. We crossed that bridge and went on to stop excesses of those in power in Alabama and across the country.

In Mali, there's a bridge as well. Remember, the people of Mali had to destroy the French who had them in bondage. And then the military—those that had come to sup at the table with the French, [those] who knew only what they'd been taught by the French—became the new dictators. And the people rose up after seven years. But to get to the military, they had to cross a bridge, a wide bridge across the river. People marched across the bridge with nothing in their hands [that could be used] to destroy but a power in their hearts and a will in their minds and a sense of soul that drove them, for freedom and justice, against those who garnered wealth and power.

And thirty of them died. Many of them were pushed over into the river, but they didn't stop coming. Oh, we only marched across our bridge three times, talking about the power of democracy when you use it. Ours is easier to use than any [other such power] in the world, if we would only but use it. It took those people of Mali three months [of] walking across that bridge. We got nobody killed walking across the bridge. They got thirty people killed, young people. And finally, from the middle of January to the middle of March, they marched on across that bridge, and they took over their government. And the people were no longer cheated. They had been robbed, and it'll take them a century to completely get over the robbery. They waited too long. But a line came out that I want to share with you. Somebody was saying to one of the older people during that time, said to them, "You're behind the times now."

And he said: *We were the front line that made it possible for you. We were the shield against evil that made it possible for you to have a decent life. You say that I'm old-timey. That spiritual was not old-timey. The Scripture was not old-timey. The prophets are not old-timey. They are the lifeline upon which we begin. They are the shield upon which we grow and develop.*

Delivered: February 9, 2003
Providence Baptist Church
Atlanta, Georgia

COMMENTARY

Michael Louis Pfleger

C. T. Vivian draws on the prophet Amos to challenge the very government and culture of America over the hypocrisy of their words and actions. Vivian goes beyond the surface of Scripture to the substance of how people in power have used their money and influence to do whatever they wanted while exploiting the masses of the poor. He exposes a world in which the wealthy and powerful have gone rogue and trampled the powerless and impoverished, destroying lives and using a system designed for that purpose to keep the masses down. Vivian describes how the system of America has been set up to play on vulnerability and use the law to keep people captive.

Vivian reminds us that violence is not done just by picking up a weapon but also by creating a structure that keeps people in bondage and prevents them from reaching their God-given purpose and destiny, that violence is setting up systems and creating laws that promote and sustain poverty, that rob the masses of their potential to succeed. Vivian proclaims to us that the masters of the poor are, at every level of society, throwing crumbs while building up billions for themselves and their families.

Vivian challenges us to have the courage to pull back the curtain and expose the hidden hands that are pulling the strings to create and sustain an unjust and unequal society and world, and to acknowledge that we are being puppet-mastered by those who don't know how to do right, even as they speak hollow words of caring and justice. Vivian proclaims that the very system which has been entrusted with protecting the rights of people has determined that only certain people have rights, and the others have been sentenced to captivity by the arrogant and entitled. And until we identify them and dismantle the laws and system they've put in place to keep them empowered, they will continue to control every aspect of society. And they will continue to seek to brainwash the people to make them think injustice and inequality are okay.

Vivian tells us that the problem has its roots in the thinking that the problem is the poor when, in fact, the root of the problem is the rich and powerful who have lost their conscience and moral compass and have sought to hijack Jesus and His teachings to support themselves. That in fact, the real Jesus, the revolutionary Jesus, is a threat to them because the real Jesus demands exposing the very ones who have created the poor and use power to keep others poor and powerless.

Vivian does not leave us to our anger or hopelessness. Rather, he challenges us to have courage, determination, and commitment to come together and bring down the walls of injustice. He warns us that when a nation loses its conscience and moral compass, it doesn't know how to do right, because it no longer knows right from wrong and can no longer even see its own evil. Perhaps most importantly, Vivian challenges us to recognize that if the church gets hijacked by that nation and becomes part of it, it becomes silent to the evil and abandons its responsibility to be the prophet it has been called to be. But when the prophets rise up—such prophets as Amos, King, and, yes, Vivian—just as evil has a rippling effect, so does righteousness, and that righteousness can and will overcome, because the word of God is still true.

6

The Evil of Racism

STRANGELY ENOUGH, AS much as I've talked about the issue of racism, and for as many years—way back when the earth's crust was still cooling, I was still talking about racism, right?—and the thing is, no one has asked me what Mack[1] asked me. He says: Talk about the evil of racism, the depth of the evil of racism. And one of the reasons no one has asked me is because we so take it as a social phenomenon, and we talk about it in psychological terms as though that's separated from, and we talk about it in sociological terms as though that's separated from... But we really don't talk about what racism really is. And that it is probably—at least I want to say—the most devastating evil in American life today and has been—not just today.

And the way you do this, of course, is you do a little prologue, and you talk about what has gone before. But I just want to give you one quote because I want you to see that in American life, we've always seen it as a matter of sin, right? For instance, Frederick Douglass says, "Can American justice, liberty, civilization, and American Christianity be made to include and even protect alike and forever all—American citizens and the rights that have been guaranteed to them?"

And I mention the Pope's statement today.[2] And I'm going to repeat it because I think it is so basic, all right? That there can be no truth until we eliminate the very vestiges of racism. Truth—we're talking about moral and spiritual terms, we're talking about the very essence of our humanity, of the things that cause this community to be worth it. And Jesus, of course, should always be on your mind as we think together: It's the truth that sets us free.

Now we haven't too much time, and so I'm going to only hit the tops of things, and leave the fact that you, with your background and understanding coming up out of a Christian understanding of life—I don't want to use that term so that it's so broad: *Christian understanding of life*. I want to think of it in terms of you looking at people, and what Christianity is about [being] more about your relationship to humanity, and what we do, and how we appreciate and understand human beings as God's creatures. That's what it's all about, right? And you can't even begin to talk about evil until you see the humanity, our humanity interrelated, working together. That's where evil shows itself. And as we think about it, that's where we have to be.

And what I'm really saying is that racism is the ultimate evil in human community. And that the ultimate evil is organized, institutionalized, nationalized disunity of humankind based on something that is part of our common humanity given by God but redefined by man. We take the matter of color, which is one of these [parts], and then reinterpret it so that, in fact, it is destructive and is a denial of what God's talking about. Using race as racism is the reason that our disunity means that it can never really be stopped. As I was saying to the brother, I was praying to hit these things quickly—but I want to say them well—that we seldom even define evil. But until we can even define it in some meaningful way, it's difficult to even understand what it is when we're looking at it. A way I like to think about it, because of the depth of it, is that you can always tell evil because it always destroys itself.

See, and when you begin to look, it becomes destructive of everything that you would consider decent and good. You take it on as an acceptable social form, and it ends up destroying your very ability to socialize. You take it on as a part of that culture, and it ends up destructive for that very culture. And that racism—for instance, because of who we are, let me just start with one of them. If the Bible is to be accepted as the standard, as love fulfills the law and the prophets, that racism is the denial of all love, hmm? Racism destroys every one of the Ten Commandments, for instance. The racist—the First Commandment, "Thou shalt love the Lord. . ."—the racist person places himself before God. He denies God His own creation. See, he defines for himself what is God's relationship to him, the racist.

Furthermore, he decides what laws of God to obey. He refuses to obey God and decides his relationships with all of God's creations. And then he denies the sacredness of all other people but those that look like him. It's the depth of this thing! And at the same time, he demands God still treat him as though he is a special being. How evil can you get? And then, when he organizes God's church, [he] places his symbols on it and says that's him.

Just because of time, shall we say as homework, take Exodus 20, set it up in front of you, take the commandments, lay them out one at a time, and decide for yourself, just one, two, three, for yourself, and see how racism destroys each of the commandments. Go right on down to covetousness. [When] we really think of it, we think a good deal [about] how racism is used in breaking the Tenth Commandment. Right? The North Atlantic slave trade, which is a crime against humanity, [as it was] just declared by the UN—we had to go over and fight for it, but [that] made it true—but the point being that those [who] controlled the UN were all part of the North Atlantic slave trade. That's why it's been so hard. Now, when we look at that, is that what was really involved? Because slavery was pretty normal all over the world. It's the North Atlantic slave trade that has been the greatest crime against humanity, but it was the greatest misuse of man, because it was the one [that] for the sake of profit and greed worked people to death. I'm talking about racism.

[So it is] that, in the islands, for instance, the average life of anyone brought there was fourteen years. They were worked to death in fourteen years. You find the bones and—I don't really want to spend time on that—and you can see how they were worked, because of what's left in the bone and how the bone has been misused in various parts of the body. We're talking about the depth of sin. The central concept—and we have to think about each one of those persons in terms of the dehumanizing of a whole continent. That's when slavery isn't just slavery and something that just happened over here. It dehumanized a whole continent. An entire continent that's four and a half times bigger than the United States by itself! It's the depth of it all! And, just for quickness, isn't [it] that the central concept of Christianity is love? Without love, you do not have Christianity! Talk about it any way you want to. In terms of what you can do, Christ's very importance is love. Otherwise, all we do is look at him and say he was the son of God. From where we are, the concept is love, and the ultimate is love, all right? Racism has totally torn apart our community; never has there been an American community—because of racism. *The depth of it all.*

Now, let's look at some lines. We'll take the lines. I don't want to spell them out, because of time—that racism has and does destroy more people than any other factor in American life—has been doing it longer, has been doing it both psychologically and physically. Furthermore, its victims have no reason to believe that it's ever going to end, that it's ever gonna end. Think of what that means. Remember when we talked about the pressure of just being in here a few hours? Hmm. And what it does to your mind, what it does to your psychology, what it does to your levels of endurance? We have no reason to believe it's ever going to stop with our children and our grandchildren. I look at my grandchildren. I have no reason to believe. All I'm hoping to do is to halfway protect them from white racism, my grandchildren. And I can look back at five generations before me, and then I know what they went through, hopefully that I wouldn't, and five generations later I am [still going through it], six generations [even].

Let's look at this again. See the violence of America—and I could leave this out, in one sense, but I just want you to see it—the violence in America towards nonwhites as accepted and approved violence of the Ku Klux Klan. It wasn't just the Klan; it was the whole society. That's what I mean by approved by—you didn't have to be a Klansman just to kill Black folk. If you wanted to, any white man could kill any Black [person], and that was that.

What was it about? To make us work at the lowest wages, live in the worst housing, be easily raped and beaten, be subservient to even the lowest level of white people to make them feel good. And the society would be quiet about it, that's what it meant. And it meant that if you were Latin, that you could be shot off of your ranch, murdered by any white boys that came along and wanted your land. And you had a culture superior to theirs, and did. The Aztecs were superior to the Europeans coming in.

Okay, let's look—I want you to be able to see what sin is. For over a half century after slavery, this nation made blackface comedy their basic humor. When it was so low and so degrading and so dehumanizing that Black people wouldn't do it, [white people] blackened their faces and did it. And for over a half century, that was the way of deciding what a Black man is and ought to be. Now, who is going to take such people—buffoons—seriously? Right? But what that does is to say that you can decide the image of God's people. But of course, you automatically then can't say they're God's people if they're that low, but we who misuse them are. What this does to us in the sense of God.

Let's look at another one of these [costs]. As a result of racism, no minority person—except a very few, and I have to say I know this is true of Black people, but it's broadly true of others in this country—will ever know what they might have been, might have become, might have done for themselves, their family, their own people, or their country. We'll never know what they might have done, might have been, might have become. It is the destruction of human personality. What we're talking about is what God has given each human being destroyed by other human beings and by their minions, so that God's world, God's hopes, God's dreams for humankind cannot be fulfilled on a meaningful timetable.

You know, do you see God? That's what this is all about. This is all about God. It is about suffering with God, it is about seeing God, it is about the mind of God, it is about the heart of God. Do you think we can think that God is simply up there, somewhere, roaming around, and has no appreciation for the fact that multimillions of people suffer because of his so-called people? And that he takes that lightly? And that it doesn't really matter; it's just history rolling along? But we love thee, Lord. And we'll even place a music behind it and sing it to you, Lord.

Thirdly, America cannot solve any social problem until we deal honestly and forthrightly with racism. See, the problem with stuff like that is it sounds bad to us because, hey, we're all college-educated in this room. Take it from the standpoint of spiritual life and worth, and we're not simply talking about a social problem. We're talking about housing for people, hunger of people and little children every day. We're talking about education. When she sat there and said, *Children starve to death in my neighborhood*—huh? We're talking about wherever you go in the world, that would be a sin!

And the Christian church sits there, preaching every Sunday, and is willing to be basically no more than the garbageman for those that control the culture, instead of putting [a] finger in their face and telling them, *You are a murderer of God's people.* Because we don't have the guts to do that, because we go along, because to go along means that we're going to be socially acceptable, and to be socially acceptable means maybe we can raise enough money to keep the bricks in place. I—no, I shouldn't. I was going to say "pardon me," but I'm not gonna pardon me. You think of all the problems of urban life, all the sprawl, the use of human resources, the suffering, the waste, and the wealth that could be used to help people.

Now, fourthly: Every value in American life is compromised by racism. Every value. We can never become, as individuals or a collective three hundred million people, what we say in our hearts we want to be. This is not just a compromise of those that are destroyed because our values are compromised, right? We allow other people to suffer. It starts with our allowing our values to be compromised. And others suffer as a result of it. And we can't escape from that because—how believable is it? It is believable because the church itself is racist. It is no longer a matter of being nice.

I want to pause for a moment. We need breaks and pauses, so people can see the importance of it!

It's no longer a matter of white people being nice to Black people and brown people. Even if you weren't Christian, it's no longer being nice. It's a matter of saving the very soul of white people. Remember, the only reality is in the mind of God, and he doesn't care that you're white. Maybe down here, but not up there! The only reality is in the mind of God. God's concern is not that we're white or Black or yellow or brown. His concern is that we are his children. He, and we, can destroy ourselves, and God can hurt, but He doesn't save you if you're not willing to save yourself. We can argue over the theology of it, as someone said this morning, right? But hey, please, let's never think that, with our theology, God is a fool, and don't ever think that we'll outthink God because of the words we write in books. We might think that, but our theology books are God's comic books.

It is necessary to see the sin of blaming the victim. It's immoral to throw stones and hide the hand. To create the conditions that destroy people and then act as though you had no part in it. To do nothing to change those conditions and act like you had no part in it, all right? It's immoral to break a man's leg and blame him for limping. It's immoral to create a double standard and then blame the victim. It's immoral to blame a man for being on welfare when you created the work policies that created his poverty. It's immoral to tear couples and people from each other because of sexual racism. It's immoral to say we're all the same and then organize our society so that we don't have the same freedoms and are treated differently, and then organize the church in the same way. It's immoral to know that white racism is the problem that has created the Black condition that millions and millions of people have been forced to live in for hundreds of years and act as though you know nothing really about it. It is in fact immoral to know that you have white privileges not given to other groups, and to act as though the spatial privilege doesn't really exist. It really doesn't exist. We're all alike here, are we not?

They become questions, but they never become statements, because we know it's [all] a lie. The church lives with racist immorality as a way of life. That is the thing that sickens me most, huh? And that we come together to pray to God in the midst of the immorality that destroys His people, and it's supposed to be the place where we get refueled to go out and help people. No victim of racism can be less than dehumanized in a racist, controlled society.

Among the deep sins of racism is that racism is structured to demand that we are strangers and demand that we remain strangers. And that we remain that way. Pull your Christian text out, and talk the text, and even preach the text of who is my neighbor, and add Jesus's answer. Now, we've done that for three hundred years, but in American churches—we're still strangers. And it's something that, out of the Christian church more than the other, we should have learned, because Moses understood: that you open the gates to the stranger, open your doors to the stranger. Moses understood that! How many thousand years ago? And we haven't caught up with it yet? Something's very, very wrong, but the depth of the sin that keeps us from understanding, that's what I'm talking about.

Let's look at another, because I'm trying to jump ahead—but this is my recent favorite, because you see, what has bothered me that neither the press nor the church, nor the institutions of this society would get to: What is the bottom core of the civil rights movement? Read the literature. The central core of the civil rights movement was not political or economic, even though that's what America wanted to do—answer back politically, answer back economically. When you start looking at what is it that people don't want to do when protesting, and you can gain more truth [this way] than you can any other way. The central issue of the civil rights movement was—and I'll say, under Martin King—whose God is God? Is God a god of racism, is God a god of separation, is God a god of disunity, is God a god of prejudice, or is God a god of truth and justice and love? And it can't be both! Cut it any way you want; He cannot be both! That was the issue, and that was the issue you could never get in the newspapers. But until the issue of whose God is god is settled, you can't ever get there. You can't destroy racism until you deal with the issues of God. Whose God is God is the central issue of the civil rights movement.

We have to ask ourselves, Is God a god of glass ceilings, is God a god of cheap education for some and good education [for] others, is God a god of [the] ghettoized, is God a god of sexualized racism? See, what we have to understand is [that] God had it so that we worked it out in the South, where it's worse. See, we separate things, but the senators and the governors and the mayors and the policemen and the citizens who elected them to their evil, racist work were church people. I think God worked it out so well, he had white Baptists dealing with Black Baptists. Because we were the problem in the South. And if you're in the South, the Southern Baptist church rules it; oh, others exist there, but the [Baptists] rule it. And they decide who's gonna be the senators and the governors and the mayors and all the rest of that. But I want you to understand [that] God's working it out when I say that. Let me skip a couple pages. And remember that all those voters were church people, trained by the church. And the church people going out there to vote would have not voted for them if they were not racist. We're talking about the institution that is the value-producing agency of the society. And until that's clear, the rest of it is conversation. Let's just add right quick the sin of lost opportunity.

Racism has robbed the American church of most of its spiritual credibility and vitality. I was at the World Conference Against Racism, I was one of the speakers there—just drop that in there—and the thing that stood out for me: We had the whole world there, of NGOs, of people representing people's leadership, not just elected officials up here somewhere. And they agreed that racism and the North Atlantic slavery and colonialism were the worst things that happened to the world in the last five hundred years. Nongovernmental organizations. These are people's organizations, not put together by government and supported by government. They're supported by the people.

For many of these countries, to send somebody to South Africa is an extremely expensive affair, but they had their representatives there so they could make their voices heard against racism. I'm telling you how bad it is, yet we're talking about our mission, and we're going out to save the world, and the world's just saying, *If we can save ourselves from you, we'll be all right*. So that you really have to see the depth of this thing.

In fact, let me ask you a question, just to end this part of it. You must understand that the Christian church is the church of racism, it is the church of slavery, it is the church of colonialism. The most destructive force in modern civilization. That's our church! And we are the church of American culture. And seen as such, we're tied to it! Either we save it, or we shall go down with it. Which is most important to you? American culture or Christ? The central issue is Christ or culture. And God has given us every opportunity to save American culture, and it's up to us to do it.

Let me just ask you a question right quick. Because this is the question the world is dealing with as we go out into it: How large would the Christian church be in ten years if you took away the white Jesus and replaced it with any other color, particularly brown or Black? How large would the Christian church in America be in ten years? Maybe I should have said how small would it be in ten years, huh? Maybe easier to count. You see what I'm saying.

But the racism of the Christian church is mostly responsible for the fact that, in the Black community—let's put it this way. The Muslim church is now the fastest growing church in America—the fastest growing religion in America, that's what I should say. Thirty percent of that growth is Black alone, and we're only 10 percent of the population. I want you to get that. Both of those are important. But I know, in the Black community, we wouldn't have lost our cause if it wasn't for racism. In Detroit, Black people will tell you in a minute, Muslims in particular, of the racism of your church, am I right? And they will say to you, *Who wants to be a Christian? Those white people are racist, and you are doing no more than following around after them.* Isn't that the kind of language you hear out there when you try to, in fact, evangelize in the Black community? Am I right, bro? Whose problem—not us! White Christianity! Remember, we got a world out there we're dealing with. That's if we're serious.

So, let me ask you another question. We've come to the point that racism has put us in the position where we've got to ask this question as minorities: Can the future of American Christianity be entrusted to the leadership of white American Christians? That's a serious question. Not just something thought up. And it didn't just roll off my tongue; it's been building.

Now the great sin of racism makes one group feel superior—another great sin in itself. But while one group feels superior, it makes the victim hate themselves. That's sin, that's evil! That's evil! And yet, as an American church, we've talked of evil as being drink, smoke, and dance, right? As long as you didn't smoke and drink and dance, and maybe run after someone's wife occasionally, you're all right, and we can forgive you for that, if you come and kneel down at the altar. But you see what altar are you gonna kneel down to here? This is the stuff that counts, right? Racism tries to create a world where there's no way to end the suffering of the victim, nor any way for the class that in fact victimizes them to allow the victimized to be free. How evil can you get, hmm? And that can go on for centuries—not fifteen minutes, not five years, not ten years, not the fifty years that the Jewish synagogue talked about. It goes on forever.

I want to give you an ultimate piece. Time's running out, but I want to give you an ultimate piece. I was saying to a friend who's a speaker at the Fourth World Conference on Non-Violence—and so, a couple of us were at the speakers table, and we went off in a special place so that we [could] discuss. And they give you special pins and ribbons to wear, but the point [is] one of the guys there—Bill Moyers is his name—he's not *the* Bill Moyer you're familiar with. He's a writer, and he's one of the best people ever to deal with the topic of community organizations, by the way. So, we're sitting around talking, and so I mentioned something about developing countries—because I've been to South Africa three times last year, so it's been on my mind—so I mentioned developing countries, and he laughed, and so I wondered why he was laughing, and I said, "What do you mean?"

And he said, "Oh, you mean the 'never-to-be-developed countries.'" There's the language, by itself. Do you have to say anything else when we live in a world where 17 percent of the people, white, control 53 percent of the materials of this world and use them up faster than they can ever be replaced? And the rest of them, Europe, has already used up its [materials], and America's next. We're holding up the oil from over there, and taking the oil from over there, and most of it is coming out of Africa. Do you think they're going to allow those African countries to develop, when we're spending three hundred billion dollars on guns and weapons, et cetera, and when we have the power to either heal AIDS or cause it to happen?

In Africa, that's a real question. When I say, "cause it to happen," they do not think it's all accident. See, they're seeing us think ahead, clearing off a continent so that we can have the goods out of it. See, I'm trying to tell you the depth of racism! Because Christianity does not see the value of other people's lives, and they know it. They then can begin to see us as we could never see ourselves. But when we look at those that control our culture, we're not for certain whether it's not true either. So that, when you look at it, where does that place us?

Finally: We have to understand that this sin is seen by the fact that flesh is made more important than our faith. That's what racism does. It makes our flesh more important than our faith. It decides that color is more important than the church. It decides that Western culture is more important than Christ. It makes race more important than our religion. It makes money more important than mankind. This is the evil and [the] consequences, and it's against any understanding of God. And that the Christian church has never been able to fully accept the humanity of nonwhites. Truly accept—I'm not saying they won't let them be a member. Of course, there's always a few of us who can infiltrate here and there. But the American Christian church has never really accepted other people as fully human. So, the question has to be asked: Can the Christian church fully live with anyone that is not white? We can send missions, but can we live with them, right?

What hurts me personally is that the church has failed Jesus, the church has failed God, and the church has failed people, all humanity. We had the answer, but we refuse to give it the commitment that makes the difference. And for cowardly reasons, that's what hurts. We go worship and look at a cross of the committed and the crucified and suffering, and then we are in denial about the obvious, and that denial causes us to be passive about the evil, and we discriminate in the body of Jesus himself. And the cock has continued to crow for three centuries, and we act as though we can't hear. And that's the short form.

Delivered: November 28, 2001
Location Undetermined

COMMENTARY

Earle J. Fisher

As a people, we miss this type of preaching—the depth, insight, acuity, and audacity to address core issues instead of galivanting around a gospel of greed, self-help, and superficiality. We need so much more of what C. T. Vivian presents in "The Evil of Racism." This sermon is both philosophical and practical. It is topical but still deeply theological.

Vivian is in a rhetorical quandary as he tries to exegetically contextualize racism—a modern phenomenon—using an ancient text, the Bible. Although he doesn't go as far as anachronism by imposing contemporary realities on ancient contexts, he does take liberties in drawing parallels between then and now, ones the average churchgoer can relate to.

The homiletician in me desires more of a grounding in a particular biblical text. Exodus 20 is presented as a backdrop. I wish it were foregrounded at the offset and woven throughout the fabric of the sermon more clearly and concretely. That said, I still appreciate that it's not a surface-level exposition of a Scripture dripping with white-evangelical sentiment. It can't be. Because this sermon is about the evil of racism—it's the precursor to Willie James Jennings's epic *The Christian Imagination: Theology and the Origins of Race*, Barbara Holmes's essential *Race and the Cosmos*, and J. Kameron Carter's treatise *Race: A Theological Account*.

What I celebrate most fully is Vivian's unflinching confrontation of an explicit and enduring evil: racism. He names it. He dives directly into its deep waters while wading in the wonders of divine revelation. He calls it sin, unequivocally. No meandering. No vacillation. No compromising or negotiating with evil. No quintessential Negro-tokenism or white evangelical theology in blackface. "The depth of it all."[3]

Oh, how we miss this type of preaching in most (Black!) churches in the twenty-first century. And Vivian is right to call the church to account for its/our complicity and duplicity. Because until we transform and reconstitute our churches toward Black liberation, the evil of racism will continue to be swept under the rug. It will keep flying under our religious radar in exchange for more pious prosperity, pastoral and congregational popularity, and individual and institutional pleasure.

Vivian is right: We seldom define evil—in times past or in present. In the book *Black Christian Nationalism: New Directions for the Black Church*, Reverend Albert Cleage contends thatwe define our enemy.[4] This is what Vivian does sermonically. He defines racism as the ultimate evil that is an "organized, institutionalized, nationalized disunity of humankind based on something that is part of our common humanity given by God but redefined by man." Preach. Black. Man.

Part theologian, part Theo-therapist, Vivian displays oratorical acumen and philosophical fortitude. He evokes what Frank B. Wilderson III will term *Afropessimism* while yet holding on to the hope of a loving, living, and liberating God that transcends human category and comprehension.[5] That God is God.

As a people, we miss this type of preaching—even the quintessential Black Baptist-multiple-conclusion closing(s). That form of Black preaching endures.

As a people, we miss this type of preaching. We need so much more of it. God knows we do.

7

Peter: The Profound Nigger

(Also titled The Profound Peter) Acts 5:29

IN THE FIFTH chapter of Acts, we see Peter before the Sanhedrin—a simple fisherman standing before the power structure of his time. Yet this man was dominating the encounter. This simple fisherman proved to be the profound Peter.

As we think of this encounter, we must realize that it is related to our own time. We need to see Peter. If we are to speak to this nation, we must see vividly the picture of Peter before the Sanhedrin. In this encounter, Peter laid down a principle—a principle whereby dedicated men could break conventional patterns and bring vitality to their own time. His statement that we must obey God, rather than men, puts forward a basic principle which enables us to gain a functional understanding of the encounter between secular and religious man. In this short sentence, Peter offers us an insight into what it takes to break the impasse between a person's understanding of his own culture. The basis of the struggle for freedom that transcends the state is revealed.

Peter recognized the great issue of his time, and he saw that this great issue had to be settled for the Christian conscience. The growth, development, and validity of the Christian church depended on it.

The church in every age must meet the great crisis of its time or it is not worthy of its time. Whenever the Christian church does not confront the crisis of its time, decline follows on its inaction. We win men by having the answer for the problems of men. We can win the masses of men when we have come to positions on the problems of the masses of men.

If we can find within our Scriptures the means to answer the great issues of our time, then we will speak and act with conviction. Then we need not tell men [that] Christ is the answer. Men will tell us [that] Christ is the answer.

Let us look at Peter standing before the Sanhedrin. Peter was defying the court. But the Sanhedrin was taking its orders from Rome. Rome was behind [the court], with the short Roman sword, saying to all Israel: "Step in line. Obey the Sanhedrin, or we will cut you down in the streets of Jerusalem." So, Peter was not only defying the culture and the cultural establishment of Israel; he was also defying the laws and the lawmakers of Rome. He was defying those who set law and order.

Why was he doing this? If we look closely at Peter, we see that he was a man on fire. He had seen an idol being raised up—an idol that had been raised up to destroy the church he loved. He saw a law, created by the mind of man, that was dramatically opposed to the kingdom of God which his Christ had taught. Peter had to choose, and we see Peter in this passage set a torch burning in Jerusalem when he says: "I will not bow down to idols and false ideas. I must obey God rather than men."

Since Peter, there have been others who have diagnosed their historical situation and have seen the idol of their time. They knew that, if they were really to follow Christ, they had to find a way to encounter the idol, or else the idol would place the faith of millions in jeopardy. Those who were faithful declared with Peter, "We must obey God rather than men."

A few years later Paul saw the issue in terms of the separation of religion and race. The central issue of Paul's great encounter with the church of his time was whether God's message in Jesus was only for Jews, or whether it was for all men. Paul maintained that Jesus broke down "the middle wall of partition" existing between men. He saw the issue, fought the good fight, and was able to create a universal church. He lifted the Christian church from the national tentacles of a negative racial past. He obeyed God rather than men.

Let us look at another age. We see Martin Luther's Germany. Luther saw the idol of the organized power structure set against human conscience. He saw the conscience of man dominated by the power of the Roman church and the government of Germany. The issue became Christ and conscience or church and control. When he decided to creatively reform the church, he caught the torch of the profound Peter. He stood on the floor of the German parliament and declared, "Here I stand; I can do no other, so help me God." He was echoing the words of Peter: "I must obey God rather than men."

In seventeenth-century England, John Bunyan saw the idol of English laws set against man's desire to be able to seek the Gospel as he chooses. History records John Bunyan in prison, but he was preaching from behind bars. The officials came to Bunyan and said, "Bunyan, if you will stop preaching as you do and stop saying the things you say, we will let you out of this jail." Without hesitation, Bunyan replied: "I would remain here throughout my days before I will make a butchery of my conscience." The torch Peter had lighted was still burning.

Martin Luther King was in the jails of the Southland. In the Birmingham jail, he wrote a distinguished letter. It is one of the great modern Christian epistles. He wrote that there is a higher law than the laws of men. The issue is morality, not legality, and we must obey God rather than men. The torch of Peter had been passed on.

It started with Peter, who understood out of the heat of his own action, out of the depth of his own conviction, that the basis on which Christians remain in this society has something to do with a profound faith in God, a deep and profound obedience to God. We think of Peter as the simple fisherman, but there is something so profound in him that the great mind of Paul had to bow, and the learned mind of Luther had to understand, and the simplicity of Bunyan could receive it, and Martin Luther King still heard his meaning.

The lesson is clear. If we are worthy of saving the Christian church where we are, we, too, must see the issues of our own time.

Let us look at the issue of our own time, our own age, and our own country. The issue is race, and the idol is racism. If we are to confront the great idol of racism that has been raised up in our own time, we have to do what Peter did. We must assess the situation and be able to stand and say with him that we will use our energy, our time, our resources to destroy the idol, so the true Christ can be worshiped.

Let us see Peter and try to understand what was profound about this man, as he stood before the court. Maybe you and I can examine the model, gain some insight, confront the structure of church or state, and then destroy the idol.

The fifth chapter of Acts shows us the confrontation in the courtroom. The court scene is filled with tension and remarkable contrasts. Look at the contrast: Here was Peter, dressed in the robe of the streets, just a piece of cloth thrown across his shoulder, torn as a result of a beating, dirty from the prison cell, his feet showing through his sandals, which were still covered with the dirt of the street. [Against] Peter sat his judges, scented with the fine perfumes of Rome. Here they sat, in their finest silken robes with the wide borders of those who represented religion.

Contrast, if you will, this Peter, uneducated, knowing they did not care about him, with these men who had gone to the finest schools of their day. Among them were pride-filled lawyers and theologians who were very much at home in this courtroom, which they felt they owned and knew they dominated.

This court was the creation of power to complement power. Its heightened arches and architectural grandeur were designed to make a lowly Peter bow before them. Contrast these men, who had soldiers standing by to do their bidding, with Peter, who stood by himself, unable to command forces or move men, so it seemed. Contrast the Sanhedrin, with its lawyers all around it, with Peter, who had no one to represent him.

They saw Peter. They saw him as poor and ignorant. They knew him well. He was the despised, abused, powerless peon of Israel. In short, he was the Nigger. Peter was the Nigger of Israel. His poverty added to his despicable condition. He was the common worker; all he could do to make a living was catch fish. He was dark, black from being in the sun. "How could God speak through a Nigger?" they thought.

They knew what to do with him. Put the Nigger down. He claims to know God. How could God even want to give dignity to his kind? Put this Nigger down. And now! If you don't, then watch it. Other Niggers will be acting proud, talking loud, walking around, mouthing sound, getting louder and louder and louder. Put the Nigger down. If you don't, the other wretched ones will expect consideration. Why, even woman, the universal Nigger, may stop being Nigger!

The Sanhedrin saw Peter as its opposite. In the minds of these judges, the despised were the despised, never to be anything else. They built their attitudes into every schoolroom, public display, public pronouncement; into every court of law, every decision-making guideline, and every institution. Peter was their Nigger, and no power could change it. Why should they deal with this small-time religionist? Why should they have to deal with this uneducated, powerless, dirty Nigger?

But Peter did not see himself as they saw him. How they saw him and how, since Jesus, he saw himself were quite different. He had been working toward the day when the Sanhedrin would have to deal with him—personally. He wanted a confrontation with the power of Israel. The nation itself would have to deal with the truth of his existence. What they thought of him would no longer matter. What they would know he thought of himself would be of final importance.

Now, they were dealing with him personally, on his terms. He had preached and then waited in the courtyard, so they would drag him into the courtroom. Now he was there before the leaders of the high court. This was his confrontation, on his terms. Suddenly we see a light in Peter's eyes. He had planned it this way!

The confrontation was on his terms. How else could the despised gain dignity? How else could an uppity Nigger prove he was a profound, articulate human being? For them to deal with him personally meant the affirmation of Peter as man. Not because they wanted it, but because he wanted it.

Without the confrontation on his terms, there would still be no manhood for him. As long as the Sanhedrin decided the basis upon which his life was to be lived, he would always be the despised—and millions would be like him. The Sanhedrin had to deal with Peter on his terms. He had planned it this way. The Nigger had planned to become a man!

Peter the new creature is apparent in this confrontation. He was in charge of the moment and impervious to the destructive forces of Rome and Israel. Only the new creature as man can bring other men fully to the Man. There was something in Peter that made him realize what his Christ had already taught him. Christ had taught him that the long Roman cross is stronger than the short

Roman sword. Those men willing to stand with courage and willing to die for their manhood can and will be men. Regardless of the law and so-called order, manhood can be gained. A profound lesson for the underdogs of mankind and for the Niggers of this world. Peter could bring forth by his own courage, by his own learning, and by his own deep sense of spiritual being a new sense of manhood. Now the despised everywhere would gladly hear him.

It was Peter who was in charge of the Sanhedrin that day. It was Peter who had taken over the court of the land. It was he who stood. It was from him that the new force could flow. Peter saw himself in a new way and forced the Sanhedrin to see him in a new way, too. When the man who was once a slave or is still a Nigger begins to look at himself, he is about the business of salvation. Seeing himself in a new way allows him to witness to other men, so, they too, can become part of the new order and become new beings. A new identity emerges; a new birth takes place; a new man is born.

Peter knew Jesus was the new man. But now he realized that Jesus had also once been Nigger. Was not Jesus Nigger when Peter met him? Had not Jesus been just another one of them? Jesus had not been a part of the high order. Never before had he thought of Jesus as Nigger, for Jesus had such wisdom, such strength, such purpose. But was not Jesus all soul?

Was it not this Nigger who had given him the courage to go beyond himself? Now it was Peter who could take pride and also stand. Was it not Jesus who had been free enough to speak out and fight for others? Now Peter was free enough to stand up and fight for other men. Was it not Jesus who had had the insight to take the entire society and put it up tight? Peter saw himself as the man continuing the work of his master. That was why he was in the court in the first place. He had been protesting.

Jesus's protest had made of Peter a protesting Peter, a man of action. Let's look at him again. He was there because he had been provoking the populace against the cheap religionists who sought to accept some people and leave others, to elevate the rich and forget the poor. He had led a demonstration in the temple. Peter was in court in the first place because he had been demonstrating, he had been organizing. Such actions were a challenge to the authorities, and for this reason Peter was brought before the court. Those who were in power thought they could destroy this man in their court. Everything in the courtroom was designed, calculated, and planned to make criminals of the people who appeared there. They would challenge his character, blemish his being, and push him back into niggerdom.

But Peter is no longer the Nigger Man. Peter knows how to take the initiative from the power people. Peter stands and declares that he must obey God rather than men. In this obedience to a higher power, he affirms his manhood.

But there is something else about Peter that must also be mentioned. Look at him in the courtroom. Here the word had become flesh. Isn't it unusual? All of us know that we should obey God, and we go around saying so occasionally. But listeners take it lightly because we who say it take it so lightly. That tells us something about the man Peter. There was something about Peter's profound presence that forced them to take him seriously.

Someone once said the problem with their minister was that such great things were being said by such a small man. One of the problems of the Christian faith is that we say such great things but we offer such little service. As a result, the society cannot take us seriously. The confrontation is not there.

The confrontation between the church and the secular world comes only when we are serious. Because the secular world is as serious as murder. The secular world is as serious as repression and isolation. The secular world is as serious as death. But we can only meet it when we are as serious as life.

There is something else, I believe, Peter teaches us. Peter understood that the gaining of manhood is more than an individual matter; it is a group experience. Peter had been leading a demonstration; that was why he was in jail and in the courtroom in the first place. The demonstration had become the means of revealing to the people who they were and what newness was inherent within them. The people were looking for something beyond niggerdom—a new manhood and sense of values beyond the religions of the day.

Peter had preached from the housetops until enough men had understood and were willing to demonstrate for other men. Peter made men free enough so that they were willing to struggle for the freedom of others.

To fight for yourself alone never allows you to become fully yourself. Not to help your neighbor to become, is not to live in fullness. To allow yourself to be, and not to help your neighbor to become, is in fact an act of treason against mankind. It is to keep men niggardly and to deny them the fullness of their manhood.

The story of Peter's appearance before the high court of Israel concludes with what looks like a defeat; he is beaten. But there is a mystery in life. Those who challenge the power of the culture see God act in strange and mysterious ways, his wonders to perform. It seemed necessary to the Sanhedrin, as an assertion of its power, to have Peter beaten. But the beating allowed Peter to prove to the people that he bore the mark of the Lord Jesus. The Sanhedrin's act of petty power became Peter's passport to credibility.

It may seem that Peter's work was in vain because the court did not repent and the conservatives were not radicalized. Not so. Peter and the other Christians now knew the power of Jesus could take them anywhere. The encounter had given them new status and power. Every Nigger had become closer to becoming a man. The question "Will you obey God or man?" was to be echoed in many ways through the years. Two thousand years later, in Mississippi, they were to sing, "Which side are you on, boys? Which side are you on? Will you follow Christ Jesus or Governor Ross Barnett?"

Peter may not have won over the Sanhedrin, but his words and action did have tremendous consequences. Peter had acted without fear; he could now live without fear of power structures. He had acted on faith; he could live daily by faith. He was free to proclaim a higher law, not because the court said so but because the power of Jesus enabled him to do so.

Peter's love was so great! He placed himself in peril for the saving of all Israel. His love caused him to try and save even the principalities and powers of the world. His love for the people in the street was so great that he offered his own life to lift them from niggerdom to universal manhood. Profound Peter. No matter what the cost. Peter's love became an active confrontation on behalf of the wounded neighbor. Peter's love and risk of life were not sentimental. He demanded conversion. His love demanded that the iron brace of discipline be placed on the twisted limbs of the soul of Israel. Peter was radical. He cried "Repent! Liberate! Power to the people!" The conservative leaders of the secular religion cried, "Repress! Kill! Put Niggers down!" The liberals said, "Compromise! Put it off! Time will work it out!"

To whom will we listen? It is still Peter who speaks to us today. His words apply to the church today as much as they once applied to Israel; they confront the American power structure as forcefully as they once confronted the Roman power structure. Peter's words remind us that God continues his work in history today, and there are some things that cannot be put off.

America must be made to realize her central sin: The prophets are being killed as surely when they are shot on a motel balcony in Memphis as when they are crucified in Jerusalem. The steel braces of obedience to God must be placed on the twisted limbs of America, or she will not be able to stand the company of international man. For America to speak of democracy, she must find a way to allow all Niggers to become men. The church can lead the way in this when it listens to Peter and chooses to obey God rather than men.

Then we can go beyond law and order to obedience to God. We can go beyond secular mandates to a serious commitment to the Christ. We can go beyond religious services to the profound actions that allow men to make a choice to obey God rather than men.

Delivered: Date and
Location Unknown

COMMENTARY

Otis Moss III

> *It is the American Republic—repeat which created something which they call a "Nigger." They created it out of necessities of their own.*
>
> —James Baldwin[1]

James Baldwin, the prophet of letters, and C. T. Vivian, the prophet of the pulpit, in this quote converge as colleagues and ancestral sages to declare a simple truth. The term, the description, and the antebellum myth of Black people as "nigger" is just that—a socially constructed myth. A myth devised for social control, economic benefit, and spiritual deception. Vivian, in his brilliant sermon "Peter: The Profound Nigger," dares to upend our notion of what is proper in the pulpit and acceptable in the civic arena through the use of a word many utter but few understand. This homiletic of Black liberation and personal examination is designed to make conservative ecclesiastical leaders grab their robes and clutch their crosses while simultaneously causing the disinherited to stand up and shout, "Glory to God!" I can only imagine the reaction Vivian received from uncomfortable church leaders juxtaposed with the riotous applause and "amens" from young people who hollered back to this civil rights icon, "Yes sir, we are niggers no more!" It is within this frame that I want to discuss the magnificent subtleties, double entendres, and immense scholarship bubbling over from the words, phrases, and repetition in this message.

What cannot be ignored is the context of Vivian, a child of Missouri who was reared in neighboring Illinois. He was educated at Western Illinois University and the American Baptist Seminary in Nashville, Tennessee. The American Baptist Seminary was a hub for one of the many tributaries of what is now called the Black Social Gospel, championed by intellectuals like W. E. B. Du Bois and such ministers as Howard Thurman. This tradition jettisoned the southern evangelical idea that faith was only a personal endeavor, separate from the social economic conditions of a community. Even as the school highlighted this progressive theological tradition, it enacted a conservative culture of what some today might call respectability politics. This cultural tradition demands that Black students, and Black people in general, be twice as good as their white counterparts, elevate standard English as superior, regard code switching as problematic, and present at all times with the fashion sense of a conservative southerner.

Vivian was well acquainted with the nuances of southern institutions, the diversity of activist spaces, and the contradictory ideals inherent in bourgeois sensibilities. What makes this message remarkable, beyond his creative rhetoric and scholarship, is his awareness of these middle-class norms. He emphasizes and employs the authority given to him by his community to intentionally shatter unwritten codes of respectability, to preach a truth about the social construction of race and use the word *nigger* openly in the sermon.

If the preacher preaching this message had been a young activist still matriculating through school, the impact of the message would be minimal. The rhetorical strategy would be easily dismissed as a tactic to shock. But Vivian understands the weight of his position and voice. He forces the congregation to wrestle with the difficult as a way to put us in a position that sets us free. To use more academic language, Vivian exegetes the community and the preacher, and he puts the taboos and vocabulary of the community on trial.

The opening section of the sermon offers a typical theme and message. We are lulled to sleep, thinking maybe he will not use the charged terminology of *nigger*. Maybe it was a rhetorical device for the title, and now our bourgeois and ecclesiastical sensibilities can return to a sense of calm. With "Peter Before Sanhedrin,"[2] we are given a description of a religious man standing before secular authorities. Peter is lifted up as a symbol of what the church is called to embody. Peter confronts institutions of power that seek to diminish human flourishing, and Vivian makes the case that his doing so is the call of the church. But the American version of the church has failed to be the conscience of the nation and has hindered human thriving.

Please do not miss the genius of Vivian's work. He has already announced an uncomfortable topic but transitioned in his introduction in such a way to put the gathered religious leaders at ease. Then, he slowly raises the temperature in the room by making an indictment, not of another group outside the walls of the church, but of the very people listening to the message. The message then highlights not just the failures of the church but also the oppressive action of Rome. Rome, as conceived in the sermon, is a euphemism for America or any institutional power that reduces human thriving and God-ordained flourishing.

Vivian is a premier communicator of Black moral imagination. Edmund Burke is attributed with the first use of the phrase *moral imagination* in his book *Reflection on the Revolution in France*. The words refer to creating space in a commonwealth for human beings to seek and practice actions that elevate the individual and society. When Black people get ahold of this notion of moral imagination, it is transformed, like all things we hold. We transform this philosophical idea into a spiritual practice of merging the blues of Black experience with the Gospel of creative self-agency and imagination.

Vivian's life was shaped by this philosophical and sacred ideal, which asks several questions: *How do people blessed to be Black thrive in a space that calls itself a democracy but rarely practices democratic ideals? How do Black people thrive in a world of anti-Blackness?* Vivian's work, as that of a prophet and preacher, embodies these questions. The Freedom Movement was a spiritual revival of Black moral imagination that cast a vision upon the canvas of America's not-yet-democratic experiment. This sermon sits squarely at the epicenter of this tradition.

As we walk with Vivian in this message, we hear the echoes of the language employed by Vernon Johns, by Howard Thurman, and in the creative exegesis of James Bevel. The echoes of these giants can be heard in his use of the phrase "encounter the idol."[3] All three preachers use the technique of comparison between two opposing forces to communicate spiritual ideas. Vivian has offered—in interviews, on several occasions—his deep respect for these communicators, and their influence echoes in his message like good seasoning placed in a pot of delicious gumbo.

Step by step, we are given historical examples of activists, prophets, and preachers facing the idols of the day, including his friend Martin Luther King Jr. Vivian brings us along slowly, turning up the temperature, until we realize the water is getting hotter. He finally offers racism as the idol that the church must face today—or Christ cannot be worshipped. Again, his brilliance is on display as he leads us to a conclusion that we know is true, but that the empire—Rome and America—does not want us to face: Racism is essential for an empire to flourish.

Now, with water simmering almost to a boil, the heat is turned on high when we hear the word *nigger* employed once again. Peter, who is an outsider. Peter, who is disinherited. Peter, who is oppressed. Peter is defined as a nigger—a person of low status, hated by Rome. We are forced to look at Scripture through a Black lens of liberation, and we see Peter as a marginalized brother. We see the destructive nature of an empire called Rome. We no longer see Scripture through the lens of Western eyes.

Christ is now centered; suffering is elevated as a central challenge for all believers to engage as the Black moral imagination is on full display. I wish I could have been in the congregation the day this sermon was preached. In my imagination, I see conservative preachers looking shocked, unable to wrap their minds around what they just heard. I see Bishop So-And-So looking dazed and confused, and Apostle Such-And-Such frantically calling his armor-bearer to bring him water and a handkerchief. I see young people, influenced by the Black Power movement and the African independence struggle, rising to their feet, shouting with joy that a man of such authority knows about our struggle. I see, in my imagination, Jesus in the back of the room, wearing simple clothes, with a smile across his beautiful Black face, nodding in affirmation, speaking softly under his breath: "Well done, well done, my good and faithful servant, well done."

8

God of History: Five Stones

1 Samuel 17:40–47

HELLO, GOOD PEOPLE. I'm very thankful for that reading and thankful for the ministers of the pulpit and people I've known for many years. And as I look at this church, there are people I remember [here] from a long time ago. It's a great church. I remember even when you were at the other church, you had a dean of the Sunday school and his wife, and his father before him, all great men of our churches. Now you have a vice president of the convention, one of the reasons I happen to be here this morning. He had other things to do. Then, of course, on a day like this, one cannot come to think about a Memorial Day, think about the victories and struggles of this nation, without thinking about a combination of men.

You cannot come here as a Black Christian living in our time without understanding that one of your pastors, Rev. [Ralph] Abernathy, along with Dr. King, really fought the greatest single battle of our times. And it was not a physical battle abroad, but it was a nonviolent battle, here, [on] our own soil and in our own place and time.

Because this is the memorial time, and because I don't hear anybody else talking about it on TV or radio, I thought we should talk about our own struggles in this time for the fulfillment of democracy in a way it never desired to be fulfilled. But a way to fulfill all of our meanings in terms of the Scriptures which we have before us, and the church [of] which we are a part. Because if there is to be a memorial, and if there is to be some memory of meaning in our time, you have to go back to who we are, and what we have done, and what we've accomplished, and what the generations that represent us gave to us that we have extended into another century and another time.

When we think about it, I want us to look at this famous story. We all know the story. It was just so good to have it read because the details get forgotten. And it's the details that have the greatest meaning for us on this Sunday morning. For when we look at it, we begin to see this is a confrontation between a huge foe and a small one. We know the story, do we not?

So it was in that century, and so it is in this century through which we have lived. The struggle between a huge foe and a small one. The Philistines represented an entire army of trained men; they had everything behind them to win with, or so it seemed. They had all the force that was needed to defeat any country in the world; so it was in our own time. They knew they had scared the Israelites, so that they were winning psychologically in the beginning.

Look at our own condition—for is it not so? We are not for certain that we even believe in ourselves. We're outnumbered ten to one. They had police in great numbers, and they deputized whoever they wanted. All you had to be was one of them, and you could be deputized to destroy us. That was the story. And the courts, the prisons, judges—they owned them all. There was no way out of their concept of justice, and they had everything in hand, or so it seemed.

And when we think of ourselves for over a half century in this nation, to in fact be certain of their victories, is that they belittled us with blackface comedy. Not just for fun; that was to belittle a people that was discarded and understood as less than, to keep their labors in the fields. Let's not forget that what appears on the surface always has deeper things underneath. It is that ability to penetrate and to understand what the church has given us. When we think about it, we weren't even allowed to define ourselves or even know ourselves historically. It was a matter of how [things were] then.

And Israelites were put down as less important, as not having a history that was necessary. Do you think that the Philistines would have praised Moses? And do we think that, on today, a Memorial Day, they would praise Martin King? You see, there's a holiday for him, but on a Memorial Day for violence, he is forgotten. It's his nonviolence that defeated their violence.

We have to understand something that Lerone Bennett put so well. If we had fought violently, we would have been destroyed violently. We cannot come to this story without understanding that. However, LaRon said something else—[that] if we did not fight, we would be destroyed morally and spiritually. They did not think they were going to win the physical battle, but they knew not to fight would make them unworthy of their own manhood and ancestors and for any possibility of a future. There are struggles you must fight. The issue is, Do you want to win or do you want to fight? And this is what Black America's always been about on every Memorial Day, because we have always joined in somebody else's struggle, only to come out on the other end. We have fought every battle America has ever had, only to find out when we return home that we were fighting for somebody else, and it provided us with nothing.

How do you fight the battle? What happened is, little David stood up and his opposers laughed at little David. And do you think that this nation thought that a Martin King would have a chance against them? They laughed at little David. But what they didn't understand was that little David had something that they didn't know about. Little David was going to fight in a way that they did not know. David said, "I come in the name of the *Lord* of hosts."

And when we really begin to think about it, that's what Martin and the movement did. Their weapons on violence were not our weapons, and furthermore, there was no proof that they would work. That's what we have to understand. We have fought in every battle this country has entered, but it didn't work for us. Furthermore, mankind has fought war after war, and to what advantage—he's still fighting war? And for two thousand years we've had the way to stop it.

When we begin to look at this Memorial Day, we begin to understand that we're in a different age and time, and everything has changed. We've gone from an agricultural civilization to industrial to computerized. Time has changed, but our violent ways have not, but God is a god of history. God is a god of history, and that, when we really think about what should be remembered, what is worthy of our remembrance, we have to understand that God is moving all the time.

Now let's get to the center of this Scripture because it may be overlooked, and that is what David did. He picked up five smooth stones, and I'd like to make the argument that there have been five smooth stones in our struggle, and those five smooth stones have been basic to our winning the struggle, not just to struggling. And in those five smooth stones, we've found ways to end violent struggle for anyone that would listen.

And that first stone was cause of the struggle. This has been the first real stone of the Black experience. We have been struggling for freedom and decency ever since we've been here. Now, there are those that will tell you we were happy little slaves, running around and grinning. The truth is there's been no time, no day in our existence on this continent, that we have not fought for right, for justice, for decency, for freedom. Name it! If you read somebody else's history of yourself, you would think that you always did like it. If you read your own history of yourself, you'll understand there were times to play the game but only [with the hope] to win it on the other end.

When you look at it, is that the first one was the cause. Martin used the cause of our people, and the method that we had always used were nonviolent because the weapons of violence did not work. But what he did was to teach us something that we already knew in slavery: to do something by doing nothing. Our struggle was to win over racism, and we refused to use the enemies' methods, because we knew they would not work in our struggle. He brought out his buses to get us to work, but we refused to use his buses and created our own [means] to get to work. We were learning, we were proving to ourselves that we did not need somebody else as much as we thought we did. We were proving to ourselves [that] we did not have to obey someone else if we were properly obeying God.

Let's put it another way. We refused to cooperate with an evil system. And from the time we refused to cooperate, we began to win. There were always a few who win, but when we united to do it, that changed things. In fact, how we redefined ourselves made the difference, see the struggle again. For instance, they said we were involved in a boycott, and we said, "No we're not boycotting; we refuse to use what God has given us for evil." How you define it makes the difference, you see.

Now let's look at another smooth stone, the church. That's been the smooth stone that we've used. Every Sunday morning, it was the church that gave us a sense of our own selves. That let us know there must be a way out because there was a way out for Daniel. And there was a way out for Moses, and for a whole people called the Israelites. And if God was good to them, he would be good to us. If God delivered Daniel, he would deliver us. We knew it from the very beginning. It was the smooth stone that made the difference, you see. Think about it—every mass meeting was where? The church. Who were our leaders? Preachers! You see, when we look at it, our leadership came from the church, both ministerial and lay [leaders]. And the people that supported that movement were people in the church.

One fellow said to his maid in Montgomery, "I know you don't want to be around that mess that they're doing down there with Martin King." And she said, "That isn't true. Could I get off an hour early today?" She wanted to go to the mass.

And when we look at it, because of the church we then began to find that every Christian in the world that was worthy of the Christian faith came to our side. The National and World Council of Churches came to our side. Jews, Russian Orthodox came to our side because they understood we were right [in] standing against the churches of the South. It was a decision being made by the world on our side that gave us a strength that we would not have had if we were not in the church.

It is interesting—I know what it's going to sound like—but you see those organizations that were not tied to the church didn't last. SNCC started out as [the] Student Nonviolent [Coordinating] Committee. By the time it ended, they weren't students, they didn't have nothin' to coordinate, and they weren't nonviolent. But we kept on moving because the church was our backbone. The church was there. That's the smooth stone that has made the difference in our existence at every turn.

You can go all the way back. Even when we praised God underneath the trees because we didn't have our own church, they said we praised God so well that we shook the ground and could [be] heard half a mile away. What was it used for? The church was often the first stop in the underground railroad. Because you went out of the church meeting and went that way towards the river, instead of back to the slave cabin. You have to understand that, at every turn, no matter how minute or great, the church was the necessary smooth stone to developing our freedom, and this is basic to our Memorial Day.

We reached the conscience of the world. Isn't it interesting that no other method got to the conscience of the world? It was because the church, because we were morally and spiritually right, [that] we reached it. Martin said the issue is not Black or white; it's justice or injustice, right and wrong, decency and indecency. Church taught us we were right on every hand. But let's look at it another way—well, so let's go to another smooth stone.

Third stone is preaching. We had proven by using the weapons of God that we could defeat all attackers. God gave us weapons to defeat evil, and even though our enemies seemed to have the same weapons, they did not have [them] at the level we had [them]. If you want to see where the great preachers were, you had to come to our churches. It is not an accident that Martin King out-preached every preacher in the world. It was not an accident—he had the greatest sense of right and justice. He had a history of people who believed, with the very depth of their being, that God would deliver them. When other people only half believed and used the churches to serve the culture, Martin used the Christian church to serve God. The difference between the Southern Baptist church and our church is that one is the church of culture, and one is the church of Christ. Cut it any way you want. Anytime you allow your sense of being to be dictated by [forces] outside the church, you are not really of the church. You are using it, but in the process, you are misusing it. Somewhere along the line you gotta be right. I was going to tell you a story about that, but I better just let that go.

What happened is that the preaching defeated our oppressors on every hand. Wherever Martin King went, he preached. Martin gave us the direction, but all the other preachers in the world were repeating what he said, in one way or the other. They may not be able to say it as well as Martin, but we knew it was right. And when people all over the world are backing it up, you reach the conscience. We reached the conscience of the world; it was the preaching that did it.

When we really look at the central issue of the civil rights movement, and when you look at Scripture here, we understood what the central issue was between the two men, David and the uncircumcised Philistine, Goliath. This great hawk of men, with this great weapon that he had and all these people behind him, who was saying, "My God will win it." What David said was, "My God will win it." Look at it. The issue always is, Whose god is God? Not what one looks like, not who uses the symbols, not who has the political or economic power. Whose god is God? That was the central issue of the civil rights movement. That's what we were fighting about. Like these two men, they were fighting about *whose god is God*.

Look at it very carefully—it was the issue in the land of the Philistines; it was the issue in the land of America. When we look at it, that was the issue of the Civil War. And we won that. Isn't it interesting? And how long do you have to work with these people? You win a violent war that almost destroys the nation, then you turn around and win a nonviolent war, and they still didn't want to give in. It took the Southern Baptist Convention one hundred years before they even admit it? That our god was God? But they wouldn't say it like that. You understand? But you see the central issue is, Whose god is God? And we proved who God was. Is God a god of white people? Who belittles people? Who believes color is more than character? Those were the issues! Because ultimately, we were going to win based on those [things]. The opposition said it was a matter of color; we said it was a matter of character and Christ.

The difference between us was that, in fact, we believed that the church was to serve Christ, not culture. Central issue always is, Do you serve culture or [do you serve] Christ? Do you bend over to be passive and not speak up when you know that the other side is wrong? How much does that make you a part of them, not us? See, Peter tried that—they said, "Ask Peter. Weren't you with him?" And he said, "Oh no, I wasn't with him." Which side did that place Peter on? It is obvious. In fact, Christ said [so] before the crows, and then Peter realized he was on the wrong side and should have been speaking up all the time, and so were we until Martin.

I suppose we should take a look at another one of those stones. Now, you not only have to be right, you have to be just. And we were. It is interesting that the church had taught us that, regardless of how others had treated us, they were still human beings. That causes you to be just. We have won because of our sense of humanity, in the final analysis. We're never inhumane in our struggles against human beings. In fact, we have treated white people better than they deserve. And the world knows it. And everything we have done to improve ourselves has improved other people, as well as ourselves. But we weren't upset or mad about it. So, let it be—we don't want to see anybody suffer. That's what I mean about being just, as well as being right; by being compassionate, as well as being right. See, we went beyond law to human rights. Jesus told us to pray and work for thy kingdom come on earth, even as it is in heaven, because his master was *God*.

That leads us to the fourth smooth stone, the Scriptures themselves. We always knew as a people that the Scriptures were a light into our feet, and it was central to our faith. We never could be without the Word. When a preacher visited our community, we wanted to know if he knew the Word or not; not how bright he was. In the early days, not even if he went to school or not—did he know the Word? My great-grandfather couldn't read, but when you started a passage, he could finish it for you. That's the stuff that kept us going. We knew that this was right. Might not be able to read it, but it's right. And don't try to fool me with it, because, hey, I've heard enough preachers and people, and my grandma knew, and she taught me at her knee; don't try to fool me, because I know, if you can start it, I can finish it. It is in the Word. It is the Scripture from which it all comes. And as Black people, we've always known it. We heard about Israel in the bible and if they can win it, we can win it.

Where did we get our strategies? From the Bible. See, what Martin King did was something we never had the—I don't want to say guts to do it, I don't want to say faith to do it—but the truth is we never put it all together. We believed in loving your fellow man as yourself. In fact, we also believed that you're supposed to pray for those who misuse you. We also knew you weren't supposed to cooperate with evil; we knew all that because it was in the Scriptures. But we never put it all together to be used as one piece. What Martin did was to take the Sermon on the Mount and make a strategy out of it. So that all of it came together. We turned the other cheek. We prayed for those who used you, who hated us. And we went the second mile, and we went no further.

When you look at it, who believes—let's put it this way. Too many of us didn't really believe you're supposed to love your fellow man as yourself. Knowing is not believing. Hearing is not understanding. It is in the doing. But I tell you what, fifty thousand people in Montgomery proved that we heard it well enough. So that when it was put together in one piece, we did something the world had never done.

Gandhi said that as great as the victories in India [were], it was decades before we moved. The ultimate proof of these great spiritual ideas will be given to us by Black people in America. Look at it, as Gandhi knew—he fought with the majority against a minority. But we fought with the minority against the majority. And won it. The proof, that the great ideas that Jesus taught us two thousand years ago are still true, and will be true as long as we live up to them. We can be as free as we want to be. Very important.

When you really think about it, nobody who really cares about the Scriptures is finished, because they free themselves. That, in the final analysis, we desire that all people be free. It is that our great role in America has been to free this nation. In fact, had this nation listened to us we wouldn't be in this so-called war today. 'Cause we would have fed the people there, we would have remade the country when we went over and destroyed it. Isn't it interesting that, for weeks after this war started, you couldn't ask why didn't they blow it up? Why are you supposed to fight a war when you don't even know why your enemy does what he does? In fact, you don't even know if your enemy is your enemy. You got to ask why. Because, you see, we didn't want to ask why, because we'd have to ask, What did we do?

This nation has never cared enough about people of color anywhere in the world to allow justice to come for them. And when we've gone over as Christian missionaries, what did we do? We tried to make them become like us, not like Christ. Tried to make them like Americans; they already knew they didn't need that. Isn't it interesting that we have never won, with all the missionaries and all the billions of dollars we've spent? Because the world knows what we're like.

Isn't it interesting that, in Africa—I've been there five times; within a few days I get to go back again, love it—they have produced better Christianity than we have produced in America? And the best Christianity in America has been done by African Americans. And the best Christianity in the world has been done by Africans. Isn't that interesting? It calls us to something much higher.

Let's get to that final smooth stone, Jesus Christ. None of the previous stones would make a difference if it weren't for Jesus Christ. The Scriptures wouldn't have made a difference if Jesus had not risen from the dead. How did Paul say it? If he didn't, we would be the most miserable of creatures. It's Jesus Christ, because the idea of loving your fellow man wouldn't make sense, but yet he did it. Turning the other cheek wouldn't make sense, except [that] he did it. And without his having done it, we wouldn't have done it to prove it in our own time.

It all gets back to Jesus. That's the smoothest stone of all. When you come with Jesus, then you can solve all your problems. What Jesus made us know and believe is that you can't solve any problem without solving the spiritual problem underneath it. If you really want it right, you have to come [at it] spiritually. It may seem that you're going to be defeated at any moment, but if you keep on believing and keep your faith in Jesus Christ, you'll come out on the other side. It may take longer than you want it to, but you can't lose with Jesus. This is what we learned in [the] movement—everything that is meant to defeat you becomes a means of developing you.

And you become greater than your opposition. In the final analysis, everything depends upon the nature and character of human beings, not upon how good your guns are. It may run in the short run, but it won't win in the long run. Jesus is the smooth stone that makes all the rest work. A church without Jesus isn't a church at all. The Scriptures without Jesus, unbelievable. Name it at any point you want to—a struggle without Jesus will not win. He's behind all the smooth stones we've had. That's what makes the difference. There's a god of history that's always working, and God is saving us all, God is teaching us all.

What we have to see is that our religion has always been a center of resistance. That's what it is. We have used our religion, or shall we say, our religion has used us to be a center of resistance against man's evil in the world. That we have been on the side of the great general that deployed his troops so that they could save the world.

We must understand that as we go to Memorial Day and watch the programs presented that they may not mention who we are, but this is the center of resistance. It was the center of resistance of slavery that freed us. The church was the center of resistance against the evils that surrounded us to misuse us. The center of resistance against the Black codes and everything that followed after we had won the Civil War. The center of resistance that has kept our souls sweet in spite of everything around us. And when they talk about soul in the street, they don't know what it is. What they got is just what spilled over—if you want to see what real soul is, see it in the church. This is the believable place. Understand that this church has been the center of resistance. That's who we are, in the final analysis.

There's this God of history that will be with us if we obey. You don't have to believe that you overly do it. Just fight the good fight. Because what Martin taught us—that it's in the action that you find out who you really are. It's in the action that you find out what your enemy is like. It's in the action that you test the nation. It's in the action that you find out what your own sense of right and wrong is. It's not in the talking. It's in the action. When you act out what God has given you, you win. It's our Memorial Day. Not for the same reason, but beyond their reason. The ultimate Memorial Day is when we come together to speak about how justice is done.

Delivered: May 26, 2002
West Hunter Street Baptist Church
Atlanta, Georgia

COMMENTARY

René Whitaker

We begin our journey with a look at 1 Samuel, chapter 17, verses 37–47. This Scripture passage takes us into the middle of the story of David and Saul, and the Philistine champion named Goliath. Perhaps everyone who preaches from this text will come at it from a different direction. That's the beauty of Scripture. A passage can speak to us in different ways at different moments in our lives. I've never really spent much time with this passage, except as part of the larger story of Saul and David and the changing of history through the eyes of the Israelites making their way from the past to the future, again and again.

However, I do believe that the story of David and Goliath inspires preachers to talk about the weaker overcoming the stronger by holding on to faith in God, the creator of the universe. In reading the entire seventeenth chapter in 1 Samuel, the picture of the battle between David and Goliath adds to the weight of Vivian's sermon.

The contrast between these two opponents was in large part what inspired Vivian's sermon as he looked back over the legacy of the civil rights movement in this country. Vivian used the symbolic story of David and Goliath and applied it to the struggle for equality and justice for African Americans that unfolded throughout his lifetime. Dr. Vivian was a member of a group of men and women—esteemed by many but too often disdained by some—who led the push. He stood alongside other courageous people and embraced the call of righteousness as they "fought the greatest single battle of their times."[1] Dr. Vivian once characterized that fight this way: This battle was not a physical battle across the seas. It was not a traditional fight with weapons of destruction. Rather, it was a nonviolent battle here, in this country, in the places where they lived.[2]

It seems fitting that the story of David and Goliath would become the story of this fight for justice and equality, for the struggle was between a huge, well-armed foe and a much smaller group of men and women of all ages who made the power of nonviolence their weapon of choice. Like David, they brought a new dimension to the battle to, as Walter Brueggemann puts it in his book *First and Second Samuel*, "establish a new paradigm of bold faith in the face of fear, threats and violence."[3] The old pattern of intimidation, bullying, and brutality was shifted.

When David claimed his faith in the God of his ancestors, he claimed their persistence, courage, fortitude, and hope. In doing so, he was bolstered in the face of overwhelming odds. He used his skills as a shepherd to defy the stereotype that the young do not know what they are doing. We must realize that many of the participants at the forefront of the civil rights movement were young people in their twenties. These young women and men, along with their older colleagues, understood that they needed to create a new paradigm even to have the possibility of a victory. Each of them brought energy, imagination, hope, faith, and courage to the table.

In his sermon, Dr. Vivian is remembering the more recent past, even as he shares the story of David and Goliath. Dr. Vivian claims those five stones, which David had placed in his shepherd's bag, as symbols for the cause of resistance and right. He transformed these stones into the foundational pieces that bolstered the soldiers of the civil rights movement. To Vivian, these stones were the elements necessary to begin to transform Dr. King's dream into a possible reality.

Like David, C. T. Vivian picked up five smooth stones that were the basis for winning his struggle. He understood that, with these five smooth stones, they had discovered a pathway that could be shared with others as a way to transform violent struggle into something much more powerful. He and the other leaders of the movement shared this pathway with anyone who was willing to listen and follow. So, with open hearts and minds, let's listen to the lessons of the stones.

The first stone was the cause of the struggle. Dr. Vivian and his colleagues were struggling for justice, freedom, and equality just as their ancestors had done since they were first brought to this country and held as slaves. For generations, men and women of African descent had struggled to be heard or to even be treated with decency and dignity. By the 1950s and 1960s, this struggle grew exponentially in an effort to defeat racism. At every step, these men and women were willing to sidestep the traditional means of protest. They boycotted buses, integrated lunch counters, gathered in peaceful protest to unfair laws, and traveled across this country to create a new path to the future. They prayed, preached, and prayed some more.

Yet the movement would have been stopped dead in its tracks if it weren't for the second smooth stone, which represents the church. Every Sunday morning, it was the Black church that gave those who worshipped a sense of who they were as people of God. It was a gathering place that offered hope and hospitality, and it became the meeting place for the movement to unfold.

Without the Black church, the third stone would have been lost in the shuffle, for it was preachers who delivered the powerful message of hope. Dr. Martin Luther King Jr., the reverend Ralph Abernathy, Dr. Vivian, and many others shared the stories of struggle from the biblical text. They shared the promise of new life offered through Jesus Christ. They led prayers, taught nonviolence, and held on to the promises of freedom. Their message inspired and encouraged all those who would listen and take it to heart. It unsettled those who were in opposition to freedom, justice, and mercy for all God's children—and particularly for Black Americans.

Their preaching centered on the fourth stone, which is the word of God shared in Scripture, and it was grounded in the fifth smooth stone, which was and is the promise revealed to us in the life, death, and resurrection of Jesus Christ. For it was Christ's message of new life for all that inspired the leaders and participants in this righteous battle. It was and is the understanding that God sent Christ to save the world. God offered the promise of salvation as a way to continue to bring to fruition the reign of God here on Earth.

Great strides for equality unfolded as the movement grew and changed. Yet the struggle for justice, mercy, and equality continues today. Too often the effort falls short as people seem to forget that the God we claim as Creator, Redeemer, and Sustainer of all people is the same God who sent Jesus to save the world with a message of love. It seems that the larger church today has all but lost its true calling: to share a message of hope, mercy, and justice as it offers hospitality to all people, not just to a few.

We seem to be at a crossroads where many preachers today use Scripture to separate themselves and their congregants from others by claiming that they are the chosen ones. Too often, those who call themselves Christian seem to encourage their congregants to use their righteousness to distort Jesus's message, which calls his followers to love and forgive one another. Sadly, there doesn't seem to be a limit as to what harm may be inflicted upon others because they are different or have somehow been deemed an enemy who is not worthy of grace, mercy, justice, or hope.

Too often, Christ's message of new life and salvation for all is lost in the clouds of time. The church writ large seems to have forgotten or simply denies its purpose in the world, which is to preach hope, offer hospitality, call for justice, welcome the stranger, and share the good news of Christ with everyone. No one is perfect. There will be mistakes along the way, but if we continue to look to our faith for guidance, if we continue to pray for promising possibilities symbolized by David's five smooth stones, if we share our message with everyone we meet, then perhaps the world and the people in it will discover a bit more freedom. As we continue to work together to establish a world based on justice, kindness, generosity, and peace, then we may remember that, as Vivian preached, "There is a God of history, who is always working; and God is saving us all, God is teaching us all."[4]

Yes, God has been saving and teaching all of us—from David, the simple shepherd, to Vivian, compassionate and courageous leader of the civil rights movement, to me as minister of Word and Sacrament, and to all who share God's word, today and in the future. We thank you, Vivian, for your life, your words, and your work in faith. Amen.

9

MLK: The Prophet

Matthew 13:57 and Ephesians 6:14–15

When we were at the world conference against racism in Durban,[1] one of the things that all of the people of color came away from there with was that, from now on, whatever we [think] about when we are here, we think about what it meant there. And it came back to me, as I entered here, that the AME church is probably the only Black organization that has greater meaning for [Africans] and their ability to do something about it. There isn't another group in the African American experience that has been so long dealing so well and continuously with the issues of Africa. I thought that one of the greatest things that you did for Black America—not just for this church—was when you decided that the first thing the bishop had to do was get a place in Africa. You sent him over to be a part of a continuing understanding, which was there from the beginning but which we'd forgotten along the way. So many good things come [from] just being [there] and thinking about it.

I said something yesterday about the value of AME leadership for the future of Black America, and I could not help but think of John Adams. When we brought the basic Black denominations together, who did they choose to be the head of the whole group? John Adams, an AME, whose father before him was a bishop in the AME church. There is so much meaning [to] your importance in thinking seriously about the future of Black America and your leadership of it. So much [of] that was yesterday, so let me get off of that.

What I want to talk about this morning is a continuation of yesterday in a very real way, and that is that I believe Martin Luther King Jr. is the prophet of our age. Now, you see, to prove that is very important, if in fact our churches, Black Christianity in America, produced the greatest prophet in our time. That says to us that God has not only picked him, he's picked us. It tells us something about the importance of Blackness, the importance of our kind of faith. It says that we've got a message to the world that can bring us from the bottom to the top. Not for our sake but for the sake of the entire earth. That's a big kind of line.

I don't use words like *earth* without using them seriously. We have to think about what prophets are for—see, prophets put whole nations back on track, bend the world toward what is good and away from what is bad. Prophets have a special kind of thing that causes us to examine the entire context we are in.

Prophets never came without there being a major thing to do. They come up out of a struggle that changes the very essence of nations. Think about it. Old or New Testament, look wherever you want. They cause us to evolve and create, and remake meaningful life for everyone, and it is not just for those [traditions] out of which they come, it's for everyone. Think about that. A Paul may have come out of Judaism, but a Paul became a spokesman for the entire world. Anywhere you look at it.

Let's clear our minds as we think and talk about prophets. The idea is that prophets are perfect. Even Jesus said that only my Father in heaven is perfect. When we begin to think about David, he was a favorite of God, but David murdered for a simple thing like sex. [laughter] Well, let's take another murderer. [much laughter] Moses murdered because he was angry at the mistreatment of someone, and yet he found favor with God to the ability of leading his people completely out of slavery. To create for all history the possibilities that slavery is wrong [and] that one can go above and beyond it. Peter denied God to save himself. He was fooling with losing his soul, but he ultimately became [one of] God's greatest spokesmen. Both men started out as very common people, but they had contact with God. They became very important people in order to save others, and so they became prophets for the rest of society. They may have made mistakes, but they were perfect enough to please God on the issues of right and wrong, justice and injustice, love not hate. And that was good enough. They were perfect enough to change an imperfect world. That is what was most important of all. You see, the world understands that Martin is who I am talking about.

It's interesting that the prophet is better understood than we are. In St. Paul's Cathedral, the most important cathedral in the Episcopal church in the world, there is a statue of Martin King, almost life-size, of five feet, three inches, that's above the west gate. Now, that's not just there for a moment. That's to be there because they understand and realize that in our own time, not in their denomination, that out of the Christian church there rose up a person [who] was great enough to be the prophet of our age, to set us in new directions and to reawaken and remake Christianity and what it ought to be.

You see, they understand that. Understanding [it] even before [we were] understanding. Something is wrong with that. It could be much like a friend of mine who says, "Vivian, I want to tell you, I knew Martin, I grew up with him." But the point being that he always found that he was a good person, but they could not believe that anybody . . . they knew could be that important. And I think that's the way we are.

Let me give it to you another way. The president of Georgia Baptist [State Convention], he said, "You see, Vivian, I had to really argue with that one about how great Martin really was, but finally I came to it with a story." He [said] a fellow was in New York City, standing in front of the Empire State building, had his back to it and was trying to stop people in the street. But finally somebody stopped, and he said, "I hate to bother you, sir, [but] I came to New York City for one reason, and that was to find the Empire State Building. I just wanted to see it." And the man looked at him, and looked over his shoulder, at the Empire State Building. And said, "You're looking for the Empire State Building? You really want to see it? I tell you what, you walk forty blocks that way, and you look back." And I think that's where we are. We had to go ahead forty years, and now we're looking back and beginning to see the importance of a man [who] was in our midst, and [whom] God used to help deliver us until we [could] finally see it.

Now, what I did was to ask myself, "What are the characteristics of a prophet?" Of course, I do not know them, and neither do you because we don't know church history that well. So, I went to those who make their lives studying prophets through the ages. And here are some characteristics—listen to this.

First, they were called to speak for God. Now, you know the calling. We thought we were the only ones that understood the calling. Second, they were not manipulators or [opportunists]. [Third], there was something mysterious about prophets. They had the mantle of leadership given to them by people, not by power. They believed in a personal God. They suffered. How did Paul say it? I bear the marks of the Lord Jesus on my own body. They revolutionized the church of their time. [Often, they were] martyred. They were not seduced by material things. They were unstoppable. I like that. They changed their times. And the twelfth and final thing: They answered to the love of God, no matter what circumstance they found themselves. I just like repeating it. They answered to the love of God, no matter what circumstance they found themselves. They didn't place themselves; they found themselves doing the Lord's work. God places you where you don't even imagine. The real thing—do you answer his love of you? This is what makes the difference. Martin was called from an early age.

As I said before, I talked to all kinds of people [who] had grown up with him. My wife wrote the first biography on Coretta King, and in the process, we found out a whole lot about Martin that wasn't around. Finally, now, there is a book called [*Martin's*] *Big Words*. In it, Martin is described as sitting in church with his mother, and he [says] to her, "One day I'm gonna get some big words and I'm gonna tell them." [laughter] It was always in the back of his mind. That he was going to be like those people up there, when he didn't even understand what the role was, all he was thinking was *big words*.

Let me give it to you another way. When Rosa Parks sat down, Martin didn't rush forth to be the great leader. That was not his intent. Yet he was better prepared than anyone else to do it. In fact, I believe that Martin was the only PhD in a pulpit in the entire South, Black or white. [When] you think about—in truth, [others] were not there. In fact, we had so few people in Black pulpits with any education that they felt the lack of education was seen as an important problem.

Martin tried to run from the pulpit and ministry. He was a chaplain on his summer job in the tobacco fields of Kentucky. I bring that up because we don't see Martin as being a worker, but Martin had been there, every summer when he was at Morehouse, and if you want to know what hard work is, you get under those nets in the tobacco fields. You're steaming hot under there. Things that we don't know are very important to our understanding. He was ordained at seventeen, and in college at seventeen, too. He was prepared for a time like this in the history of his people. He had studied nonviolence and the teachings of Gandhi [on that topic] in seminary; he'd talked with Benjamin Mays, the first dean of the School of Religion at Howard University. You see, things were happening in his life that helped prepare him.

Remember, it says the people selected Martin in Montgomery, Alabama, although he had just arrived there. It was the leadership that called him to be speaker at that first mass meeting. He didn't think he should do it. In fact, [Ralph] Abernathy would have been the great leader in Montgomery; he was from Alabama. He had the biggest, most important people's church in town. He was president of the Ministry of Alliance. Fifty years ago that meant something. [laughter] In other words—and remember, when we're looking back in time, to be Black and the president of anything meant something—it took the movement to change that.

You see, we didn't serve on anything [similar] before that. The only board we served on was the deacon board. There weren't any real positions for us. So, when Abernathy gave up that position for Martin King, something was happening that we didn't quite understand. And [once] Martin gave the speech and all the people said, "We will follow him," you know something unusual had happened. He didn't ask for it. It was placed on him by the people, and he could have gotten out of it if he wanted to. But he did not. He served in it for our benefit. People selected him, not [he] himself, and that becomes very important.

See, I believe he was chosen by God *and* men. Now, let's give you the moment of epiphany in Martin's life. Until I went to seminary, I thought that [*epiphany* was just] a name on a church. [laughter] There was that moment of epiphany, that moment that we all really want. Many of us have had it. And we seek for it, again and again, and it very seldom happens. It only needs to happen once, if you care enough and understand the importance of it and are willing to follow through. Martin King was in his home—had come down from the bedroom to the kitchen early one morning. He was fixing a pot of coffee. He had learned he was awarded his doctorate that morning. He'd come down to study, to keep his mind alert, to keep knowing what to do and what to think. That was his hour of meditation before he went out to the streets or picked up the phone, before he did anything. And he was thinking about buying a gun. Now, isn't it interesting? The man who was to be the greatest proponent of nonviolence was thinking, *Should I buy a gun*? Early in the movement, *Should I buy a gun*?

He wasn't thinking about himself; he was thinking about his family. Because at every hour someone was calling the house, and Coretta was picking up the phone and hearing, "We're going to kill you. You have no business being here." He was worried about his family, and then he heard it. That still, small voice that all of us want to hear. And it said, "Stand up for righteousness, stand up for truth, and I will be at your side forever." Sounds like a passage of Scripture, we know. But you see, it wasn't just Scripture. He heard the voice. And from that moment on, Martin was not concerned about having guns. In fact, he went on to say that violence creates more problems than it solves. He was not concerned from that time on.

You see, in seminary we argue about personalism. Is God a personal god? But you see, Martin didn't worry about it anymore because God was speaking to him, a personal God, and all the prophets have realized a personal god was in the midst of life. And there was something else that was made clear—that God was on the side of liberation. He never had to worry about that anymore. His mind was clear. It was clear that God had called him for liberation. God had called him to serve. God was saying to him that *I will be with you forever. You never again have to [have] the doubts*. But we shouldn't even have to think about it.

He was also tested by man. [He] was presiding over a church meeting, and there was this huge boom from across town. But they went on with the meeting. Pretty soon people came over and said, "Dr. King, your home has been bombed." They left and went over, and by the time Martin had gotten back to his home, people had come from everywhere around. One man had a gun down his leg, and others had various kinds of homemade weapons. And if you think back to it, at that time the weapon of choice was the razor. [laughter] They came ready, boy. The crowd was saying, *these people don't understand decency or love*. Let's go get them. If you will lead us, we will let them know who we really are. We'll blow them away. If they want a war, let's give them a war. They were ready. And even though Martin's home had been bombed—his wife was almost killed—Martin still told them to go home. There's a better way, and that this is not what God has called us for.

Coretta visited our home a few months ago for our wedding anniversary, and the conversation turned to that event. And she said she felt as though she should go to the back of the house. And so she said to the woman that was visiting, "Let's go to the kitchen." You know when you feel something, you don't just run right quick. And they picked up the baby, and started their way to the kitchen, and a few minutes after getting to the back of the house, a bomb burst in the front. But in spite of it all, Martin still told everyone to go home.

That, to me, was the test. It was the same test experienced when they said to Jesus, "Come down off that cross," and he refused to come off the cross because he knew his work was greater than that. And that's what the crowd out there wanted: *We will be your army.* He refused to do it. This event was the microcosm of things to come because that's what was happening through all our lives as we lived with Martin. You see, now, I believe God knew that Martin was ready. And now God knew that Martin was ready to represent Him in a world of violence with criticism from every side. What if he had not passed a test? If had he not obeyed his higher calling, we would have had bloody wars for three generations, and we would have had a reason for it. How long would it have taken? Another one hundred, two hundred years? Who knows before we could have had a reconciliation.

Had Martin failed to follow righteousness, there wouldn't have been hope in sight. Remember, no one had solved the problem of the basis of this nation. Racism is the central canon of American society. It makes a liar out of our Christian religion; it makes a liar out of our ability to be human enough to obey God. It makes a liar out of democracy, [which] can never be achieved. How long would we have had to wait if he hadn't passed the test? But he passed the test.

As we look at the Old and New [Testaments], all through the Scriptures, the prophet and the king were always at each other's throat. The prophet was always engaging the king, and the king was always trying to kill the prophet because [the king] wanted to keep his power.

Now, look where Martin was placed. Martin didn't decide to come to Montgomery. Daddy King decided he was going to Montgomery. Daddy King had numerous friends there and enormous pride in his PhD son, and he wasn't gonna see his son heading an ordinary church. And there weren't any bishops to decide it. [laughter] Daddy King asked his friends to assist him [in] finding a bluestocking church for his son?

Well, everyone knew that the church that was open was the perfect one because it was in Montgomery, where there's a lot of colleges and the members of the church were mainly members of the university. So, the thing is that [it] was the perfect church, and his friends saw that it was. Martin didn't decide to go to Montgomery—woo! Daddy King thought he decided it. But Martin King had another daddy. [laughter]

What happened was this: Who was head of the opposition? Who was the spokesman for racism and separation? It was Governor [George] Wallace. One block away [from the state capitol] was Dexter Avenue [Baptist Church]. And [so], it was set up. All we had to do was think of our Old Testament and New

Testament. It was set up! The voice of freedom was here, and the voice of rejection was here. And the clash was on. It was set up. We have to see it. He had passed the test, and God had set it up. When we look at it that way, we begin to understand things that we can't ordinarily understand, and which we couldn't decide. The world has always tried to seduce the prophets. Let's look at the temptation of Jesus as [an example] of all the prophets.

The first temptation was to be of the elite. *If you join us, we will glorify you, and we will accept you, and what more could you want if we accept you?* The elite, the inside, the group that runs things. This is the great temptation, but you see, you've got to act right. Oh, you understand, don't you? *You've got to go along with us.* They thought it would work! Because, after all, they couldn't believe that a Black man wouldn't want to be white. And they couldn't believe that anyone with a PhD could reject being of the elite. When you think about it, they couldn't believe that anybody with standing, [anyone] part of the inside, [anyone who] would have wealth could live and die for poor people. That's what it came down to. They couldn't believe it.

Let's look at the second temptation. That's about materialism and money and wealth. Martin King never left Sunset Street in Atlanta, which was the edge of the ghetto, and a long way from [the] southwest side of the city. Prominent Atlanta Blacks moved to the southwest side and bought the biggest house they could get, which is why they didn't have much money afterwards. But the point being Martin never left the ghetto and wouldn't let Coretta leave. The only reason they moved the first time was because Coretta was concerned about the children's safety. Coretta just left Sunset, about three months ago, after somebody—*Harpo* spelled backwards—[bought] an apartment for her in Buckhead.

Martin never had a large car and refused a salary from SCLC [Southern Christian Leadership Conference]. I remember one time the board was trying to decide how much to pay Martin. But the thing is, they decided there was no value they could put on Martin—he was more important than the head of General Motors. He was more important to mankind than the president of the United States. So, that wouldn't do it. You couldn't compromise at that level.

But Martin wouldn't let them give what they finally decided. He said, "I will not have people believing that I'm doing what I'm doing because of a dollar." Only salary that Martin had was from being an assistant pastor at Ebenezer Baptist Church, and we know what pastor salaries are. There was no intent [in] his mind of getting rich. But he could have! He was asked to take over a white church in Massachusetts that was going to give him thirty thousand dollars a year. That's like three hundred thousand dollars a year now. But he refused, because he was called not for Massachusetts, but for Mississippi. He was called for a greater task than making money. And he was not going to go that way.

[Actor and activist Harry] Belafonte, in fact, is the only reason that [Martin] was buried as well as he was buried, and the reason the family had money afterwards was because Belafonte had an insurance policy on Martin that neither Martin nor Coretta [could] afford. Because when you're out there to be killed, insurance is very high on you. Belafonte paid secretly. No one even know it was happening. We didn't even know it until Martin died, and we were on staff. That's why the family had some money when Martin was killed. Without it, the funeral wouldn't have been the same.

The third temptation, fame, has prevented so many people from becoming greater leaders than they [might] have been. The reason for fame is to end your radicalism. So, they finally offered Martin the Nobel Peace Prize—the top of the mountain. What did the disciples say? "Let us stay up here and build some tabernacles, one for each one of us, because 'We somebody, baby!'" [laughter] You know what Eisenhower said? He said that he would give up all his medals and achievements for the Nobel Peace Prize because he understood that it was better than all the other awards. What I'm talking about is that Martin fulfilled all the temptations.

Seduced by money? No. Acceptance by the powerful? No. You want to live badly? So, the problem, as Martin put it, is if you take all of that stuff, you'd be afraid to die. You want to live so badly in order to put on the right things in the morning and go to the right dinner at night. And so that you get the right praise in between. That you just want to live because living isn't living if that's not happening. And since I'm this high, how am I going to come down? And Martin later said, "If you're afraid to die, you're not fit to live." He understood what God was about.

The world always tries to make things what they are not, particularly for those [who] are better than the society wants them to be. The bad newspapers hire whole [staffs] of people to make you look bad. They follow you and bug your room. We knew, whatever room we were in in the country, it was going to be bugged. So we talked to the bug. We knew that. And so we're saying, So tell Hoover! [laughter]

See, if you remember, all during the movement years, you never heard of Martin being talked about as one of the sons of God. You never heard him being talked about as a Christian minister. You heard him talked about as Dr. King, the academic PhD. They never talked about him as being a minister, leading in the name of the Lord. They tried to take that away from him. They tried to make him a political personage and make it seem as though his only concern was passing a law. See, but Martin's movement was not a political movement; it was a moral and spiritual movement. That's what we have to see. Because what Martin was doing was trying to reach the conscience of a nation. We hadn't tried that before. Prior to that, we had tried everything but the spiritual. [laughter]

You see, we tried law and order. That's why Howard University had the whole strategy of producing constitutional lawyers. But it didn't truly work. You see, I believe what was happening was God's way of bringing us to Him.

Delivered: 2005
African Methodist Episcopal Church
Joint Institute for Ministry
Dothan, Alabama

COMMENTARY

Gary Dorrien

This sermon glossing Matthew 13:57 and Ephesians 6:14–15 gets to work at declaring that Martin Luther King Jr. is the prophet of our age, and that he did not come from nowhere. The Black church produced King, and God picked him out, which means that God favored the Black church: "It tells us something about the importance of Blackness, the importance of our kind of faith. It says that we've got a message to the world that can bring us from the bottom to the top. Not for our sake but for the sake of the entire earth."[2]

The Black church was born liberationist, hearing a message of freedom in the Bible that was not what was preached to oppressed Black persons. It therefore grasped from the beginning that prophets have a special role to play in urging faithful people, and the entire world, to care about what God cares about. Dr. Vivian moved early to the point that prophets don't have to be perfect. The biblical prophets weren't perfect, and neither was MLK. But they have to be close enough to God to be able to speak for God concerning that which God cares most about: "The issues of right and wrong, justice and injustice, love not hate. And that was good enough. They were perfect enough to change an imperfect world."[3]

So it was with the greatest prophet of our age. This sermon is wonderfully sprinkled with insider memories and vignettes—a friend of Vivian's comparing MLK to the Empire State Building, Mrs. Alberta Williams King's remembrance of her young son's vow to get some big words, King mulling whether to buy a gun shortly before his epiphany in the kitchen, Mrs. Coretta King drawn to the kitchen just before the King home was bombed, and Vivian remembering his own reaction to the bombing and King's response to it: "That to me was the test. It was the same test experienced when they said to Jesus, 'Come down off that cross,' and he refused to come off the cross, because he knew his work was greater than that."[4] Now his mind was cleared of seminary arguments over whether God is personal because the God who is on the side of liberation had called him to stand up for righteousness.

This third remembrance is the crux of the sermon and the entire civil rights movement story, the greatest story we have in this country. There would be no hope at all for this country, as Vivian said, had King failed to stand up for righteousness.

> Remember, no one had solved the problem of the basis of this nation—racism is the central canon of American society. It makes a liar out of our Christian religion; it makes a liar out of our ability to be human enough to obey God. It makes a liar out of democracy, [which] can never be achieved. How long would we have had to wait if he hadn't passed the test? But he passed the test.[5]

Yes, King passed the test, but the racist sickness of US American civilization mutated and spread. The US finally vowed to become a racial democracy in 1965, but King was cut down for pushing the nation so hard, and that was only the beginning of the backlash. There is always a backlash that far outstrips whatever gains it hates, which has yielded the forty blocks/forty years dilemma of our time. You cannot see the Empire State Building from close up, and Vivian was very close to King. He said in 2005 that he had to move forty years down the road to really appreciate the historic importance of King. In 1970, in his brilliant and historic book *Black Power and the American Myth*, Vivian states plainly that King's mission ended in failure.

Vivian had been a James Lawson disciple in Nashville, a cofounder of SNCC, and a longtime King lieutenant in SCLC, coordinating SCLC branches. He had shared a close friendship with King based on movement bravery and a shared seminary worldview. He admired King immensely, but after King was gone, Vivian said his approach rested on two mistaken beliefs: (1) Integration is the solution to racism, and (2) legislation leads to justice. Vivian allowed that King wrung as much as possible out of liberal Christian idealism. At the time, nothing would have worked better. But King wrongly assumed that racial integration was the model of success, that white Americans believed in their democratic ideals, and that white supremacy would break when enough good people recognized the justice of the civil rights cause. By 1970, Vivian struggled to remember that *he* had ever believed it.

The only thing Vivian knew for sure in 1970 was that white liberalism was no longer a basis for making any further progress toward racial justice. White American racism was so toxic and pervasive that it drove whites into two groups.

A small tradition of white radicals shared John Brown's hatred of racism. The rest were psychologically incapable of acknowledging what Vivian elsewhere calls the "unspeakable and intolerable crime"[6] of American racial tyranny. The only true white allies were the ones who hated racism enough to purge themselves of it. They recognized their complicity in white supremacy and worked to abolish it. Vivian said there were more of them than Black nationalists tended to assume. He had white allies that he trusted, and even Brown had sixteen white comrades at Harpers Ferry. But this was a small group, and the genuine white allies did not ask Blacks for validation or a place at the table.

In 1970, Vivian said that the new separatism was finished with helping white liberals with their problems. What mattered was to build a Black freedom movement that sang its own songs. King and Vivian had pledged allegiance to integration because this concept fit their understanding of how people should relate to one another. A good society has integrationist values. But this idea, Vivian rightly said, does not fit US American society. Holding out for integration in racist America is demeaning and self-defeating for African Americans. It masks the oppressive relation of whites to Blacks, making white liberals the brokers of racial integration. Vivian declared that almost everything he had learned in the movement made integration impossible as a goal for the Black community in the post-King era.

Holding this book of 1970 next to this sermon of 2005 is a telling measure of what has changed and what has not. Vivian was the same person through all of it, standing up for righteousness and pouring himself out for it. Some things that he expounded at length in 1970 no longer needed to be said by the end of the decade. It can be jarring to recall how much we *did* talk about integration in the 1960s. What mattered about King in a changing political context changed as the backlash took over an entire political party, we endured the nightmare [Ronald] Reagan era, King was domesticated for holiday status, and we belatedly recalled that King was radical. Then we stressed that King was a postcolonial liberationist who condemned the Vietnam War, was mostly sympathetic toward the Black Power movement, was a democratic socialist who wanted to speak directly about socialism, was the founder of the Poor People's Campaign, and who opposed nearly the entire SCLC staff concerning that campagn.

Vivian was one of the few who had always known that King was radical. He didn't need the revisionist scholarship of the 1980s to remind him. But the years and blocks problems were terribly real, and still are. Vivian was the epitome of a prophet through the shadow years, showing up to give a witness and a reminder, giving all that he had, exemplifying in this context, and the next one, and then the next one, what it means to carry out the Black faith and prophetic religion of Martin Luther King Jr.

Part Three

A Theology of Reconciliation

10

America's Joseph

What Man Meant for Evil, God Meant for Good

I HAVE TOLD your minister that I would probably be as long-winded as you would expect from a Black Baptist on a Sunday morning. I have chosen this pulpit for a particular reason, to do what I want to do this morning because you are familiar with the preacher-writer-activist who, every now and then, not only preaches a sermon but at the same time is writing his next article. And I thought that you might share with me, and think with me, as I think through the basis of an idea. The subject would be America's Joseph.

It is my basic contention that America's Black man is America's Joseph. And that we are in a period where identity is the central issue for [the] Black American and those who are thinking Black today. The matter of one's personhood—who am I, not only in relationship simply to one's presence, but to one's goals and ends and importance and being? What am I meant to do, what to be, and what to become? What not simply is my ability to breathe and to appreciate beauty, but what, too, is my ultimate being in the midst of my fellow men? The matter of identity. Not simply in the terms of Blackness in color alone but in terms of the understanding of the more profound nature of one's being that is altered by the fact of his coloring, whether it be social or physical.

The matter of our identity is a central issue as we struggle. And it is not a central issue of Black people only, but the identity of any member of the Brotherhood. In fact, it changes the meaning of the identity of all other members of the Brotherhood. It is sort of like a people tree. That is, you cannot really shake one part of it without shaking all of it. The ultimate result of that [action] will determine whether the fruit matures or how quickly it drops to the ground and perishes there.

And so, as we come to worship this morning and think in terms of ourselves in relationship to each other, I would like for us to turn to this story—this story which most of you have known from your youth, which was a part of your Sunday school text. The story of that gigantic figure of Joseph, as one of the five major figures of the Old Testament, prior to the period of the prophets. For here we see a giant strolling across the Scriptures [who] not only had meaning in that day but [who also] speaks to us today. A figure [whom] Jewish people have never forgotten. [In] any writings of the Scriptures, there was a continuous reference to Joseph.

The Scriptures have a way of revealing for us the period in which we live. They provide some prototype of the possibilities for our own lives. As we gather to hear a word from the Lord, and gain an understanding of Scripture, it might be that this morning we turn not so much to a central abstract text but to the total story of a man and his struggle to be, so that we see a Joseph as that figure who is hated by his brothers, who is thrown into a pit, who is pushed off into slavery, who becomes the servant, who is lied upon, who is tempted, who finally comes to the right-hand side of power, and is the decider of policy that [saves] the nation. The story is Joseph. It is my contention that, in a very real way, just as this was the Joseph of Egypt, that America's Black Man is in truth America's Joseph. Let us look at the struggle.

The story starts by saying that Joseph was hated by his brothers. We begin to see that his brothers said that it was because of the color of his robe, but when we look a little closer, the Scripture itself, which never really allows us to hide or to rationalize or to use excuses, tells us that the true conflict between Joseph and his brothers was not one of [the] color of his robe or the color of anything: It was in the conflict of the color of character. It was a conflict of lifestyle. It was a conflict of basic life concerns. It was the issue [that] here was a man who had tremendous vision. It said that his oneness with the moon and the stars peeking out [was] in terms of Joseph's ability to become a part of the universe [by] which he was surrounded. We see in Joseph a man with a kind of vision of the possibilities of men living and working together. Over and against his brothers, who seemed to always look down, [while] breaking the clods in the earth. In fact, becoming almost a part of the clod-like nature of life, rather than the vision opening the nature of life. We begin to see brothers who are concerned about how much they can make, how much food they could gather into barns, over and against another brother, whose deep concerns were not in terms of things, but in terms of soul.

The conflicts: The conflicts between persons involved in an image that said that, because of their birth, they were in fact sons of the Father. Rather than in understanding the kinds of visions of the Father. The conflict: The conflict, if you will, between those that store into barns and those that are concerned about the development of man, [who], simply because he is and is meant to be, must do his thing. Because he was born to be. [There] are conflicts that fall beyond the matter of the color of robes, where we begin to understand the views of Joseph involved in trying to define humanity in the period [of] which he was a part. Those [who] were so concerned about that which was outside of themselves, so much so that it was difficult for them to understand a Joseph—because of [their] inability to understand a soul with style, they saw the need to get rid of him rather than to define a deep and more profound human channel, whereby they and their brothers could find each other.

When we begin to look at the Scriptures, it becomes clear that Joseph's brothers did not really hate each other over some simple artificial understanding of the color of robes, but for a far deeper and more profound understanding of what they were about as human beings. So, it says here that the brothers could not stand him because he found favor with their father. And so, they were continuously in the confusion and frustration that leads to hate. He was hated by his brothers. So, they were concerned about the making of things. Joseph's brothers were in contention and competition.

America found that, in order to get rid of the competitor on another level, it was necessary to force him out of the economic market. The brothers had a clash of lifestyle, of vision, an image of fame and soul and humanity inside, and we begin to see that the hate began there. But the glorious thing about the story is that the story doesn't end here. It does not end with one brother hating another brother. God never allows a story to end with hate.

And that's our reason for coming here this morning, our reason for worshipping such a God, for celebrating at such an altar. For we have a God that, no matter how long it takes, will not allow the brothers to end in a relationship where one hates the other.

So, the story goes on from there. The story goes on to say that the brothers, in their confusion [over] what to do with the unusual Joseph, who was different from themselves, decided that they would throw him into a pit. And so, they threw Joseph into a pit. I suppose that the contrast in America's Joseph—[Michael] Harrington said in his book on poverty that those who come from the suburbs ride through the morning with the *New York Times* in front of their face and do not look down into the pit which is Harlem.[1] And in the evening, tired from the day's making of money on Wall Street, the clod-like existence, they in fact play cards across the table instead of looking down into the pit. It is the kind of story that [Ralph] Ellison describes in *Invisible Man*, where the attempt was to make Joseph invisible by placing him on the other side of the railroad tracks, by placing him on the other side of town, to herd him into a ghetto. To give him Kenwood Oakland until the university wanted it.[2]

In fact, the pit, the pit we see everywhere we look. And I have a feeling that what really happened was that when Joseph was first in the pit, he blamed himself. But when you're in the pit, there's only one place you can look, and that's up. And really, Joseph's nature was to look up. And in that looking up, one sees the universe from a totally different perspective. When one is hemmed in on every dark side, one sees the world from a totally different perspective. When one is cut off from the things that might embellish [one's] bodily being, [one] then begins to see the world in terms of its skies, its universal understanding, its spiritual depth. And that becomes a strength.

Those who have been in the pits of this world, somehow, were more sensitive to the needs of other men than those who have been able to reach and to twirl on every side. Joseph was the invisible man. But strangely enough, that man which we turn our backs on always, somehow, becomes the man that causes us to shed a midnight tear on the pillow. That person that we misuse and mistreat and then turn our backs on, is that person who goes with us wherever we are. In ways that he could not go physically. That person whom we mistreat and misuse and turn away from is that person who goes to worship with us on Sunday morning, when we thought that he was in the pit. First Baptist churches across the southland today—we may not be physically there—but there can be no worship service in America today without the invisible presence of the brother Joseph that moves the conscience of men. It was the conduct of Joseph, even in the pit, his relationships with his God that created the relationship with other men, that had to move the conscience even of the brothers [who] pitched him into a pit.

Scripture tells us that one of the brothers was moved. Not all the brothers. They had a clod-like existence. Scripture says one of the brothers was really moved. There was a liberal in their midst. And the one brother talked with his other brothers and said, "We cannot keep Joseph in the pit." And so, he lifted down a hand, and together the brothers lifted Joseph out of the pit. For somehow, God has so made us that, in spite of our desire to make men invisible, they in fact become present in our midst, in a very moving and meaningful way. But the Scripture here never denies the brotherhood. Even as Joseph was hated, there was not a denial of the brotherhood. Even as Joseph was in the pit, it was not a denial of the brotherhood. Regardless of the misuse of one brother by the others, God never allowed for the story to end there, in the pit. For the brotherhood was always there, even in the midst of the acts of hate and in the pit.

Strangely enough though, the conscience of one brother was moved upon, and the invisibleness of the brother was seemingly made visible. The Scripture goes on to say that after they took Joseph out of the pit, they still could not live with him. So, in their frustration, they decided to sell him into slavery. While they could not make him invisible, the desire now was to destroy him, but to do it in such a humane way that they could blame someone else for what was done. In fact, maybe even blame Joseph because he could not live through the rigors of such a slavery. The tendency was not to put the blame upon the seller, but to put the blame upon he who was sold and upon [them] who were involved in that system of slavery itself and those who profited from it.

Strangely enough, everything done to destroy Joseph in slavery only developed Joseph for the future. The parallel is of the children in the wilderness of forty years that, in fact, prepared them to be in charge of the promised land. Having not been involved in the wilderness experience, [Black people in the United States] may have too quickly imitated Babylon. The need, if you will—Lerone Bennett in *The Negro Mood*—I was joking with him several weeks ago and told him that if it was republished, he would probably call it *The Black Mood.* And we were talking again last week, and he had done just that. His publishers had called him, and it's going to be reprinted. It will come up under *The Black Mood.* In this book, as I read it in a prison cell in Alabama[3], was the story, as Lerone put it, that when the Europeans came to this soil with their gunpowder and their liquor and their Bible, they fell upon their knees, and then they "fell" upon the Aborigines and destroyed the Indians' civilization until there was nothing there but rocks, high up in the mountains.

The gunpowder destroyed them physically, the liquor spiritually, or the Bible spiritually. And the liquor only kept the whole process going. As they came to the shores of America as we know it, the Indians—who were hundreds of thousands strong and roamed the land and owned it—were demoralized by those same three things severing their lives, so that now the Indian is only a remnant on a reservation here and there across the land. And [he] has no control over what was his own heritage, his own being.

Look again when, in 1619, there were only twenty slaves brought to this land—America's Joseph, America's Black Man. Now, today, there are twenty million. Everything that was done to destroy him only, in fact, developed him. While other civilizations fell and other people diminished, he remained and endured and strengthened. The Joseph of America. He took the gunpowder and turned it into nonviolence, took the liquor and drinks, more scotch than anyone in America, and still survives, and took [Scripture] and made it as pure as anyone has made it in the land, and gave it its only meaningful set of songs from the spirituals in the midst of depravity. What was meant to destroy was only a means of development.

But the story doesn't end here. God never allows a story to end with one man being another man's master, whatever the life. Whatever hope has become, that is the understanding of our lives as we bow before a cross—that God, in fact, never allows one man to be another man's slave.

So, the story goes on from there.

The story goes on to say that Joseph was then made a servant in Potiphar's house. Potiphar looked upon Joseph and said that he was too good for the field. And that he should at least be in the house as a servant. It is my contention that, for America's Joseph, that [change came in] 1864, and we went from slavery into servanthood. The Emancipation Proclamation somehow delivered us from slavery but only made us house servants in Potiphar's house. It did not make us free men. For if you [white America] want your diapers washed or your windows washed or your floors scrubbed, the ditches dug, [Black people] go on to become America's servant. The last to be hired and the first to be fired—the servant of America. There was something truthful about the Scriptures. The Scriptures did not ever say that Joseph was out of slavery. [The Scriptures] simply said that his slave's state was changed to one of servanthood.

It is my contention that we are America's Joseph. Our state has never been one of free men but merely servants, a part of the slave past of going through the long years of peonage and living in the shadows of the servanthood that is nothing more than slavery, in fact. For the control on one's life in the hands of other people: There is something truthful about the Scripture as it deals with the story. There is the servanthood of Joseph. Those who would claim to be both Black and citizens of this land are probably neither. For, in fact, those who would claim to be free in this land only deceive themselves. The Emancipation Proclamation did not free Black people, it did not free America's Joseph. I believe in a far deeper and profound understanding. It says that not until a man says for himself that he is free, knows who he is, tells the truth about himself, only then is he free. Regardless of the shackles around him, he then becomes no longer [a] slave. He becomes a captured man, but free. Those who [know] the truth are free indeed. But the story doesn't end there.

Strange thing, a very long story. But a very meaningful story in the journey of a man who could be the prototype of a people. For we find that, in the midst of that servanthood, there is a story that we've all heard from childhood. We even snickered about it. The story that was read this morning. Later on, as adolescents, we looked down and then asked each other, and then as adults we said something like, "It's like that, ain't it." But this morning, as we began to see Joseph as a prototype of a people, we're not simply talking about a sex story. We're talking about a profound temptation. Of a man of vision and destiny, who was trying to be fully what he was meant to be, regardless of the social blocks in his way. For there is something profound in the temptations of Joseph in this seemingly simple sex story that, to me, are the temptations of America's Joseph in 1970. For what Potiphar's wife was saying to Joseph was this: "Joseph, if you would love me, on my terms, you can be socially acceptable. If you will forget about the love of your God, and you will love on a more perverted level, if you will forget the bounds of dignity and sense of being and vision, that slavery in the pit and suffering which you have endured. If you will forget that, if you will accept the terms of my society, you can be socially acceptable." And I think that [some] part of his wife understood the depth of the struggle of Joseph. And I think she said something like this to him: "But Joseph, you were hated by your brothers. They told you that if you were Black, get back. If you were brown, hang around.

And if you were white, you were all right. I know that you were hated [by your] brothers. I know that no one has ever really loved you and cared for you and respected you. And if you will sell out, and love on my terms, I will make you socially acceptable."

And this is the struggle of middle-class Black Josephs living in America today. To forget the vision, to forget the good work that struggle has taught and simply to accept life in the normal status quo, and if you're in the South, status Jim Crow, American terms. Bow down, do not try to delineate a moral and spiritual future of a value that is beyond what this system now has. "And you'll be all right, Joseph. I'll take good care of you." That's a profound temptation.

Let's look again. For the temptation of Joseph here is a profound one. For what Potiphar's wife was saying to Joseph was, "Joseph, if you will do what I tell you to do, you can have all the things you want. I know that when you have seen the master of this house, driving a chariot, you, too, will want a chariot. I know that your father once gave you beautiful robes, and you desire some from the textile mills of this land also. I know also that you would love to live in a beautiful split-level house, and drive a Cadillac car, and have two-hundred dollar suits—I know you would, Joseph. So, you can have all the things you want, Joseph, if you will just forget about the rest of those like you and step on them, as Potiphar steps on them; use them as Potiphar uses them. Trick them even as I trick them. You can have anything you want."

The temptation. The temptation of a goodly number of America's Josephs today. To simply accept the economic system as it is and be an individual unto Potiphar and become an artificial Black capitalist. The temptation. Let's look again at the temptation.

For this is not simply a sex story. This is a story that is as deep and profound as man's struggle. For we begin to see that what she was saying to him—because these temptations showed that she understood the frustration in Joseph—was "Joseph, not only can get your revenge. I know that since it was you [who] made cotton king and gave Potiphar an economy that allowed him to compete with his neighbors. Since you first did that, you want a piece of that economy, a piece of that pie. I know that. I know that you have hated being degraded and you cannot help but hate those that degrade you. I know that, Joseph." And she played on the hate, and she said, "Joseph, you can get your revenge. Use me, whom he does not want you to use, take away the only things that he tries to build his security upon. Take away something deep and vital to his inner life."

Here we are, in a position being able to destroy all the myths of America. Potiphar's wife was really a myth of Potiphar's life, something that he thought he could care for and something that he thought really existed. The idea that American society tries to hold so dear, that one can make it on individual initiative and that the world is there for everyone—it's all a myth. A myth that America's Joseph destroys by his mere presence. The myth of the loved ones of life. That America tries to believe in. But in fact, the myth so destroys life every day, in the inner cities of this land, that it destroys the spirit of the suburb, that it is impossible for it to talk of a spiritual life outside of its myth structure. She was saying, "Get your revenge, Joseph."

These are the temptations of America's Joseph as he finds his full identity and his new being in relationship to all those around him today. Profound temptation. Why, I like to think that when she said to Joseph, "Joseph, love me," that he said, "I know the love of one that is greater than thee." I'd like to think that when Joseph of Egypt was tempted, and she said you can have things, he said, "I know the one that owns the cattle on a thousand hills." I'd like to think that when she said, "Joseph, get your revenge," he said, "Vengeance is mine, saith the Lord."

That will be the answer of America's Joseph in 1970. But the story doesn't end there. The story does not end simply with temptation. Though it seems as it should end here. Why doesn't the story end? Didn't Joseph act out of his righteousness? Didn't Joseph stand through the temptations? Didn't Joseph stay with God? And in our Sunday school world, our world of dream books and our world of fairy tales, isn't this enough? For shouldn't, now, Joseph live happily ever after? The contrast, however, between the reality of the world and the Scriptures that delineates life in all its reality and the storybooks of we who write to rationalize and to escape, tells the truth. It says that Potiphar's wife lied upon Joseph. This is so much a part of the story. We moved against segregation in the land, and the nation lied on us. Martin Luther King Jr. moves, if you will, to make a nation free for all men. And even after his death, they try to put the lie on him.

We do not have to look to the special lives, however, for America lives the gigantic lie of the stereotype. All Josephs lie, all Josephs steal, all Josephs gang-bang, and all Josephs stink. I know they didn't make all that Lifebuoy soap for me. And even in that, there was something of great meaning, for we live in a culture that likes to take all of its own evils and then find a scapegoat to blame. There is a basic kind of truth that we need as we come to worship this morning.

Having said that, Potiphar's wife told a lie on Joseph, but it doesn't tell us anything about Joseph. It tells us something about Potiphar's wife. When a nation can lie upon Martin Luther King Jr., that does not tell us about Martin. It tells us something about that nation. When a nation feels it has to suppress one-tenth of its population's basic drives for dignity, it does not tell us something about the suppressed and the oppressed. It tells us something about the suppressor and the oppressor. There was not a sickness in Joseph, there was a sickness in Joseph's wife. That is the basic sickness of American culture today. Potiphar could not but deal with the event in terms of the testimony of his wife. And it is my feeling that, inside of himself, Potiphar already knew that she was lying. And yet, he had to call in his police force with a charge to shoot to kill, rather than deal with the reality of the conviction. Had to lay down a search-and-seize law, rather than deal with the reality of the lie. Had to bind Scriptures in institutionalized ways rather than deal with the condition that created the bedroom scene.

Where was Joseph, who finds himself as the lied-upon, the tempted man, the slave? And yet the story doesn't end there, for it says he's a prisoner. Now, on the basis of the lie, they put Joseph into prison. There is something about a prison, that when you have done all that you can really do, when you have tried to uphold the code in which you believe, imitate the person—the spiritual understanding of the person who you think represented humanity, when you have tried to tell the truth—even as the prophets, when you have tried to show in brotherly love the lie, and yet you are pushed into prison—something happens to you that's hard to really rationalize. I remember being in Selma, Alabama, again—or was it in Selma this time? I remember the prison, rather than the surroundings. And just as we got to the jail door, and it was unlocked, and the jailer opened the door, he pushed me in, even though I was willing to walk. And the steel door clanked behind me before I could turn around. And there was something about that heavy door locking behind me that says, "There is nothing more that you can do."

I remember falling down on my knees on that metal bunk with the rolled-up mattress in the corner, and praying to the Father that he [take] it from here because there was nothing I could do within the confines of that little space. When I opened my eyes, I looked up. There was a little window over me, and I looked out at the sky. And I left it to heaven. Three days later, I was out. And Jimmie Lee Jackson was killed in an attempt to get me.[4] I understand what Joseph felt.

But there is something about God, something about God that when you have done everything you can do, when you are boxed in and are locked in and are seemingly left powerless, there is a power of God that moves. Oh, yes, there is. Oh, yes, there is. It is not the kind of thing you can know simply by the arguments of that abstraction. But it is something that happens when you come to the end of your own resources. It says in the Scripture that when Joseph was in prison, Pharaoh had a dream. Pharaoh had a dream that he could not answer. He called all of his wise men and his charlatans around him and asked for an answer to the dream. And they gave him some quick answers and did some research and study papers, but it didn't answer the dream. And finally, they told him the truth. They said that if you will simply go down into the prison of the southland of Egypt, there is a man by the name of Joseph down there that has been talking to God and [has had] a vision, all the days of his life. And he's got the answer to the dream. But you've got to humble yourself because you put him into prison. And now you have to humble yourself and ask him for the answers to your questions. I have a feeling that the pharaoh pondered a long time before he did that. A part of the spiritual dilemma of American life today.

America knows that, in order to get the answers to white racism, it has to come to American's Joseph because it does not have the resources inside itself. America knows that, in order to answer the dream of the democratic existence, it has to humble itself. To get the answers from America's Joseph. The left-out man. America knows [that], if it is ever to move from myth to reality with the great concepts, it has to humble itself. *Sometimes I feel as though America would rather be destroyed than to humble itself to its blacker brother.* Sometimes I have a feeling that America would rather never answer the dream that Martin Luther King Jr. had on the steps that was a repetition of a Jefferson. It's a matter of a spiritual conflict in American life.

And Pharaoh had to think a long time before this King, master of the house and nation, would be willing to go to a prison in the southland. And it was the South of Egypt. It said, however, in the story, that he was able to bridge that spiritual gap. And humble himself. And the price of his going to Joseph for the answer was that he had to take the powerless Joseph and sit him on the right hand side of power. And the price he had to pay was to turn over the internal workings of the nation to the sensitive nature and the vision of Joseph. And if he did not do that famine would destroy the nation. He was able to make that spiritual leap, and Joseph went from powerlessness to power. For it is impossible to answer the problems of a nation or of a people without power. So, let us not make excuses for Black Power. Let us not make excuses for this Black Power, for we must see it as a necessity in order for a nation of people, not simply of Black people, to be saved. For this is not a struggle of Joseph alone. There is a famine in the land that must be dealt with.

Now, when the brothers first came to Joseph in Egypt, they came to deal with their physical problems in themselves. The physical problem in the land. And Joseph was sitting behind a great drawn curtain, and he gave them a small subsidy that would lead to undergirding the poverty. And finally, the brothers came and asked for Joseph. For when they had gone home, their father told them, "You may be fed physically but you will never be fulfilled spiritually, [you] will never know what it means to be a full man, you will never know what it means to truly live in your father's house until you go out and find your brother Joseph that you cast into a pit, that you sold into slavery. And not until you find him and reconcile yourself can you be a full man and live in your father's house."

And they went to find Joseph. And they went again to the curtain, and the curtain opened up, and Joseph walked down. And they fell back in horror, for they knew that this was the Joseph that they had sold, the Joseph that they had hated, the Joseph they had sold into a pit. And they were afraid that Joseph would do the same thing to them that they had done to Joseph. But Joseph put their fears away and said, "You meant it for evil, but God meant it for good. I have suffered so long that I want no other man to suffer. But I have learned out of a deep spiritual understanding, out of a sense of love, how we can be reconciled together." And the brothers fell on each other's shoulders and wept, [Scripture says] with all its imagery, down each other's backs.

And that's where the story ends. The brothers loving one another. God never lets the story end until we love one another. God will never let the story end until the brothers reconcile themselves to one another. How long it will take depends upon the actions and the level of spiritual understanding of the brothers. How long it takes will depend upon the great sense of humility of all those involved. It will depend upon the great sense of forgiveness of those involved. It will depend upon the sense of understanding of one's humanity, and a willingness to be, and to become the recipients of goodness in the household of the father.

Written:
In the early 1970s

COMMENTARY

Jonathan Lee Walton

In his 1973 text, *The Hero and the Blues*, literary critic Albert Murray laments a truism about Black preaching: an inordinate emphasis on the biblical character Moses and the exodus motif. According to Murray, African Americans have overlooked the unique implications of Joseph's entry into Egypt. Although sold into slavery by his brothers, the biblical patriarch Joseph "not only uses his inner resources and the means at hand to take advantage of the most unlikely opportunities to succeed in the circumstances in which he finds himself; he also makes himself indispensable to the nation as a whole."[5]

The quote above leads me to wonder if Murray was sitting in the pews when Dr. C. T. Vivian climbed the sacred desk and delivered the sermon "America's Joseph." This sermon is a curious yet courageous homiletic account of African American history. It is curious insofar as this sermon pivots sharply from the prevailing themes of the Black Protestant tradition. Moses, not Joseph, is the archetypal biblical figure of the Black experience in America. For a blues people who spent centuries seeking to break free of enslavement and another hundred years wandering through an American wilderness of legalized apartheid, peonage, and mass imprisonment, Joseph's rags to riches storyline could certainly strike hearers as off-key. Exodus. Liberation. Speaking the truth of freedom to the Pharaohs of oppression. These are the themes that held great purchase in the Black sacred imagination. Joseph, the assimilated Egyptian? Not so much.

Nevertheless, Vivian was not like any other preacher. His life and ministry were anything but typical. Vivian was a creative and courageous spiritual genius who was always willing to push the boundaries of convention and the status quo. His theological reflections were laden with hope and moral challenge. They were grounded in history and pointed toward a better and brighter future. His sermons encouraged hearers to dream of a world anew, though he would never allow us to forget the prophet Micah's admonition to do justice, love mercy, and walk humbly before God.

True to form, "America's Joseph" reconsiders the role of African Americans in the nation's self-conception. The sermon challenges African Americans to connect the moral attributes of resilience, determination, and a deep abiding faith with a noble history of Black progress in the face of inimical circumstances. The same virtues that propelled Joseph from the pits of enslavement to the height of power, for Vivian, constitute the story of America's Black Man.

Such a modernist narrative of progress was not new, per se. A longstanding tradition of spiritual autobiography in America valorizes singular, masculinist narratives of advancement and achievement. Black folk are not immune, as we, too, sing America.[6] Think of Frederick Douglass and Booker T. Washington, who epitomized the genre of Black self-determination and virile manhood. Their respective autobiographies, *Narrative of the Life of Frederick Douglass* and *Up From Slavery*, trace their journeys from enslavement to a self-realized liberation. Moreover, like the biblical Joseph, both figures rose to the height of American power, insofar as they became representative men of their age—heroic figures who inspired others to maximize their own potential and to strive for cultural acclaim and mass acceptance.

"America's Joseph" sought to resuscitate such a spirit of hope and optimism when it seemed Black folk were locked in a Dickens-like paradox. Consider the numerous uprisings that broke out across the country in the wake of Martin Luther King Jr.'s assassination in 1968, even as the Civil Rights Act outlawing housing discrimination was finally signed into law. That same year, Shirley Chisholm became the first African American woman elected to the United States Congress. Furthermore, in the period between 1968 and 1973, more than two dozen cities or towns across the nation elected African American mayors. In the words of Curtis Mayfield's 1970 hit song, Black folks were set to "Move On Up!" Yet, as the 1968 Kerner Commission ominously reported, America is "two societies, one black, one white—separate and unequal."[7] Indeed, depending on one's view, it was the best of times or the worst of times. It was an age of progress, but also of despair, of Black striving, and of concentrated poverty.

With this sermon, Vivian seems to be wrestling with that paradox himself, from the pulpit. In one respect, Vivian is full of hope and even optimism regarding the progress of Black people. His words of hope speak to Joseph's resilience, which is evidenced within the Black community. As with Joseph, Black success in the face of evil and oppression is the ultimate vindication. From cotton sacks to Cadillacs, the truth of Black dignity and humanity marches on.

This argument goes beyond mere materialism. Vivian is making a moral claim about the ways African Americans, like Joseph in Egypt, have helped to deliver an unjust nation from itself. "He [the Black man] took gunpowder and turned it into nonviolence," Vivian declares.[8] From the abolitionist movement to the Black freedom struggle, African Americans continue challenging the nation to live up to its promise of dignity, freedom, and justice for all.

More than fifty years later, many are familiar with this hopeful storyline of Black achievement. It constitutes the substance of political sloganeering and quixotic appeals to racial exceptionalism. Not to mention that it fuels a cottage industry around Black history which offers up paraphernalia with sophomoric phrases including "King marched so Obama could run." Sigh. Nevertheless, whether framed as God's blessings, moral fortitude, or some combination thereof, one can and should be proud of Black achievement. This point was the one Vivian sought to impress upon his hearers. Black progress is a result of a shared struggle and sacrifice. Like Joseph, in Vivian's retelling, "Those who have been in the pits of this world, somehow, were more sensitive to the needs of other men [sic]."[9]

In another respect, Vivian was acutely aware of the implications of fetishizing upward social mobility. He even questions the value of Joseph's integration into Egyptian society. In this sermonic retelling, the allure of progress is premised on a lie, a great temptation. Likening America to Potiphar's palace, Vivian contends, "The idea that American society tries to hold so dear, that one can make it on individual initiative and that the world is there for everyone—it's all myth."[10]

Vivian then likens the temptation of Potiphar's wife to the seductions of bourgeois life:

> I know that you would love to live in a beautiful split-level house, and drive a Cadillac car, and have two-hundred-dollar suits—I know you would, Joseph. So, you can have all the things you want, Joseph, if you will just forget about the rest of those like you and step on them, as Potiphar steps on them; use them as Potiphar uses them. Trick them even as I trick them. You can have anything you want.[11]

Thus, he condemns those who view their middle-class existence as merely a means to individual acceptance. Beware of Potiphar's palace and all the promises it entails. This argument is one that Vivian fleshes out in his book *Black Power and the American Myth*, which was published the same year he delivered "America's Joseph." The book is a tender, tear-soaked lament from someone publicly mourning the death of his dearest friend and co-laborer in the struggle, Martin Luther King Jr. A wail of frustration and heartbreak emerges from its pages. Vivian indicts the lies that he believes America offers about itself, the self-satisfying myths of American exceptionalism that he admits to having once believed. These myths include the notion that Americans will do right when they know right. That legislation leads to justice. That America is an open society. And that a love ethic is at the core of American conscience. The civil rights movement fell short for Vivian because its aims were premised on these mythic assumptions.

Thus, he is seemingly using this sermon, "America's Joseph," to sound the proverbial alarm. There will always be a pharaoh who knew nothing of Joseph. Why? Society never cared to know Joseph in the first place. He was, and will always be, a stranger in the land of Egypt.

Therefore, Vivian offered the listener a paradox: a belief in progress and what is possible on the one hand and a lack of faith in the virtue of the dominant society on the other. How can America's Joseph transcend this double bind? How does Vivian reconcile these paradoxical impulses? Here is where Vivian's deep and enduring faith in a sovereign God matters the most. It is not up to us to reconcile our competing passions, nor to overcome our fallen humanity. It is up to God. "God never lets the story end until we love one another," he declares. "God will never let the story end until the brothers reconcile themselves to one another."[12] Indeed, our humanity, humility, and ability to forgive—they matter. Vivian believes, without a shadow of a doubt, that God will redeem the suffering of America's Joseph, just as he redeemed the suffering of the biblical Joseph. This is the moral of the story for Vivian. African Americans can testify, like Joseph, that "what man meant for evil, God meant for good."

Knowing that this sermon was delivered in 1970, it comes as no surprise that its language and theological content suffer from severe gender limitations. Vivian conceptualized "America's Joseph" an entire decade before Black woman theologians, including Jacquelyn Grant, Katie Geneva Cannon, and Delores Williams, began developing what we now commonly call "womanist theology." Vivian preached this sermon well before these towering women began bending the arc of the theological academy to take seriously the experiences and perspectives of those who lived on the underside of Jane Crow.

Consider how Vivian takes the notion of redemptive suffering for granted. Joseph had to carry the hatred of his brothers, endure unjust imprisonment, and suffer under the weight of exploitation and servitude. Vivian concludes, "What was meant to destroy was only a means of development."[13]

This line of thinking—a theodicy premised on the redemptive nature of human suffering—can have dangerous implications for the most vulnerable in any given society. If Joseph's brothers meant it for evil but God meant it for good, it becomes difficult to distinguish where the sinful behavior of the brothers ends and God's sovereign will begins. This theological problem is at the heart of redemptive suffering. It can absolve unjust structures and pernicious behaviors by elevating evil to God's pedagogical will. Thus, endurance and acceptance of such injustice become a badge of piety and fidelity.

Moreover, that women have historically borne the responsibility of carrying the sins of others around them as a mark of true womanhood only exacerbates the problem. Domestic violence. Sexual abuse. Labor exploitation. Too often, we expect women to endure as long-suffering servants to maintain family structures or even protect Black manhood. The idea harks back to slaveholding Christianity and its emphasis on submission and obedience (Ephesians 6:5–9, I Peter 2:18). In her 1993 essay "Wading Through Many Sorrows: Toward a Theology of Suffering in a Womanist Perspective," theologian M. Shawn Copeland calls out this notion.[14]

It is ironic, perhaps, that a theology of suffering is formed from resources of resistance. It is not womanist perspective that makes it so, but the Christianity of the plantation. In its teaching, theologizing, preaching, and practice, this Christianity sought to bind the slaves to their condition by inculcating caricatures of the cardinal virtues of patience, long-suffering, forbearance, love, faith, and hope. Thus, to distance itself from any form of masochism, even Christian masochism, a theology of suffering from a womanist perspective must reevaluate those virtues in light of Black women's experiences.

Christian faith communities must continue to wrestle with where we locate the source of suffering. The risk of amplifying rather than undercutting a theology that reinforces the power dynamic between master and servant is too high.

This critique notwithstanding, none could ever believe that Vivian holds a glib view of human suffering. His courageous life and witness negate this idea. He held a political theology that called for us to confront evil. Name it. Stand before it, just as he stood before Sheriff Jim Clark in Alabama. His head may have been bloodied but it remained always unbowed.

This was the spirit of Joseph that Vivian channeled. He was a servant of God who refused to let the accident of birth or the injustice and wrongdoings of others define or determine his freedom. Maybe this is what Murray meant when he wrote that the biblical character Joseph, "a fine figure of a man was once not only a slave but a convict. . . . He never regarded himself as being anything other than a Prince of the Earth."[15]

Herein lies an apt description of the life and ministry of. Vivian—an American Joseph. Whether in an Alabama prison or dining at the White House, Vivian made evident to all that he was a man set aside for a special purpose. Indeed, a Prince of the Earth!

11

What Does It Mean to Be a Christian?

Ephesians 6:12 and 2 Corinthians 11

You know, to be here on a Sunday school day is, I think, so important because when I think *ministry*, we who preach would not even be understood if it were not for those who taught in the Sunday school for years before people got to us. When we speak of various phases, ideas, when we bring up such great concepts—if they hadn't already been discussed at another level, if there weren't teachers there before, half of us wouldn't know what's really going on. One of the problems of the Christian church today is that so many of our members didn't go to Sunday school, and so they really don't know what's happening.

It is an interesting thing. If you look [back] about thirty years ago, we came to hear the preacher preach. Today, in practically all the huge churches, we see the pastor with a Bible in his hand, going carefully through, step by step, with everybody with a Bible in their hand. The real reason is that they never had a Bible in their hand before. We have the same problem when we say "turn to. . ." and it takes us five minutes to do it. Because we weren't in Sunday school and didn't learn where the various books of the bible were, right? So, we don't know how to quickly find the difference between the Old Testament and the New Testament, et cetera, et cetera. What I'm talking about is the importance of the Sunday school, and without a Sunday school you won't end up with a very good church. If you have a strong Sunday school, you'll end up with a strong church. And it doesn't matter how many people will be there. You will know that they understand you work for the Christ.

Well, as they say, there's another Scripture I would like to read today to complement the one that was so beautifully done by our sister here, who does everything so very, very well. In Ephesians, the sixth chapter and the twelfth verse—and you don't have to look for this one, it's just one verse and I'm going to read it to you: "We are not fighting against humans. We're fighting against the principalities and powers, against forces and authorities, and against rulers of darkness and powers in the spiritual world."[1] See, without that, we may not get the importance of what was read in Second Corinthians, eleventh chapter. Because you see—and this is the focus—because Paul is saying here, "I fear," he said, "that you will be tricked," and he uses the first trick of Satan against Adam and Eve. He said, "you will be tricked," like Satan did with that snake. Now, the fear that the average church member—now remember, he's writing a letter to a church, and he says, "My great fear is you will be tricked, and I fear that you might stop thinking about Christ in an honest and sincere way, because if you begin to listen to the wrong stuff, you won't get the good stuff."

And it goes on to say, you will let some people tell you about another Jesus. Says, they will be using the term *Jesus*, but they'll be talking about another Jesus. They will be talking about the church, but it's not the church that I've been telling you about. It's not the church I'm writing you about. Oh, you'll have an institution, and you'll be using the word *Jesus*, and you'll be sitting in a pew. And then, he says,you will be receiving another spirit, rather than the Holy Spirit. It says I'm afraid you may accept another message, the wrong interpretation of the very words that we both share, but they'll mean something totally different than what we, who were the missionaries" And he doesn't use [that word], he uses *apostles*—the apostles—those who knew Jesus and those who were sent out by Jesus. That's what made Paul an apostle in the first place. He resented all his life that he was not there to be sent out by Jesus, but he knew he was knocked off that horse and was called to go to all the places in the world. That's what gave him his standing. He knew that his saying it didn't make any difference, it was doing it, going all over the world, writing the letters, until finally, about a third of the New Testament was written by Paul. Now you see, then he really goes into it and is very hard on—there's no group that he's harder on, if you will read Paul's books, right here, he says: "Such as do these things that make you believe differently. They are false prophets." And then he says, "They're dishonest workers, they are pretenders. They are pretenders who not only speak for Jesus but pretend to look like Jesus's followers. They pretend to do what is right, they pretend to be what is right," he says. Then he goes on, and he even says, when we look at it, they are going to get what they deserve at the end. And if you read it carefully, he goes on to say, I'm not going to let them change me, I'm going on and [will] preach what I preach, even though I don't win you with this letter, because they will have to end up imitating us in order to have respectability in the world. So, you keep on doing and keep on hearing and keep on interpreting like you know [to do]. This is important.

Now, why is this so terribly important for this morning? It's terribly important to this morning, one, because we're in Sunday school. But it's important for another reason, and that is the reason that most of the problems of the Christian church in America [come] because they have not dealt with the meaning of these verses. The battles that have been lost and the condition of the Christian church in America comes down to right here. It's not every day you get a chance to pick up the newspaper of the week and give the sermon of the week. But you see, what's important is, when you look at it, if you read the newspapers this week or if you watched TV, the newspapers didn't deal with it as much as I thought, but you know, that's me. Preachers think a whole lot of stuff. What I'm dealing with is that Pat Robertson, a preacher, a man who owns a college, teaching people what's the Gospel about—you gotta watch the message. And who runs for president, so we can have a Christian president. He says he thing to do is to kill this newly elected president down there because he won't do what we say.[2] That's what he's really saying. He will not carry out our policies. He's down there getting the vote of his people, but we know his people don't know democracy. Can you hear it? "We are going to tell everybody what democracy is 'cause we know. It's not what they want, it's what we want." When did that become democracy? When did that become decency? When did that become divine?

So when we begin to really look at it, we have to understand that what the man is saying is—a preacher, a gospel man—is [saying] "Go kill them." Not "Go convert them." Go kill them. Not "Go allow them to speak for themselves," [but] tell them what they're gonna say, and if they don't say it, kill them. Gospel. Now, can you hear Jesus saying, "Right on, Pat"? And he doesn't stop there. He says the real reason for doing it is because it'll cost less than our going down and having a war on them. Cost less? When was money more important than man and dollars more important than decency? And cash more important than Christ?

We really have to ask ourselves—a basic question comes out of all this. Here's a man talking about starting a war. Let's look at it first, as Paul is talking to three people here, and that's what we have to see. Paul is talking to three people here. But he's talking to the authorities in high places, the principalities and powers. And secondly, he's talking about the rulers of kingdoms that are of this world, but they're the rulers of darkness and work with the rulers of darkness that are not of this world. Oh, listen to Paul, that's the way he explains himself. It's not a matter of what you think, it's a matter of what Paul said, and he's the one doing the writing. And then he talks about the third group, which is the false prophets. Those in the church, not those in politics, not those in [finance], not those that are supposed to play the dirty tricks. He's talking about those that are in the house of Jesus Christ and subvert it so that the message is not clear. It becomes very clear that the [one] he is hardest on here is the false prophet within the church.

I was so surprised that the newspapers hardly picked it up. When a preacher cries murder as a way to solve problems and murder people on foreign soil, in the name of Jesus and your nation, and that it's not dealt with except for here and there, then, you see, I know there's something wrong. And what's particularly puzzling is that he does this after a high authority—the president of the United States—did just what he wants to now do in South America, he already did it in Iraq. Now we can see that you can go jump on people and bomb people that you can't even prove were involved, just because you want to, and then talk about American values and Christian values. You see, there was something very, very wrong, when we can spend billions of dollars in order to kill people, rather than billions of dollars in order to save people and feed the hungry and clothe those that need clothing—Christianity is not involved! One of the preachers of Jesus was trying to support him—an evangelical. This is, like, so funny to me—this is an evangelical—those that are always telling us how great they are and how Christian they are and how pure they are, and that the rest of us should be like them. Well, you see, "them" is the reason we got this president now. You see, there's something wrong about it all. This represents Jesus; this represents the church of Jesus Christ. Is this what we should be like? Something is wrong.

And remember, because I can't get this out of my mind, they voted for Pat Robertson when he ran for president so they could have a president in the White House. They couldn't get him, so they voted for [President George H. W.] Bush, and then they voted for him on the basis of values for a second term. There is something wrong! The question has to be answered: When is a Christian a Christian? No, let me put it the other way: When is a Christian *not* a Christian? What makes a Christian? How do we decide that? Do we listen to Pat Robertson and decide? How do we decide that? When do we see people fronting off Christianity and call them Christian? How evil is the misuse of the faith? And yet we never call it evil! But Paul does—oh boy, he really lays it out, doesn't he? Now the point is, what's wrong with us that we can't call it evil? Are we so much a part of this culture that we can't hear Jesus plainly? Are we so much a part of what has happened around us that we can't separate ourselves?

We have to really ask, this week—now for me, this week—so if I break down halfway through, don't listen to my voice, try to listen to my ideas. Paul is right—he calls them false prophets. Now you see, let's put it this way: There's a question here that has to be answered, and that is, What does it mean to be a Christian? What does it really mean to be a Christian? And until we answer it, we cannot answer any of the other problems that we face. We will not even be able to tell false prophets from real prophets. And that becomes tremendously important to us, because every day you turn on the TV set and you got six people to listen to every hour. And you don't know which is who and which is what and what they mean, and in fact are they interpreting—you don't know. And you know why? Because we have not been clear about what makes a Christian! All a person has to say is, "I joined church, so I'm a Christian." Are you? Are you really? One of our great poets said: "This young man said, I'm a Christian." And she says, "Is that right?" And, "Yes, I'm a Christian." And she said, "It took me sixty years before I was arrogant enough to use the term."

What does it mean? To be a Christian? But until we deal with it seriously, we cannot convert, we cannot have a church [so] that we know what it really is, we don't know who we're talking to and who we're not talking to, and we will be afraid to bring up or evangelize the world around us—because for years I've said, with doing race workshops, I've said, if God asked me, "Vivian, what would you like to happen now to solve the problem of race?", I would say, "Oh, Lord, thank you, convert the white church! And stir up the Black church!" Because the problem is not out there, the problem becomes in here. How do we do it? We can't do it by passing people off as Christians who are not, who don't care, who don't do any work, who don't do anything but see that their children get to Sunday school but [are] really not serious themselves. You see, let's look at that again, because nobody should know better that the definition of *what a Christian is* is important—nobody should know better than we.

Now, the real reason is, is because our ancestors were made slaves, our ancestors were beaten down, our ancestors worked for nothing. A continent was cleared by Christians. People were hung every week in America by Christians. What is a Christian? Who do we let get by with that? When do you call a liar a liar? When do you stop being nice? Paul wasn't nice. It becomes terribly important, and we are the ones that should be doing it, because we know that if you don't know what a Christian is, you will accept anybody, and they'll do anything to give them praise they don't deserve. Had they answered the question—*the* question, 'cause the question is, What does it mean to be a Christian? They would, if we'd made white America—if we'd made America, white, Black, pink, or polka dot—if we who are believers had made America deal with that question, then we wouldn't have had generation after generation after generation of racists who continue to set the policies, the principalities and powers, of this world. We would've brought them down! But we allowed them to remain. We allowed our people to be hung and nobody go to jail. It's the principalities and powers! We never attacked—we wanted to talk about saving those who were hungry but not saving those who made them hungry. Answering the question because the Christian church was not converted in the first place. Look at America! America has an entrepreneurial church—it's a personality matter. I don't have to know nothin'. All I have to do—and I don't really even have to be anything—because if I preach to you, you'll let me do anything to your women and your children. Do you hear me? And if you got enough money, you can decide what's right and wrong in this nation, and God won't have anything to do with it. Because if you don't obey me, I'll send you off to get you killed. What is a Christian?

How is it that, generation after generation, we have allowed this falseness to go on? Because America was an entrepreneurial church, never really a Christian church. The whole South made it very clear that they didn't give a care what God thought about slavery. It's what they thought about slavery [that mattered]. And they did it so well, they told the United States, "You will shut your mouth and let us do what we want to with niggers or you won't be president of nothin' else." So all of 'em just grinned and said, "That's all right." "But we will go to church every Sunday," they said, "because you got to know how good we are." When is a Christian a Christian? It reminds me, since I mentioned [the] president—one of the great presidents of the United States—or, one of the presidents of the United States. I don't know him well enough to know if he was great. He came home from church one Sunday, and he started up-steps with his wife. And his wife hadn't gone to church, and she asked, "What was the sermon about, Reverend?" He says, "Sin." And he said, well, what did he have to say? Said he wasn't getting it. He was there but he didn't know what was going on. It really didn't matter, because nobody was going to do [any of] what he preached about anyway. So, why get all upset, why worry about it, since he was the president, and he represented principalities and powers, and he showed up to look good. He showed up, said something about sin, and then went on upstairs and up to bed.

What I'm talking about is, What does it mean to be a Christian? [When] we really look at it, it becomes important because the Christian church will never be a Christian church that can answer the problems of people in this society until they know what a Christian is. Because if you don't know what a Christian is, you won't know what Christ is about. How many sermons have we heard when, afterwards, two hours later—and they telling you, "Great sermon," and they say, "But what was it about?" Well, I don't know, but it was a great sermon. What they're really saying is, they don't know much about Jesus. That's what they're really saying, is that their lives are a false life, and that they need more emotion than they actually need knowledge to participate in spiritual life.

What does it mean to be a Christian becomes very important. The Pat Robertsons of this world can run for president. They can own colleges in the name of Jesus. They can be heads of great denominations and groups of faiths within this nation because we don't make them answer the question: What does it mean to be a Christian? Paul was saying, "I will not put up with false prophets who get you off track, who confuse you as to who you really are and what you're really about, who interpret the bible wrongly. Won't put up with it, and you shouldn't!" And he says, "No matter how big they get, I will not change. Because I know, in the final analysis, they'll have to pretend to be like Jesus, whether they are or not. And one day, the pretense will wear out. One day. The rest of us will say, 'You are a false prophet.' And when that time comes—pray for it."

All they have to do—it's so simple—[is] pick up the red-letter Bible. All you have to do is to read what Jesus says. He says, "By this will all men know that ye are my disciples, not false prophets, but that we love one another!" Oh, it's so simple, so simple but so necessary that it is the very essence of the faith. Somebody said that Christianity is so deep, that the stream of Christian thinking and activity is so deep, that he said geniuses must swim. [He] says it's so shallow that idiots can wade. Woo! I love it! Isn't that powerful stuff? God made it possible for all of us to be able to have the goodness of God. Some of the simplest people know what a Christian really is. They just look at people and say, "They ain't right." They can't explain it all. They may not quote Paul, but they know there's something wrong with that man.

Think of a woman at one of the great cathedral churches of New England, back in the 1800s.When the sermon was all over, she turned to a lady friend who had come with her to church, and she said, "Such big things to be said by such a little man." That's like a knife to a preacher, isn't it, sister? The point is that we know, but nobody has to *prove by doing* that they are a Christian today. The great thing about the movement was, Martin King not only had a PhD in theology, he proved it on the ground. You understand what I'm saying. Could he preach it? Oh, he could preach it. A whole lot of folk could preach it, but they couldn't do it. Can you do it?

See, that becomes the issue, and if we don't have enough Christians doing it, nobody will know what a Christian is. We'll be talking the talk, making those arguments, talking about who's smarter than who and did we use the right words when we said it, all right, and was that what any of the disciples were talking about. Oh, and I'll give you three Bible verses to back it up. But *what does it mean to be a Christian* still is there. The Christian church has lost on every major issue in American history. Isn't that interesting? We dominate American life in numbers, and yet we've lost and been wronged on every major social issue in American history. How could that be? Because we weren't clear on—that's exactly right, bro! So, we let anything go.

If you had the right size church and you could pay for the right pew—in early America you paid for the pew, so the only people up in the front were the rich, and the poor were in the back—you understand what I'm saying? We were wrong on the issue of the church itself! The great social issue—the most important single issue in American life—has been what? Race and racism. And America was wrong. And you know what? You know who had to change it? Black church had to change it. Those at the bottom became worthy.

Let's look for a moment. I'm a little off. Just be with me until my voice runs out here. But you see, there's some deeper stuff, and sometimes preachers have—they don't deal with the deeper stuff. But I just feel like it this morning, at least on one issue. So let's deal with it. You see, it's this issue of nonviolence. Why was it effective? You know why it was effective? It's because those who thought they were mighty were being humbled by those they thought were not. The issue wasn't civil rights, the issue was moral and spiritual rights. It was a moral and spiritual movement. It wasn't a legal movement because you see, in the final analysis, law doesn't mean much. It sounds like it, but underneath law is custom and tradition. Underneath custom and tradition and *beyond* it all is the spiritual understanding of God. And if God isn't there, people won't obey it! Woo! Not for long! And when I say people won't obey it, I'm talking about those who are the principalities and powers because they know they don't have to. You know why we won the civil rights movement? It's all about God! It wasn't about law. It was about God. When we made them understand that you've got the big church, but you're going to hell if you don't deal. We made them understand that you've got lots of money, but you can't spend it in hell. So you might as well get with it.

But even deeper than that, you know what we did is that we made them realize that, inside, they were hollow. That anybody that can stand and watch people be beaten and hung and keep their mouth shut has already been dehumanized. Sooner or later, man is so made, particularly women, 'cause they are the first to awaken to spiritual understanding. But it's true. It's not an accident that our churches are filled with women. It seems like, by very nature, women are more spiritual than men, all right? But that's another sermon.

But the point is that when we look at it, it was our spiritual life that made them shrink back. That's what changed the law. We made America understand. You see, let's look at something that we take for granted and need to understand. Is that how you subdue the principalities and powers of this world? Who does that? Common people do that when they are together on what greatness is. Do you understand what I'm saying? It's so important. Because we who are the Christian church, we are the manna. We are the food that counts. We are the power when we become Christians.

That's what hurts so badly—is that God has called us, and we play with it. He's allowed us to be inside the knowledge, and we talk about it but don't do much about it. This is what hurts so badly. That the principalities and powers of this world don't care about God, no more than Satan did, which Paul mentions two times in this Scripture. We bend to them. Isn't it interesting that there's four denominations in America called the *peace church*. They will go to jail rather than go to war. They're the smallest denominations in America because they won't kill. We will, and send our sons off to it. We lost the issue of war and peace in America because we don't know what a Christian is.

Is it interesting? What's hurting me is that I believe we're going to lose the issue of hunger. Everybody now is talking about, we must feed the world, and we must. But you see, I'm afraid we're gonna lose it. Because the principalities and powers are not concerned about feeding the world. They're just concerned with how much profit they can get. Martin King put it so well when he said,

"There is something wrong with the nation that creates poverty in the midst of plenty." What's being said? Where are we? I can't preach forever. I'd like to. Most preachers would.

But let me give it to you another way: We are having to make a choice right now on whether we're going to be led by Pat Robertsons and George Bushes, or whether we're going to be led by the prophet of our time, Martin King, and Jesus, the King of all. That's what goes on. That's the real question. Because Martin is saying *the end of war*. Bush is saying *war even to create an empire.* Jump on people who aren't saying anything to you. Martin King is saying the end of race and racism and the differences in people, and we are now pushing a line that says if you're Arab or anything but white, something's gotta be wrong with you, and you've got to obey somebody who's white. That's still what's being said. Listen to it. Martin King said we have to have the end to poverty. But what I'm hearing—listen to [President George W.] Bush. You know what Bush said? He said he wanted to raise money for people who were destroyed in the tsunami.[3] And he did, but you know what his reason was? His reason was because we're doing things so badly in Iraq, we must do something for those people so they won't think we're bad.[4] The right thing, wrong reason! The issue is, who will we follow? Is Jesus that important to us?

You know what? Two weeks ago, I was eighty-one. I've been here a long time. And I used to hear the old preachers say that I've never seen the just and righteous, the lovers of God, forsaken, and I've never seen their seed begging for bread. And I used to hear them say it, and I thought they just memorized it and learned that it sounded good. But you see, now I know what they're talking about. And then, in the final analysis, there's something greater than all of that. All of my life, I've been fortunate to have lived for Jesus. Oh, yes. I was four years old, I went out and laid in a rut in the road. Gonna let the cars run over me. There weren't many. Gonna let the car run over me because why? Because they wouldn't let me go to church. I started early, and I sat in the church. And I heard the old folks say I have not sinned all week. I was just a little boy sitting there, and my feet couldn't touch the floor. But I knew somebody was lying. As a result, I've lived my whole life either fighting Jesus when I was young, in my early youth, but that was making me understand him. Woo! So, all my life I've been living for Jesus so, even when I was wrong. I was right because He was there!

And in the latter part of my life, I just began in the last thirty, forty years, to understand the depth and the goodness and the meaning, just to be able to understand how to be thankful to God. I've learned you don't have to be a genius, and I've learned that we don't have to be perfect, no matter how hard we try. Learn something that will get you there, and you won't fall into any one of the negative categories of Paul, but you will fall somewhere with Paul. And it's so simple—trust and obey. See, I know the song is old, and the tune is corny. I know all that. But you see, I also know that if you just trust and obey, you can be—oh, I know we talk about joy and happiness, but you see, you can be an effective Christian. It's not about how happy I am. It's not about how much joy I get. It's about God's kingdom!

Delivered: August 28, 2005
Providence Missionary Baptist Church
Atlanta, Georgia

COMMENTARY

John K. Stoner

It's 2005 in America, and C. T. Vivian is preaching.

It is no accident that Vivian's sermon title is a question. That's the way he engaged his listeners. Before he says a word, you are wondering, "What does it mean to be a Christian?" Now, that is a question!

Vivian reminds us where we are and what time it is. We're in church on Sunday morning, the day of Sunday school—the time when we learned life's real, important truths. Or, at least, should have. But did we really? Or did we miss a thing or two? Do we even know what it means to be a Christian?

From here the preacher takes us to the Bible, to the writer named Paul, and says, "You heard Scripture read today. You were warned that there are false teachers out there, and they will mislead you." Vivian paraphrases another verse from Paul, an obviously familiar and favorite one: "We are not fighting against humans. We're fighting against the principalities and powers, against forces and authorities, and against rulers of darkness and powers in the spiritual world."[5]

Then, suddenly, from the Bible to the newspaper, to a report about Pat Robertson, a famous preacher who ran for president, who said that "the thing to do is to kill this newly elected president down there because he won't do what we say." Vivian does not name Hugo Chavez, president of Venezuela, but his listeners know. We can hear them respond, "Well, now. . ."

We're in a life-and-death struggle, with false teachers spewing toxic ideas and false ideologies, says Vivian. Look at our world and ask yourself, "Who is a real Christian?"

Here is the courage and honesty of Black preaching—at least of Vivian's Black preaching. Look at Jesus, and look at the world, as you ask, "Who is a real Christian?" We're living in an empire that thinks you can be Christian and assassinate your enemies.

> I was so surprised that the newspapers hardly picked it up. When a preacher cries murder as a way to solve problems and murder people on foreign soil, in the name of Jesus and your nation, and that it's not dealt with except for here and there, then, you see, I know there's something wrong. And what's particularly puzzling is that he does this after a high authority—the president of the United States—did just what he wants to now do in South America, he already did it in Iraq. Now we can see that you can go jump on people and bomb people that you can't even prove were involved, just because you want to, and then talk about American values and Christian values. You see, there was something very, very wrong, when we can spend billions of dollars in order to kill people, rather than billions of dollars in order to save people and feed the hungry and clothe those that need clothing—Christianity is not involved! One of the preachers of Jesus was trying to support him—an evangelical.[6]

From excoriating empire and American supremacy, Vivian goes to racism and white supremacy.

> For years I've said, with doing race workshops, I've said, if God asked me, "Vivian, what would you like to happen now to solve the problem of race?", I would say, "Oh, Lord, thank you, convert the white church! And stir up the Black church!" Because the problem is not out there, the problem becomes in here.[7]

Like a true prophet, Vivian always brings the critique home. American's problem is not Iraq or Venezuela, it is America. The church's problem is not Muslims or communists, it is the white church and the Black church.

Vivian turns to Martin Luther King Jr., great prophet of antiracism and nonviolence, and to women of courage and spirituality, to show what it means to be a Christian. All of that in 2005—twenty years ago. American supremacy and white supremacy—both condemned in one fell swoop to show what it means to be a Christian. The peace churches named as examples of the Jesus way. One wonders where the church and America would be today if this path had been taken.

He, being dead, yet speaks.

12

Law of the Spiritual Life

Habakkuk 2:4

It's great to be back with such wonderful people. No church I ever have known had as solid a group of ministers as this church. As they say, let's get down to it—T-U-I to it. Do you know what it means to be just? To be just—not just to be just. But to be just. I really want you to know. I'm not going to really ask you, but I think it's important that you know because it means so much to your spirituality to know. It means so much to your relationship with God to know and define it. And the definition of *just* is one who is righteous before God. If that doesn't move you—you hear what I'm saying? One who is righteous before God. [That] may not make you shout, but it ought to make you happy. There's something about it if you're in the way. If you're trying, if you're going beyond the normal trials and tribulations, and still want to grow and develop, it's important to know what it means to be righteous before God, and he makes it very clear.

But when we think about it, the issue is, how do you get righteous before God? And you see, it is used in the Scripture, throughout various points, and throughout history we change the translation of the word so that it gets lost. But nevertheless, I want to use it with Habakkuk because Habakkuk is the first one of that great group of ethical prophets to talk about it. If you notice, in your Scripture, you will find the ethical prophets. If this was important [enough] to be important to Micah, [to] Amos, it had to be important to you. And he tells us how. Habakkuk tells us how [right] here. He says, "The just shall live by faith."[1] I want to emphasize something. The just shall live by faith, but he says the just will live by their faith. If you notice the words, they say *the faith*, but it's really *his faith*. You see what I mean? So, it's not a matter of the Christian faith per se. It's also that you have to live by your faith rather than simply have one. It's a distinction.

[He] is saying that the just, in fact, live by their faith. In that, to be just and [to] have faith are combined. And the prophet who has God's vision tells us [that] only when you live by your faith can you then satisfy God. Only when you live by your faith can you, in fact, be righteous before God. The logic then says only when we are just are we righteous before God. And, in fact, I told you that the word has been changed a little. We hardly use the word *just* anymore. We simply go with the word *righteous*. But you see, there's something about the word *righteous* that throws us off. We're so used to it that we can be self-righteous and not pay much attention to it. We can get mixed up spiritually, is what I'm talking about. Whenever we get mixed up, it's up to us to change it.

Micah and Habakkuk make it clear that the just live by faith, and that they live by that faith. And that's the only way we can know that they are just. And we have to understand the context—three little chapters right here, and they are so terrific—that we have to see the context in which Habakkuk comes to realize God's vision for him and for us. For the same god that Habakkuk has, we also have. And the same rules and regulations in his century are the same in this century. I don't care if the clock has turned or not; God hasn't turned.

And when we see what we're talking about here, we have to see the context in which he discovers the law of the spiritual life. It's one thing to have the law of the universe. It's another to have the law of spiritual life. Because God will take care of the universe, you've got to take care of your spiritual life.

Law of spiritual life. So now, let us see the context. Habakkuk puts it so well here. You see, he sees the evil and violence around him. And he sees how his people are oppressed by his own people, too. They treat us like fish, he says. I told you it would speak to our century as well. The only concern the evil have is to satisfy their own appetites. And he goes on to deal with it. They catch us in their nets, and we all are the same to them. The righteous are devoured the same as the rest of the fish. That they make no distinction between those who are good and evil. They want to say because there are evil fish in here, all of you are evil.

The stereotypes of simply catching people in nets, when we really think about it, God says it—read it, it's important you see this dialogue between God and the prophet. The prophet cries out, and God answers. And then the prophet cries out again, and then the prophet cries again. And when God answers—knowing he's in misery and seeing the violence we suffer—answers back to him and lets him know that I understand it better than you do. Habakkuk says, "They store up stolen goods and cheat others. And they made their families rich at the expense of others. And they have said, by their action, I am above the law." Habakkuk says that the wicked prosper while good men suffer. He says that even his own people imitate those that were destroying their people. He saw the lives of the masses of people who could never be fulfilled. And he questions: Do we have the same God? And in that case, he knew they didn't have the same God.

But it's up to us to understand we [can't] be talking about the same God. So, he cries out, "Lord, why?" Habakkuk is caught in the middle. He loves the people and loves his God. But God, too, is caught in the middle because God loves his people. But he must also find a way to deal with the evil forces and hopefully redeem them, too. Whether he be a prophet, or in [a] pew, or God himself—how to deal with it. If God just wanted to crack down on everyone [who] is evil, it would be easy. But God says his role is far more difficult than ours. That's why we question, just as Habakkuk questions: Lord, why do you let it happen? Get rid of them right now! We say, they are not worthy of you! But God seemingly has a different kind of understanding because they are his children, not our children. [That] makes it difficult. So God answers him. God says, "The just—those who really stand before me—the just, those that are acceptable to me are those people [who] live by faith." And he goes on to say, "I know it is difficult."

We have to always know that God knows it's difficult. And he goes on to say, "I know you don't understand." But he doesn't let us off the hook. "You will have to be just, and to be just you will have to have faith. And you will have to have faith that, one day, my promises will come true. That no matter how things seem, I am still in charge of the universe." He was saying, "Look up and remain just, regardless of the circumstances."

I say to you that, if you don't live by God, you are destroyed by the fact that you didn't live by God. You don't break the Ten Commandments; you break yourself on the Ten Commandments. You don't break the spiritual laws; the spiritual laws of God break you. When you break the rules, there will be suffering. I know your pain, but if you can be just with me in difficult times, it's the test to strengthen and purify you and prepare you for the time I will use you more mightily than you think.

I think it's true of our people and our church. No matter which way you look at it, it's to purify and prepare. I can't help but think of Gideon when I think of things that [way]. He won the battle with a few men, but they were just people, committed, disciplined. God works with the just for the benefit of all people. Look around us. That's where the joy is. That, regardless of the evil around us God has us for a purpose. God is not a god that moves without reason. We don't always understand it; that's why we have to live by faith to be just.

But what I've learned is this—and even if God doesn't have a reason beyond me, it's all right. Because I find that obeying God is the best life anyway. [applause] If the change doesn't come in my own time, that's all right. It took forty years in the wilderness to prepare Israel, and those who lost the faith, died. Those who made it over the just were delivered. And all Israel was safe. Forty years? Doesn't seem long. It wouldn't matter if it was eighty years. Because if you're not in contact with God, you're in the wilderness anyway. [applause]

To be just—acceptable to God—you must live by faith. The just live by faith. The just have faith that life is a moral and spiritual adventure. There's a moral and spiritual world where the adventures are far more important. Those who want adventure find God. Those who want adventure obey the law. That's where you have the adventure of your life that takes in your mind and your spirit. And when you're wrong, you find yourself descending, and then you want to return up to God. That's adventure.

When we see that kind of adventure—one of my great adventures with God is not to double-guess Him. I had Him all figured out. I not only prayed but I had the answers. I wasn't waiting for God to answer. I had the answers and how He was going to do it. If that doesn't break the First Commandment, I don't know what does. But you see, why pray to Him if you already got the answers? But, of course, we have to go through the ceremony. And when I still think it's that way, and then if it doesn't work, I blame God. After all, I prayed to you, God, and you didn't do it like I thought you would. There it goes. But you see, when you watch, when you're in the darkness, and you watch God bring the light, that's joy. You notice that the world talks about fun, but when you pick up the New Testament, it talks about joy. And the world doesn't know how to have [joy] because [it doesn't] live by faith. When God pulls you out to be just and enjoy the adventure—God created people as moral people, and the just understand that. That people are moral people.

Let me give an example not even about the church. You can go to the baseball game. Sixty thousand people will shout and throw things when they think it's [an] unfair call, a bad play. Everyone jumps up on their feet. And even the guys on the other side don't like it because they know it was wrong. We are moral people. We are made to be moral. We are spiritual beings as well. God made us, and he can deliver us. The just. To remain just, we must know that moral people, united under God, will overcome the violence and evil of an immoral world. God is in charge, and he's in charge of a moral society. [So] that when we choose, we can make it a moral society because we're a moral people.

And when you think about it, you and I who are oppressed, find it harder to do, but we must live by Habakkuk's God. As God says, it may take a long time. That's a translation. But it will happen. But we say, "God, what about the meantime? I know about the long time. And I know about the short time. But what about the meantime?" So, he answers you, "In the meantime, regardless of circumstances: Be just and know that I will deliver." That's your faith. [That] the just live by faith. That beyond the cry of the world, there is a deeper, greater wisdom that is always working. That the just can, and must, live by faith, regardless of the circumstance. That's what we're called on to do. And he says, "I know that is difficult for you because of everything [that] is dumped upon you." Nevertheless, it is the faith of the just—knowing that when you act and keep on acting in faith—who know that only God can pull you through it. It is the faith of the just, who stay consistent with the gospel, even though you don't have the answers to your problem. It is the faith of the just, who do the right thing for no other reason than it [being] right. That's the faith of the just. And for the just person, the race is not to the swift, nor to the strong. It's [to] those who hold on.

When you're in the darkness and can't see the light, but you know that God's going to bring you around a corner pretty soon, just hold on to the faith. It's that kind of understanding, that it may take a long time, but it will happen. What do they say? [pause] I thought somebody was going to tell me. I thought you grew up with a grandma like mine. [laughter] He's not there when you want him, but he's going to be there on time. But what we have to understand is that God has his own time. If you're just a soldier, you might say, "Let's storm the opposition." If you're a general, you know that they have [a] canon that you don't have. You see what I'm saying. We're just soldiers. God is the general! And all I have to do is trust and obey, and I will be just before God. It is that kind of deeper wisdom that makes it very, very important.

[I've] been to South Africa twice this summer. Each one of [the visits] was an unusual spiritual experience for me. First time I was there, I shook hands with [Nelson] Mandela. That wasn't the spiritual experience. But he spoke and talked about prison. That he thought that he had to murder all the white people in South Africa, push 'em out, get rid of them, make them flee. He saw no other alternative. But he was in prison year after year. On Robben Island there was a chemical that is pure white when the sun shines down on it. It's not used anymore. The persecutors had the prisoners dig it up and put it in wheelbarrows, and wheel it over to the side of a pit, dump it out, and go back and get more. In the meantime, the sun is coming down and it's flashing back from all this white chemical. And as a result of it, the prisoners go blind. So, when you see Mandela with glasses on, it wasn't simply because of age. It was because it was decided [that the apartheid regime] would destroy the people that were there. But in the midst of it all, even though the enemy is mistreating [him], this man was searching. And he came to the point where he didn't want to destroy anybody anymore. All he wanted to do was save South Africa, and [he saw] that there was an alternative in the midst of it all. And he began to believe that, even though these evil men were persecuting [him] every day, even they can be changed. And by the time twenty-seven years was up, he was able to walk out a finer soul within a finer frame. He walked out to be president of all the people and take the first step to saving a nation. They just lived by faith! No matter what's happening around them. If they learn about God, even if they don't know him, [they] get in contact with him. Even if you don't see a way out, God will find a way out.

Second time I was in South Africa, I sat in the church of Bishop [Desmond] Tutu. I haven't always been a great admirer of Tutu. He and I had a little misunderstanding. But you see, I thought this time, how could a preacher ask a people to forgive another people who could stand in front of them and talk about rolling a man on a rotisserie [over] a fire while they ate lunch? How could you ask a people to forgive people like that? The South Africans had been on a rotisserie of circumstances since 1913. How could you ask them to forgive? It was this kind of thing that caused me to realize that no matter the circumstances, the just must live by faith. That no matter how evil man is, [the just] will obey God. And that they will structure their lives based upon God. That's what Habakkuk said. He said that God told him to write it so that it's plain. Put it so that the people can't miss it. Don't put it in jargon that people can manipulate. So plain, one little sentence, [so] that they can't get around it. So that the oppressed will know that the just—those that stand before me and desire to be on my side—live by faith. That there's no other thing worth living by but faith.

And as I stood in Africa, I thought about the America that I had just left. I had taken a plane out of Atlanta where Martin Luther King had lived, grew up as a child, and where he lived by the faith of the just. The just believe that you will reach the conscience of people, that they have a conscience. That God created them, and inside of them, somewhere, you will find what is necessary.

God has given us three great examples to let us know that He is working it out. To let them know that sin—no matter how great—will be worked out. For those in prison, regardless of whether their name is Mandela or not, God is working it out. And for those that live in fear that they won't be able to feed their family, or their job will be taken away, know that God's working it out. And for those that sit passively and watch evil, don't do that. Be active because God's working it out. Let those know who don't see much light, that God's working it out. God was working it out in Jesus Christ, with his prophets, his apostles—he's working it out in past and present. God is working it out. That's all we need to know, is that the just live by faith.

Delivered: September 24, 2000
Providence Missionary Baptist Church
Atlanta, Georgia

COMMENTARY

Robert Christopher Wright

Like the apostle Paul gushing over the church at Philippi, C. T. Vivian expresses his love for Providence Missionary Baptist Church in Atlanta, Georgia: its pastor, its people, and its music. "No church I ever have known had as solid a group of ministers as this church," he says in preliminary remarks.[2] As you read along, you feel the warmth of this occasion. You feel the congregation open the doors of their hearts to this wise elder and moral colossus.

He leads with a question on this occasion: "Do you know what it means to be just?" His question is pulled from the second chapter of the book of the prophet Habakkuk. This question is central to our spirituality, he says, and to our relationship with God. Ever interested in Christian maturity, Vivian is pointing his listener toward growth and development beyond normal trials and tribulations, and toward what it means to be righteous before God. Masterfully, the preacher organizes his words so that we don't think about righteousness or being just as some extraneous philosophical musing. This isn't learning in general; this is individual soul-making preaching. "It's not a matter of the Christian faith per se," he says, but that "you live by your faith. It's a distinction." He keeps the opportunity for change and transformation close to each hearer. To be just and faithful are combined, he suggests. And then he moves to a position not taken by most modern preachers. For Vivian, the answer to the question of *Why bother with any of this?* is to satisfy God. Vivian understands that the church is not supposed to be a bastion of perfection but of imperfect people endeavoring to respond imperfectly to a loving and merciful God. God is the lead actor in this sermon. All we can do is respond—respond with faith-inspired justice.

Vivian's theological imagination is what drives this sermon. God is sovereign, available, knowable—at least in part—and ultimate: "I don't care if the clock has turned or not; God hasn't turned."[3] And, in another place, "God will take care of the universe; you've got to take care of your spiritual life."[4] This of course sets Vivian up to do the heavy lifting of good preaching, and that is to answer the perennial question of the faithful: Where is God amidst the violence, injustice, and chaos of the world? Vivian's real gift to us here is that he doesn't rely on euphemisms, academic explanations, or anecdotes. His tone and his word choices point to decades of life lived at the intersection of that question. He has seen the unrighteous thrive and the faithful suffer, and his faith in God remains intact, gentle, joyful, and bold. Like Habakkuk, he does not hide his eyes from the abuses of the world. He acknowledges the oppression. He personally identifies with those who have been, or are, oppressed. His concise definition of evil—"The only concern of the evil is to satisfy their own appetites"[5]—demonstrates an intimate insight and an athletic eloquence in communicating this reality. Still, when he tells us the prophet cries out to God and yet submits even his outcry to God's sovereignty, he teaches us something critical for daily living with God: "If you're just a soldier, you might say, 'Let's storm the opposition.' If you're a general, you know they have a cannon that you don't have. . . . I'm saying, we're just soldiers. God is the general!"[6]

As we read onward in the sermon, it's easy to lose track of who is speaking. Is it Habakkuk or Vivian—or both—who tells us that God understands the misery and suffering of the world better than we do? And then Vivian demonstrates a rare gift in introspection and preaching. He moves us from simply thinking of our own travails or the trouble of the world to the trouble it must surely be to be God. "Habakkuk is caught in the middle,"[7] he says, between the people who suffer and the God he loves. "But God, too, is caught in the middle, because God loves his people but he must also find a way to deal with the evil forces and hopefully redeem them too."[8] For the students of nonviolent direct action, this paradigm is familiar. The ultimate work of the so-called civil rights movement was never as straightforward as the simple revision of laws. Upstream of the desperate need for social and economic justice was always the necessity to transform enemies into brothers and sisters. The goal for the prophets of old and those who speak for God now must continually be redemption, individually and nationally. For Habakkuk and Vivian, simple retribution for evil is complicated because the doers of evil are children of God and the siblings of the oppressed.

It is with this point that Vivian moves us squarely into the spirituality of Jesus, whose considerations and answers were always larger than the questions posed to him. In just a few sentences, Vivian effortlessly brings the matter back to the lap of the average listener, who is simply trying to live a faithful life: "I know you don't understand. [God's] promises will come true, [so] remain just, regardless of the circumstances."[9]

There is a defiant humility to this sermon offering that is compelling. Vivian is on guard against the modern notions of life that are predicated on the primacy of individual ego or obsessive material satiation. For Vivian, the best life is life lived in evolving trust with and for God. This life he calls a spiritual adventure. This adventure is experienced by endeavoring to be just and therefore acceptable to God. He combines the idea of adventure with obedience to God. "Those who want adventure," he argues, "find God."[10] And just so we are sure that the preacher is one of us and not our moral superior, he reveals a bit of his own journey as a soul adventurer: "I had Him all figured out—I not only prayed but I had the answers."[11] He concludes, "If that doesn't break the First Commandment, I don't know what does."[12] When you are wrong, he notes, "you find yourself descending, and then you want to return up to God. That's adventure."[13] This sermon equally could be titled: "The Spiritual Laws I Have Learned by Living with and for God."

One of the laws implicit in this sermon is that Vivian believes human beings are moral and are made to be moral. And that "moral people, united under God, will overcome the violence and evil of an immoral world."[14] Here is an invitation to come back to your better self. This is an altar call for every listening heart. The real spiritual gift of sermons like this one is that the preacher gives voice to an understanding of humanity that listeners personally and actually believe. Vivian believes, after having personally seen the worst in us during his work in the American South, that we are all good and created to accomplish good, if we will only choose to be exactly what God has made us to be. The shelves groan under the weight of books that tell us the techniques of effective preaching. But rarely are we treated to a preacher who knows us better than we know ourselves and can, like Jesus after the resurrection, find his way deftly through the locked doors of our thoughts and hearts. Vivian finishes this rousing sermon—short, by traditional Baptist standards—with a beautiful finish that keeps God central, and you and I as respondents. Vivian tells us God is working it out. Through the evil and indifference. For those who sit in darkness. Down through the history of faith. In past times and in the present. So, "be active," he encourages, "God [is] working it out."[15]

13

Creating the Promised Land

The Book of Joshua

As we come to the pulpit this morning and come to the pews and come to the house of God, and as we think about and contemplate the work of God with his people, and as we reach to the Old Testament, in particular, to gain our text, it becomes important that we understand that the theme of the Old Testament is about the liberation of a people. It is important that we understand that whoever and whatever we reach to and whatever names we lift are important, not by names in and of themselves, but because they were about fulfilling the deepest desire of the heart of God, working with his people. It is important, as we look at this text, to begin to think about it because the Old Testament and our lives are about the same thing. The theme of the Old Testament and the central theme of African Americans in this land [are] the same thing, that basic reality of the liberation of a people from oppression, finally to freedom, finally to the creation of a promised land.

Let us think about this text not in terms of a Scripture or a chapter, but let us think about it in its totality, because you see, here are the people who wandered through the wilderness and finally came to a land that they could call—well, let's look at it another way. You see, there is a distinct pause. There is a separation. There is a space between their coming onto the land and the time they call it the promised land.

See, let's look at the Scripture because you see, I think we've so long heard *the promised land*, we think God delivered a promised land. No, God promised a land. God promised a land. *They* had to deliver the promised land. There's a great space between the word *land*, in lowercase, and *The Promised Land*, in uppercase. And what happens in there makes the difference. You see, it is not difficult to be thinking of having a land. God sort of promises that to everybody.

How I know that is because we all live on the land. Men don't walk in the air, and they can't live on water *without the land*. See, the issue is not the land, the issue is what do you do with the land. The issue is what is your purpose in having the land—whether I'm talking about me walking on this land, whether I'm talking about me having a little house on the corner somewhere. What I do with the land—not *The Land*—is important. And it's not only true with an individual; it's true with a people. God delivers a land to people for a particular purpose. [Fulfilling] that purpose is going from stepping onto the land to, in fact, creating a promised land. God said, "I won't create it for you, but I'll be with you in the doing of it."

I think it's important this morning that we look at that because so often we pray, talk, act, sit around as though God is just gonna drop it out of the sky for [us]. It didn't happen in Israel, and it's not gonna happen to us, because God is the same God yesterday, today, and tomorrow. So, as we look at it, we have to understand that it's up to us to do it. God sets us on the land, and there it is. He tells us how to do it. Look at verse 9, [which] makes it clear—in these first nine verses, we repeat three times the basic understanding.[1] He said you must be strong and be of good courage if He was gonna deliver it and drop it out of the sky for you. You don't have to be strong, all you have to do is have an appetite. You don't have to have courage because He's gonna do it all. You don't have to do nothin'. But He made it very clear you must be strong and of good courage. Courage is the hallmark; strength is the hallmark. It took strength to take the land. It took strength to cross over Jordan. It took faith that God was gonna be there. It took courage to live in spite of [not] having any proof of what you were gonna deal with.

It took great strength for us to come to the cities of America. It took great courage for us to throw off the yokes of yesterday's oppression and find ourselves at the center of every city in this nation. I am talking about the land! God gives us all land. You cross over into a land. It took great strength to be able to fight against the racism of this nation. It took great courage to overcome the hate that was here. Work took great strength in America, to leave your house in the morning, knowing that everybody who showed up for the job had a better opportunity on it than you, and yet you stayed there. That took strength! You're gonna take the land. You've gotta have the strength. You've got to have the courage to know. You just think about—I think about my wife, and I think about the wives of all, as we walked out those doors as men hoping that we could fulfill the role. It took courage for our wives to be back there, waiting for us, and to take care of us when we got back, wounded from the day and from the week. You see, it took courage, it took strength to be able to make it, and we are standing on the land because we had the strength to take it!

We had the strength to pay more for the rent than other people were paying. Pay more for the house than other people were paying. To be in the neighborhood where you knew you were being cheated, but there was nothing you could do about it. It took strength to take the land! We didn't cross over at no cost. It was not given without pain. There was always suffering there. But we worked our way through it because we had faith in an eternal God that would bring us out on the other side. It is that matter that I'm talking about. What I'm saying is that the inner cities of America are our land.

God has placed us at the center of Western civilization. This is our land. What we do to make it the promised land becomes our issue. God has given us the land. Can we take it? See, the Native Americans had all the land. Couldn't take it. In fact, let's put it another way. They moved them to a place, trying to discard them, and there was found oil on the land. But they couldn't take it. You can go people after people—the Latinos were in California and had the gold before the other people came. Read your history. Very important. And then they were taken off the land, and the gold became someone else's. I'm telling you that the inner cities of America [are] our gold and our oil. The issue is, are we prepared to make it a promised land? The wealth of a nation is here, the wealth of centuries is here. The controlling points in the pivot center where a whole civilization is, [is] here. We have the faith. Do we have the strength? Do we have the good courage, as the Scripture says, to make it our own? And make it our own not for ourselves alone, but so that God can be praised in the midst of it all? But you see, it does not come without a price. Are you willing to pay the price?

Now, it would seem, in our annals of normal thought that once you had fought the battle—well, I shouldn't say that because the battles are yet to come. But that once you have crossed the River Jordan, everything's gonna be all right. But you see, God doesn't have it that way. Read your Scriptures. Don't read it a verse at a time, read it in terms of its totality—that no sooner had they crossed the Jordan, no sooner had they been on the land, no sooner could they say that what God promised us when we were in slavery now has come because we own the land. They found out they didn't really own it yet 'cause the battles had just begun.

That's what I want us to understand. The battles had just begun. You know the story of Jericho. No sooner had they got there, they had to take Jericho. And then they had to [face] a battle, they had to fight five kings who were finally defeated in battle. And then seven more kings were defeated in battle before they could come to the point that they could talk about the promised land. And they had to go all the way to Solomon before they could have the promised land! You understand what I'm saying is that right now, in Atlanta—well, let's put it in another way right quick for you. Because you see, I think there are some of us that think, Where does that fit with us? Jericho was taken with spears and battle flags, and we don't fit that. Because we're nonviolent, so we don't fit that. And this [Scripture] doesn't really apply to us because we're not equipped to do battle. Let me tell you, if you're gonna have a promised land, you're going to have to do battle. And you might as well get equipped for it.

The battle may not be the same, but you will do battle. See, because the story of Jericho is really not about taking a city state, [it's] about having political control of your life. Do you understand? If we're talking about Israel, we're talking about Jericho. We're talking about seven kings; we're talking about five kings;

we're talking about battles where men die on the battlefield. But if we're talking today, we're talking about battles, but for the same purpose of political control of where you live. 'Cause if you don't have political control of where you live, you don't belong to you, you belong to somebody else. The first thing that had to happen was that the battles had to be fought so that there could be political control—your dreams, your hopes, your needs. The future of your children, the future of your grandchildren, is ultimately decided by you, *if* you have political control. It will ultimately be decided by whoever sets public policy, and it better be you. Because nobody serves other people's needs like they serve their own, and nobody can do for you what you must do for yourself if you're gonna fulfill the potential of a people on the land. Ultimately, as we go toward this [goal]—well, let's look at this in terms of the newspapers last week.

Newspapers in Atlanta said, We don't need city hall. It should have been saying to you, We have too much political control and they don't intend for you to keep it. Are you ready to do battle? That's the issue! Because they're saying [that] they are. If you think that we're not gonna have to defeat five kings and seven kings, when you look at all the little communities around here—they want to give Atlanta to Fulton County or to Decatur, and put it all together, in one piece, so that you will not have control. *Are you ready to do battle?* becomes the issue. Do you want a promised land? And do you think that you're worthy of being in control of your own life? I don't think anyone else in America is worthy of being in control of the lives of African Americans but African Americans. It has been proven. See, politics is a struggle for power, and power is about the struggle for jobs and income—not necessarily wealth, but economic independence. Look at this city. Mainly, the jobs that are here that keep us independent, that keep us talking, do not come from normal kinds of business. [They come] from—what? Governments at one level or the other. Lose control and you lose your life! See, I think that when the guys in the street talk about being cool, I'm all for it. But what *cool* means to me is control of our lives.

Joshua understood that to take the city was to take control and create an economy. If you're gonna have a promised land, you have to have an economy that allows you to have a promised land, and they understood it because they had just given all their work to Egypt, but they didn't get anything out of it. [Whoever] controls the economy controls their lives. You understand? You can't have a promised land without having control of an economy. Isn't it interesting that every group of people who come to America, the first thing they start doing is setting up their own economy? The Southeast Asians walked in, and now they own half the little stores around. That is not an accident. It's a necessary element of a people trying to control their lives, and there's nothing wrong with that. And that's not to put down the Southeast Asians. We need to learn from them, not put them down! Understand what I'm saying?

You have to create an economy because, you see, Joshua would not have stayed in power very long if he had not been able to feed the folk. There's a rebellion when you can't feed the folks. You may have taken the land, but you won't be on it long if you can't feed the folk. Now, it was not too difficult in the time of Joshua because if you got the land, they can plant what they want. But it never is quite that simple 'cause ultimately power is based on [land]. And whether you can keep it or not has a relationship to whether the people are satisfied. And people are not satisfied without income and the control of it.

What we're talking about is creating a promised land. And when we see the Scripture in its totality, we realize there wasn't a struggle. There was a series of struggles toward a promised land. There is no one spot in which you can look at the history of Israel. You have to see it in its totality to be able to gain what we need as a people because it parallels our own experience. See, Joshua said, "First, take over." Then he was about control, and then he was about creating. Because you've got to create an economy. You see, this is what we've been about as Black people for some time. We've not been able to create an economy of our own. We've not been able to be in control of our own money and our own lives. We have been the ones [for whom] the dollar comes in on Saturday. How do we say it?—an eagle flies! Saturday's our time to play! Sunday we go to church and pray, and Monday we go right back [to] working for somebody else because the money didn't stay where you were. Ultimately, we have formed a group of people who cannot create a promise land by having a few millionaires. Oh, you can have half a dozen millionaires in a city like Atlanta, and they can be Black. But so what? So what? 'Cause the issue is not whether we make some millionaires and imitate a capitalistic culture that has put us down. The issue becomes whether we can see that every family in Black America is independent enough to stand up and know what tomorrow will bring. That's what it's about. To the extent we can do that, we can have a promised land.

So, we didn't get [together] a half a dozen people with a million dollars. We got 336 people together that just [have] a job. And when you can do that, then you can lead on toward the time that those 336 can have more than a job, and can create jobs for those that don't have [any job], so that they can come to the time they can become independent. You have to create a means whereby there's a new economy in the midst of the old. Or those who control the economy control the old.

Think of Africa. I think of Africa, and I think about being with [Kwame] Nkrumah one afternoon and found out to make a telephone call to Africa, you go through Europe. Understand what I'm saying? We're talking about control. We're talking about having an economy that is yours. We're talking about seeing that. We'll look at it again. The richest continent in the world is Africa. The raw materials are taken out at one cost and the finished product is brought back at another cost. And though you had everything it took to make the new world, the new world is not coming to you because you don't control the wealth of the world. To be independent, you have to control where you are. There's not a group in America that doesn't bounce from a base that they created and control the economy. That's what I'm talking about.

Now let's look at something else because it doesn't stop there. If we're gonna have a promised land—a land, yeah, everybody walks on land. But will we have a promised land—something that fulfills the hopes and dreams and desires, that makes those [who] live on it know and realize that the maximum, that the fulfillment of human potential, is theirs. All they have to do is to put themselves out and try. That's what makes a great society. When you wake up in the morning [and] know that the odds are in your favor, not against you. When you wake up in the morning [and] you don't have to have fear. When you wake up in the morning knowing that, if you desire it, you can have the moon.

Their labor, their energy, will be used to create a promised land for somebody else. Now let's look. See, Moses was a very wise man. Moses didn't enter the land, but he led the people to it. But Moses was a wise man. And God had told him he would not see the promised land. Do you understand what I'm saying? But He started [Moses] on the right track because you see Moses understood something very important: You can't keep the land, much less make a promised land with somebody else's history. I want to repeat that. You can't keep the land, much less create a promised land, with somebody else's history.

So, Moses started [writing] them early. He wrote the first five books of the Bible. And if you get beyond Exodus, you will begin to realize that that last [chapter] of Deuteronomy is a summing up of the history of Israel. You see, it becomes very important because how you interpret everything makes a difference. Moses made them the chosen people. How do we know they were chosen? Because Moses told us. You understand what I'm saying? How does every Jew know that he is special of God? Because Moses told him, all right? You hear what I'm saying? If you don't have some concept of self based upon your own interpretation of you, you will end up working for somebody else. Whose history you encompass will decide who you serve. That's why we know about Jesus, because we want to know who we serve. In the same sense historically, because the sociology of religion is just as important as the psychology of religion. We just don't talk about it.

And we begin to look, and we see that Moses understood. And Moses wrote the book of Deuteronomy, and he made it very clear that you write the history on your forehead, that you learn it by rote. That you teach it at the tabernacle, that you preach it in the streets. It was important if you want a promised land. Moses started them in slavery, understanding the promised land. You see, [if] you interpret the fact that you're a slave, [that] makes a difference. If you interpret that, yes, I was a slave, but we were on God's side, they were not—oh, it makes a difference. It's because how you interpret slavery, how it gets interpreted to us, is [why] we could be even ashamed of the fact. We don't need to be ashamed of somebody else's evil if you're on your way to a promised land.

See, my great-grandfather, they called him a slave. But you see, I knew him! My great-grandfather wasn't a slave. He was a political prisoner. Who does the interpreting? And they called a man who paid a price for him—'cause you really can't buy a man—who paid a price for him, they called him a master. Now, if you will take on somebody else's history, he wasn't a master, he was a murderer! How do you interpret? You can't create a promised land [by] using someone else's definition of your history and who you are. It can't be done.

You see, the major reason—because you gotta come to a close sometime—I want you to go on and read the whole of the Old Testament. You see [there], as God takes his people from slavery to a promised land. See, we get caught and say it was from slavery to freedom. No, it was slavery to freedom, but what you do with your freedom creates the possibilities of a promised land. The purpose of being free is to be completely free, and you can't be completely free unless you have your own education system and, ultimately you control the religious life. This is why churches on the other side of town, particularly conservative religionists, come into the Black community with their school-bus-looking-thing on Sunday morning and pick up little Black kids and take them to the other side of town. So that they can say God meant it this way.

Do you understand what I'm saying? Because what you think God is about will decide what you're about. And what you think God meant you to do and to be and to become will be ultimately what you become. But if you think you're less than someone else, if you think someone else knows more than what you know about God, you end up wanting to be like them. And if they don't have your best interests at heart, you end up becoming secondary.

I was talking to a young, Black electrical engineer in Minnesota. Not many of us there, but brother was. And he told me that he became an artist. And he said, "You know, the first thing I painted when I became a good artist was a picture of a Black Jesus." He said, "Because I didn't know that the people in the Old Testament were as dark as I am." And he said, "All my life growing up in school and going to Sunday school and church in a predominantly white culture," he said, "I thought God did not love me as much as he loved others because He was white and they were white."

I'm talking about the effect. If you want a promised land, if you want a sense of who you are, if you want self-esteem, ultimately you have to control your religion. And the greatest struggle that we have is, Why do we do it? Because underneath all reality is spiritual reality. Underneath all that is physical, that you can see and feel and touch, is that which you cannot see, and you cannot feel, and you cannot touch. But [spiritual life] makes it possible for you ultimately to touch, and to do, and to become, and to own everything that you ever want to be. Underneath it all is a spiritual life. You have to have materialism to have a promised land, but if you do not have a spiritual life, your materialism will be so important to you that you will lose both the promised land and the material.

See, it has to occur to you that you can own the world and yet not live in a promised land. You understand what I mean? You can have all the things you ever wanted and still, because you lack something inside, you won't be, have, or lead anything anywhere. Ultimately, underneath all reality is spiritual reality. And if you don't have that, your land will be sold out to cheap religion. If you don't have a spiritual life, you may have things, but you won't have self-esteem. If you don't have a good religion, you may have the land, but only for a short length of time.

That's the story here, is that they defeated the others because their spiritual strength was greater than the others'. We live in a land where we're both Christians, at least so it is written. The issue of who will win the land, ultimately, is who has the greatest level of spiritual life. Do you understand what I'm saying? Ultimately, who wins the issue with God will be the deciders of the destiny. Whether it's First Baptist on that side of town or First Baptist on this side of town. What I've always been thankful for was that they closed the doors on me at First Baptist over there, but we always had the doors open on First Baptist over here. And it was interesting to me, as I looked at this church, that they held onto a building while they were losing their faith. To find that they couldn't hold it anymore.[2] Because those who had the greatest faith took it over! So it is with the land, so it is with the nation. That those [who] have the greatest spiritual understanding of life will finally be those in charge.

We got a God that lets us see that man is more important than money, that dignity is more important than dollars, that human personality is more important than property, and those [who] put those first [things first] will ultimately have all the others, and I don't mean in heaven, I mean here and now. We've walked through the wilderness. We've walked through the wilderness, and our parents and our great-grandparents before us. It is time for the promised land. We've walked through the narrow places of self-hate. We've walked through the wilderness of an imitation culture. We've walked through the narrow places of miseducation. We've walked through the wilderness of self-deception. We've walked through it all; it's time for the promised land. We're ready to live in a promised land.

How did they used to sing it? Crossing over from Canaan's land. . . Are we ready? Are we willing to pay the price? Do you have the courage? Are you ready for the battle? Not with sword and spear but with spiritual understanding? The battles of self-esteem, the battles of dignity, battles that will lift you beyond your yesterdays into your tomorrows. The battles that make us worthy of those that have gone before us!

Delivered: December 8, 1996
Providence Missionary Baptist Church
Atlanta, Georgia

COMMENTARY

Susan K. Smith

One of the telltale signs of a good preached word is that it causes one to fall out of, or away from, commonly held beliefs about Scripture and makes one probe for deeper meaning and significance in one's own life. Such is the effect of C. T. Vivian's sermon "Creating the Promised Land," preached in 1996 in Atlanta.

Vivian reminds us that we have been taught for generations that God delivered a promised land. But that if one looks closer, it is clear that God only promised a land to the Israelites, and they had to deliver it. Once on the land of a safe place where God led them as they fled from enemies, it was up to them to create a land that was figuratively flowing with milk and honey.

Vivian's interpretation of the beloved Scripture delivers a message of challenge and empowerment, not of smug and false complacency. Perhaps it has been because Black people in this country have looked for so long for a release from cultural, political, and spiritual captivity that we have sought easy answers to difficult questions, but Vivian makes it clear that God promises no easy way out. God promises only direction and guidance for people to get out of and from under the pressure of oppression, but then expects the delivered to use their gifts to produce the purposes for which God has equipped them.

The promised land story unfortunately has contributed to what I am now understanding to be a sittin'-on-the-dock-of-the-bay theology, a sentiment expressed in the song by Otis Redding. The lyrics of Redding's song tell the story of a lonely and broken person who is waiting for answers to roll in with the next ship. Black people and other oppressed people who are also Christian have been encouraged, scripturally and theologically, to sit and wait for good to come to them. "Wait on the Lord" is a common message delivered, and it has led to a practice of an eschatological faith, longing for relief and vindication once one has died.

But Vivian, who walked the streets of racial hatred and stared into the hardened eyes of those who have been infected with white supremacist beliefs, does not offer such a sit-and-wait theological perspective, but rather one of a faith driven by works. "God delivers a land to people for a particular purpose," he preached.[3] Fulfilling that purpose "is going from stepping onto the land to, in fact, creating a promised land. God said, 'I won't create it for you, but I'll be with you in the doing of it.'"[4]

In recent years there has been some pushback against the way Scriptures have been taught to Black, brown, and other oppressed people. Some liberation and womanist theologians have suggested that the way Scriptures have been taught has been crucial in keeping people chained to their religious colonization, i.e., to a theology that was created to keep the oppressed in their place. Religion, for them, has not been about liberation but rather deeper subjugation.

Based upon this sermon, it seems that Vivian would agree with that critique of the dogmatic Christian paradigm of religious education. His view is clearly that God created us all to understand that God never said God would drop deliverance for us out of the sky, but that we would have to work for it. And he is clear that African Americans need to know, embrace, and understand that same God, not through the actions of white oppressors more wedded to capitalism than to Christianity, but through us, in this country: "God has placed us at the center of Western civilization. This is our land."[5]

Vivian reminds us to be of good courage, as Yahweh told Joshua, and do the work. We are on a land. God put us here. It is up to us to make it a land that flows with milk and honey, for ourselves and for all who will come after us.

14

America: A Christian Nation

ANYWAY, LET'S GET down to it. We come this morning at one of those special times that has been set aside. Each denomination has a particular time that they set aside—maybe every Sunday for some—as we commune together. For most of us, it's once a month. For some, it's once a year. But it has a particular and specific meaning to us. Because when we come together for communion, it's a matter of our saying to God that we really believe that You suffered for us, and that we then should suffer for others. That we really believe that You died for us, and that You gave up your life so that You could have a greater life for all of us. It says something to us that nothing else says. And that's why there are only these things—baptism and communion. And so, when we come, it's a special time, and we should be dealing in-depth with very special things.

Let's look at the world we live in for a moment. And I could have used the subject two or three ways. But I wanted to say, "America: A Christian nation." But I also could have said, "[America] needs a Christian nation." You know, the greatest futurist of our time said that the greatest thing that will be most needed in the coming century is spiritual leadership. Never has a futurist talked about spirituality as being an important part of our future, yet we are in so much trouble today that it cannot be avoided. It cannot be taken for granted that spiritual leadership is needed because we've come to the point that it's very clear that we're not going to [survive] without it. It is not something that we think of as Black people or [that] we think of as a Baptist church. It is that the world has come to an understanding.

The head of the UN called a world conference of religious and spiritual leaders because he works with the politicians of the world and knows that they don't have the answers.[1] He called for a world conference of religious and spiritual leaders. All of them were there. The great hall was so filled that there were people out on the [UN's] plaza. They had a third of the people out there and the first people inside. We begin to see the need, and they knew. That's why they were there. It was no normal thing to come to because the need for spiritual leaders is that great. And the head of the UN was saying that the future of the world is too important to be left to politicians.

We have to see that this didn't happen a year or so ago. This happened two years before 9/11. It was coming. The people who were at the top of [world leadership] knew it. We could not believe it, and yet it was on the desk of the leadership of the nation. But they wouldn't talk about it. But you see, something unusual happened. When it really came down to those airplanes going through those buildings, we say that's Ground Zero. Meaning: That's the beginning of things, that the whole world has changed. And that what we understand, that day, that hour, is going to make the difference in our lives. And then, we put that together with the fact that our future must contain spiritual leadership and make it a top priority. Then, we begin to understand that we need to understand what that means for our religion, our church, and our faith. Is that because when we get to realistically deal with it—as Martin King said—the violence creates more problems than it solves. And when that happened, we reacted. And we reacted immediately, but we reacted violently. We reacted with revenge, which reminds us of the verses we just read. How we responded to it says something about us.

There comes a time, ground zero, when a person, a nation, a culture, or a religion can no longer fool itself. There comes a time when we can no longer lie to ourselves or anyone else. There comes a time when we have to face reality in order to remain sane. We have to face the reality and the responsibilities that come with it. And that central responsibility is not only to accept it but to ask God for forgiveness for our part in it. Because if we can't come to that point, we can't find a cure for it. If we're not willing to abide by what the Lord has for us, then it's too late to right the wrong, and that's what we have to figure out now. Is it too late to right that wrong? All right? Is it too late for this nation, for this democracy, for the leaders of the world? Is it too late?

We think that we can sin and walk away and say, "All right Lord, take care of it." Life isn't quite that simple, all right? And the greater the sin we commit, the longer it takes to get over it. Greater must be our response because our responsibility is greater. It wouldn't be such a horrible sin if we weren't so deeply involved. But at that moment, it was ground zero on our character. It tells us who we are and who we are not, and what our religion means to us, and whether God's involved, and whether we're involved with God in the creation of his world. When those towers were bombed and fell, this nation that proclaims Christ responded in exactly the opposite to what we just read in the Scriptures. We wanted revenge, and we wanted an eye for an eye, exactly what Jesus told us not to be about. See, our response was not to even ask why. Our response was not to use the great resources that God has given us in order to feed or help. Our response was to kill, and under this response, we not only went in to kill but we also went in to rob. And we have not yet, out of our Christian faith, counted the dead on both sides. We were concerned about every American that died; they didn't even have to be Christian. But we weren't concerned about those we murdered.

Is that a harsh word? I don't know, but I think we have to think about it. You see, we couldn't prove that they had anything to do with the 9/11 attack. What we could prove was they had a lot of oil that we wanted. We didn't respond like a Christian church that was formed at the start of the Roman Empire. We responded like the Roman Empire. We have to realize that this got started some time ago, and what was needed to save the world was not revenge, mass killings, or going to war on a little nation. But in fact, we should ask ourselves, Are we worthy of our faith in a world that needs us? This is the central thing we have to ask, whether you're in the pulpit or the pew. We didn't act like a Christian nation. We have not yet found a solution. Because we didn't act like a Christian nation, things have gotten worse, not better. We thought that guns and money could solve it all. We could see the arrogance in our president. God is in charge of the universe [applause], and arrogance comes before the fall. And what we're having to really deal with is how close to the real fall we are.

Can we save ourselves? See, we're further from the solution and don't even have one in sight. Every time we think we have one, it walks away from us. I remember a preacher told me one time, he said, "I did things wrong, and I found that I was on God's chain gang for a year or two. When you get on God's chain gang, you can't get it figured out. You think you have solutions, but they don't happen that way. You think God's just going to pick you up because you got down on your knees. You haven't stayed down long enough on your knees for the size of the sin." [applause]

What's so horrible about all of this is that, in the process, we ripped the mask off of ourselves. We ripped the mask off of the Christian church. Now we have to walk in front of the face of the world, admitting that we're not what we were. And yet, instead of saying it, we just want to walk around as if the world can't see it. But the world saw us as we really are. You see, we showed a religious world that we don't really obey God or care about what He has told us to do. That's the horror of it all. We can't even hide from each other. Our response to violence tells us who we are. That's what the Scripture is about. Read the Sermon on the Mount when you go home. Our response to challenge is "Who are we really?" Our response to need is "Are we really concerned about what God's concerned about?"

As a Christian nation, we should have responded to this kind of world need. But we didn't want to see the need because we helped create it, and we didn't want to talk about our role in it. This pulpit was one of the few pulpits in the nation that, the next Sunday, preached about colonialism and the matter of theft that goes on with whole nations of people. We didn't want to talk about our need.

In fact, we did not respond as Christians, nor did we respond as decent people. We responded so violently that we took the world back to the primitive ways of settling an argument. America had a big stick and the primitive way is, if you got a big stick, you're the winner. We moved past that primitive state thousands of years ago and had come to a far more decent understanding of life. That was, until we had come to what Saint Augustine gave us as the just war theory, which says you must have just reasons for misusing an individual, much less a nation. If you didn't have a just reason for it, you were automatically condemned by the world, and we were. But we didn't want to listen. We didn't want to listen to the other Christian nations, much less the non-Christian nations. We did not want to listen to decency in the world. We thought we could cover it up because we're so big and powerful with our countless guns, but it didn't work. We are now without honor in the world. You cannot disobey God and make it. You may think you can, but you cannot do it. [applause]

In fact, there are two or three steps in between, if we really talk about the history of how we've come to deal decently, religiously, and spiritually. But let's look at the final one. We couldn't even wait two weeks to hear what the rest of the world had to say. In fact, a general who is now secretary of state said, "Can't you just wait two weeks until you kill somebody?"[2] He's trained to kill but knows better. He knows that is not the solution. He went into the president's office and said, "If you break it, you own it!" [applause] So it's interesting to me; we couldn't wait two weeks.

It got worse and worse and worse, and things are continuously getting worse, and we're sinking deep into our own quagmire. Listen to the lies. Boy, I don't have time to lay it out for you. But you know it because you've been reading it in the newspaper. We started this with a lie, and continued with a lie, and we've lied and lied and lied. Right? [applause] What we needed was the response of a Christian nation, but we didn't have a Christian nation to respond. Two thousand years of church services, two thousand years of sending out missionaries, two thousand years of ordaining to preach, and we couldn't wait two weeks. See, we found no weapons of mass destruction, but that didn't stop us. We had no reason to go to war, but that didn't stop us. We said we were a Christian nation. In fact, the president said that he was called by God. He's had a chance to prove it, but we're not a Christian nation. You see, what we have to understand is [that] we failed God, and things are going to get worse until we, in fact say, "Lord, we are guilty, help us to remake this world." [applause]

When we look at the Bible, we look at the Old and New Testaments. [It] becomes clear that it's all about a clash between the prophetic voices and the kings. It's a clash between governments and religious institutions. It's a clash between evil disguised as good and good that desires to do good, right? We have to ask ourselves when we come to it, "Is that who was really acting for Jesus?" So, I say that to us: Who was really acting for Jesus before, during, and afterward? Who's really acting for Jesus? Because, you see, the Christian church has been silent. And if you're silent, you're part of it. We've been passive. We are—what are we? Did we turn the other cheek? Have we reached out in hope? Have we reached out to help? In fact, the Christian church has acted like it doesn't exist.

There is a need for a Christian nation. We have failed to do it in two thousand years, and the silence of the church, this going along, helped make things worse. Not obeying God always makes things worse. And it doesn't matter if you're an individual in a family or the biggest nation in the world. It doesn't matter if you have more money or more guns than anybody else, the pit is so deep that it'll swallow both you and your money. [applause]

Let us look at what we're really deciding as we come to church and communion on Sunday morning. Are we Christian enough to save Christianity? It's been placed in our lap. Our role is to build Christianity, to develop it, to do outreach, and bring more people to it. That's what saves a religion. Are we Christian enough to save Christianity? Are we believable enough to make Christ believable to the rest of the world? Can anybody really believe? Let's get a little deeper. Is the American Christian church an extension of God or [of] government? Ground zero is where we have to look to see who we really are, so that we can go beyond the pretenses of Sunday morning church and prayers and all the rest of it and ask ourselves, Are we worthy of that? Are we really about the business of praising God—or obeying the government? And see, if we obey the government [and] not the God of the New Testament, we have to ask ourselves, Are we disciples of Christ or disciples of the culture?

Ground zero—the basic most important things have come up. We've been at it for two years now. They said we shouldn't respond quickly—we haven't been responding quickly, we've been waiting. But the answers aren't there. We have to ask ourselves, Are we really a New Testament church or are we an Old Testament church? Now, I say that because there are those who believe there's really no difference, and you can pick out Scripture anywhere you want to and everything's going to be all right. But isn't it interesting that every time they want to go to war, they don't quote Jesus, they quote the Old Testament? Are we a New Testament church with Jesus in the center, or are we an Old Testament church that believes in a Jehovah of war? Or do we believe in a Christ that gets rid of violence, and refuses to let us go and kill for the sake of a government?

Ground zero—where we go from here is going to decide if we're worthy of having a chance to become a Christian nation because this is the need of the world. You see, the Old Testament idea of an eye for an eye is not as good as loving one another as Jesus has loved you, because by this will men know that here are my disciples. And it isn't just members of your church, family, or country. It goes beyond [them]; it's even true of my enemies. We have to understand that we've been given the highest order of spiritual life that has ever been given to humankind in the world. When Jesus walked, two thousand years ago, he lifted us to a whole other level of understanding our humanity. He was creating a new world in which to live.

Now, two thousand years later, we haven't one nation in the world that we can call a Christian nation. Two thousand years later, we have not done the work or [considered] it worth doing. You see, why is it when the New Testament talks about war, it's one thing? When the Old Testament talks about war, it's another thing, and yet we think that the two are the same. We really have to ask ourselves, Is there a New Testament? Because that's what Jesus was talking about—that we love one another, that's the New Testament. Do we believe in God or do we fear the government? Is our fear of government greater than our love of God? We ask this of ourselves a thousand times, but we don't talk about it. When our sons are ready to go to war, we ask ourselves, Should we in fact allow him to go die for these people that don't even care about us or him? [applause]

How many Christians do you have to have to be a Christian nation? You see, we talk about war, we talk about peace, but we're afraid to define it. This is one of the reasons I loved Martin King, because he defined peace. We walk around thinking [that] as long as nobody is shooting anybody, it must be peace. But Martin said that peace is the presence of love and truth and justice, and if you don't have them, you don't have peace. You're just playing life. Until you have love, you don't have life. Until you have justice, you're mad at yourself because you allow yourself to be misused. In fact, one of the popes in my own lifetime said that there is no truth until we get rid of racism.[3] But he could have said that there is no truth until we get rid of war. There is no truth until we stop sinning. There is no truth until we stop the systems that cause us to come down to a lower level. [applause]

When I think about this fear thing, over and against the love of God, what comes to my mind, and I can almost hear the rooster, is poor Peter. He thought that God was dead, but didn't he see him hanging on a cross? He couldn't interpret it correctly; he didn't understand, and he lived with him. So often I think, "Isn't that the case with so many of us?" We've lived with Him all of our lives, and then here comes the time, and we say, "We deny him time after time." And the rooster crows. If we are really Christians, we don't have to have fear because the question comes, Whose disciples, are we? Isn't it interesting how we handle things in terms of old and new? We have the Ten Commandments in the courtroom, yet the Ten Commandments say nothing about love, and that's the central concept of Christianity. And there's [no one] but Christians saying you have to have the Ten Commandments [in court]. How mixed up are we? When we say come to Jesus, when we say love your enemies, when we say turn the other cheek, they say: Does your Christian nation believe it? Do they do it? Because if we don't do it, they don't believe it. And you might think you're fooling God, but you're not fooling us. So you see, we have to ask the other question that's ground zero: Are we Christian enough to save democracy? All the questions, you can't dodge them anymore. It's ground zero. Do we really believe in democracy?

What I see is that we've converted it into: "I got mine, you get yours." We say democracy is the proper government for a Christian nation, but are we Christian enough to perfect democracy or do we really go along and desire everything, just like the guys at the top? Just snatch, and get, and take. Set it up so you win, and they lose, and you laugh and talk about the ones that have the most toys.

Martin says that there's something wrong with the nation that creates homelessness and poverty. We allow people to be hungry even though we are the richest nation in the world. Yet, we go to church on Sunday talking about, "Aren't we good?" We spend more money for armament than all the other armies in the world put together. Martin said any nation that spends its resources on war and allows people to go hungry is already on [the] way to spiritual death. See, there's something about it that we have to see. We tell the world that it's a matter of individualism, and yet they know that when we talk about free markets, it's setting them up to be robbed. We talk about free markets, and they don't have to pass any laws that will control us coming in. And we come in with bags of money that nobody can defeat. What we're really saying is that we're not Christian. We believe in an eye for an eye. What we're saying is that we believe that violence will determine it. What we really believe is this: He who kills the most is in fact the best. That's what we're saying.

We're also saying, "He who robs the most people is good." That's what open markets mean. The world knows that. But they won't tell us that, and we act like open markets is a good thing. Try to start a business with somebody that's got ten billion dollars, and you've got five thousand dollars. If he doesn't want you to exist, you won't exist. Let's see how evil it gets when you use agricultural science. We now have the means to grow more than the regular seed, but it can't reproduce itself. So, if you use it, you have to go back to the one with the patent. And you see, we have the patent, and we have guns to protect it, and billions of dollars to put it in other people's ground, and the force to pass a law that says if the wind takes our seed over on your ground, then I have the right to buy your whole field. Do you think that they believe that we are Christian? Would anybody? Do we believe that's a Christian act? And when we think about it, we have to ask ourselves, "Is this the world we live in?"

What does this do for evangelism? Isn't it interesting that we've sent missionaries all over the world but haven't had much success? They know what we are like. They know that we're not Christian. They know that we've not lived up to Christian ideals. They know that the means by which our nation moves has little to do with Christianity. We have to understand, as we come to communion, that it is time for forgiveness. [applause] We have to see that, somehow, we have to ask for forgiveness, to start from ground zero, and to begin to create a Christian nation. The need of the world is for Christianity. How do we do that?

Delivered: June 6, 2004
Providence Missionary Baptist Church
Atlanta, Georgia

COMMENTARY

By Gary Percesepe

On June 6, 2004, C. T. Vivian rose to preach at his home church in Atlanta, Georgia. It is certainly true that a prophet is not without honor except when he is at home, but this instance proved an exception. He was introduced by Rev. Gerald Durley, pastor of Providence Missionary Baptist Church in Atlanta, where Vivian was a beloved member. The audience that night welcomed Vivian with an open heart. And he did not disappoint, delivering a sermon that was a tutorial on the art of the prophetic interrogative in preaching. He used finely honed questions to interrogate a nation, an ideology, a system of domination, and ultimately a faith.

What the preacher places in question is the ideology of white supremacy and the fate of a nation that embraces it—at its peril—that dares to call itself Christian when it is anything but. He asks us to examine our hearts, to see if this heresy has sown its deadly seed in our soul, and whether a nation or a Christianity built on such a foundation can endure—or, indeed, deserves to endure. Ultimately, the sermon leaves white listeners pondering the profound question of this current moment in America and in Christendom: Do I want to be white or do I want to be Christian?

Vivian did not invent what I am calling the prophetic interrogative. He merely perfected it, as evidenced by the witness of his friend and co-laborer in the Southern freedom movement Martin Luther King Jr., who once called Vivian the "greatest preacher to ever live." It is instructive to remember that King issued this glowing estimation after hearing Vivian preach what is unquestionably his greatest sermon—his go-to sermon, the one he reached for when the moment called for clarity of action and strengthening of resolve, the sermon he preached so often and in so many keys of life that it was the music in his bones, a sermon rooted in the history of the oppression and enslavement of the Hebrew people in Egypt, and skillfully translated into the experience of nearly twelve million Black people in America, a sermon built on a simple question: What are we going to do about Joseph?

It was said that Jesus was a God who came telling stories. To which I would add, telling stories *and asking questions*. All the great Hebrew prophets employed the interrogative, from the first book of the Hebrew Bible, where it is God who asks the woman, "What is this you have done?" (Gen. 3:13, King James Version) Who confronts Jacob after wrestling all night with the fundamental question of identity: "What is your name?" (Gen. 32:27, KJV) The same God who asks Moses, the timid liberator, "What is that in your hand?", (Ex 4:2, KJV) asks a suffering and self-pitying Job, "Where were you when I laid out the earth's foundations?", (Job 38:4, KJV) and issued the question that creates a sense of vocation in every person who needs to know the meaning of the universe and their place in it: "Whom shall I send? And who shall and who will go for us?" (Isaiah 6:8, KJV) Jonah, the fleeing prophet, was pointedly asked, "Do you have reason to be angry?" (Jonah 4:4, KJV) Whereas Ezekiel was asked of the dry bones that signified the end of a movement and of a people, "Son of man, can these bones live?" (Ez 37:3, KJV) Jesus himself, standing in the long line of Hebrew prophets before him, asked difficult questions of his disciples, or seekers, and a watching world:

> Who do you say that I am?
> What do you want me to do for you?
> What good is it for you to gain the whole world but lose your soul? Why are you troubled and why do doubts arise in your hearts?
> Why do you call me Lord and do not do what I say? Those that were healed? Where are they?
> Are you betraying the Son of Man with a kiss?
> Which of you by worrying can add a single hour onto your life?

The one whom Jesus called the greatest of the Hebrew prophets, John the Baptist, had asked the crowds, "Who warned you to flee from the wrath to come?", (Matt 3:7, KJV) even as Jesus interrogated those who blindly followed John a withering question about their motivation: "What went ye out into the wilderness to hear?" (Matt 11:7, KJV)

Vivian stands in this long lineage of prophets who ask uncomfortable questions in "America: A Christian Nation." Consider some of the questions he posed to his audience and, by extension, to America, that night in 2004 at the Providence Missionary Baptist Church in Atlanta:

"Are we worthy of our faith?"[4]
"Can we save ourselves?"[5]
"Who are we really?"[6]
"Did we turn the other cheek?"[7]
"Have we reached out in hope?"[8]

And then the preacher unleashes a veritable cascade of questions designed to provoke, reorient, and summon his listeners to action:

> "We have to ask ourselves: Are we a New Testament Church or an Old Testament church? . . . Are we a . . . church with Jesus in the center . . . or are we [a] church that believes in a Jehovah of war? . . . Do we believe in God, or do we fear the government? Is our fear of government greater than our love of God?"[9]

And then the stinging question, draped in irony: "How many Christians do you have to have to be a Christian nation?"[10]

And now the solemn set of proclamations, as the great preacher nears his peroration:

> "There is no truth until we get rid of war. . . . No truth until we stop the systems that cause us to come down to a lower level. . . . Whose disciples are we? . . . Are we Christian enough to save democracy?"[11]

And as if to demonstrate the theme of this essay, Vivian closes his sermon with a question: "How do we do that?"[12]

"America: A Christian Nation" is a sermon built on a lifetime of asking prophetic questions, for Vivian, like King, came from the people. The questions he posed were not questions that he framed out of thin air; they were burning questions that came from the common folk, the folk who marched and were beaten and hosed and bludgeoned, the folk who fueled and fired the questions, the folk who, in that great sacrificial call and response, gave their answers by placing their own bodies in peril in a demonstration of the power of nonviolent resistance to evil and oppression.

Perhaps the greatest questions a watching world ever heard asked came that day in 1965, on the courthouse steps of Selma, Alabama, when Vivian stood in front of Sheriff Jim Clark and demanded that the people be allowed to exercise their franchise, to register to vote. Turning to his followers, he asked them, "Is this man Sheriff Clark stopping you? Is Sheriff Clark stopping you from registering to vote?"[13]

The people, as one, roared back their answer, "Yes!"

And when Clark (who, in a final irony of history, was later convicted of mail fraud, embezzlement, and drug smuggling) punched Vivian and knocked him down, the preacher sprang back to his feet and continued his courageous interrogation of the rogue white sheriff, symbol of white lawlessness, admonishing the bullying Clark that he was afraid of democracy, whereas Vivian was willing to die for democracy. It was a moment of pure moral courage, built on a commitment to the power of prophetic imagination and inspired by the prophetic interrogative. First came the meeting, with the posing of the questions of the day, and then came the movement.

Vivian practiced fearless speech and dangerous preaching. His inspiration came from Jesus, the radical Christ, and the Hebrew prophets who spoke truth to power in the form of the prophetic interrogative. In the years since Vivian died, democracy has not flourished and is in greater decline, as authoritarianism has risen. The right to vote that Vivian and so many others fought for is under siege in America today. Vivian's book *Black Power and the American Myth*, published more than fifty years ago, is as true today as it was when it was first penned. And his sermons hold the power to inspire a nation again, for those who have ears to hear. As he did on that day in 2004 when he first preached this message, the preacher is still asking us all today: *How do we do that?* Rereading this sermon today is bittersweet for me, for I was once in that church, sitting next to Vivian, both of us in the front row, listening to the voice of Durley, the preacher who would one day preside at Vivian's funeral.

15

Using What You Have

I Samuel 17

IF ANYBODY WANTS to know who we are, you don't say it with words; you say it with music. If you really want to know how we made it, well, we never have to give direct answers because all we have to do is sing the song. Direct answers don't quite get it; direct answers just deal with the mind. If you want to understand us, you have to deal with the soul. This sister represents so much of us; she got up and did that thing. [laughter, applause] That's who we are, all right? As she was singing, she shook her head, and everyone was moved. That's who we are. The way she sings; that's who we are. That's made us able to stand, regardless of what else was happening. We know that there's more to it than meets the surface.

I just want to thank you. I want to thank you, Reverend [William E.] Flippin, for having a church like this one. Churches like this don't come by accident. You don't have a place to worship just simply because you have a building. If you've got the right place and if you've got the right worship, you'll have the building, and you'll get an extra building. I saw it over there as I came in. I saw the new building and said, "Something is happening over here that's more than the norm."

As a churchman, I keep reading articles about the demise of the Christian church, but at the time that I read them [I thought] they're talking about white folk and not talking about us. The purpose of the preacher is to take what is ancient and interpret it for what is modern, to take what is old and make it contemporary, and to find the wisdom of yesterday and make it the wisdom of today. We're not really concerned about what happened to Moses and his wilderness if we can't make it apply to our own wilderness. It's nice as a Bible story, but it has to be more than that. I have a friend of mine who told me, "Reverend, you're so intense. You are always talking about what has to happen right now. Why don't you relax? As a preacher, you ought to do more thinking about the hereafter, and you could relax." I told him that I think about the hereafter all the time. Every time I walk into a room, I'm always asking, "What am I here after?" [laughter]

Our subject is about claiming the prize. When we think about claiming the prize, you must look at the connection that is historically understood. We are Black, out of slavery, and those that were Jews are out of slavery. That's our connection. We understand the Old Testament because we are living what they lived. Those Scriptures then apply to us, and those stories have meaning. This is why we understand the lion's den, and this is why we understand all the stories. It's because we not only have been there, we are there. This is what I chose to talk about today. The purpose, I suppose, is to claim the prize. I want to [address] the subject of "Using What You Have."

You see, when we put together that great thing between Jewish history and Black American history, then we can look at the great stories. I asked the Reverend [Flippin] to read, and he was kind enough to read the story of David. The important thing for the story of David and the Jewish people, in all decades and all ages, has not simply been what he did, per se. It wasn't that David killed this giant; that's really not it. The essence of the story is that he used what he had, against all odds, and it seemed impossible. For it seemed as though everything was going to go down in defeat. For was not there a giant, for was not there a sword too big for men to lift? Wasn't there a man, with troops behind him, who had great armor? Then David comes up, without armor, small in size, but goes away with a victory. He simply used what he had. He had a few polished stones and a skill that he had developed.

Sometimes, we think it just happens by accident. We just run out there, and God's supposed to drop it on you. You see, the truth is, you develop the skills as you move, and God allows you to use the skills for the victory. You take the raw materials that you have, just a few stones that had been developed by nature. David used them with the skills he had, and the giants didn't have a chance. You use what you have. When we look at our problem today, we are faced with giants greater than the giants David faced. We're faced with the real giants of modern-day life. We're faced with dope that is destroying us. We're faced with the fact that we do not have the economics we need in a capitalistic society. You know, it's interesting. In school, we don't even have a course on capitalism. That's what it is. They have no teaching on how to get capital, and if you don't have capital in the capitalistic society, you're out of luck.

The issue is that a good deal of our poverty leads to a good deal of our crime, and leads to a good deal of the destruction that causes all of us here to have relatives to somehow or other—if not ourselves—to have suffered because of it. God never did sanction poverty. Let's get that out of our minds right now. God never did sanction poverty. In fact, if you love somebody, you don't want them to be poor. You try to help them out of it. You might not be able to help them all the way because you're not able to or they won't listen. How many of us know what that's like because we didn't listen? When we look at it then, we have to begin to understand what it means to get out of it all. We not only have to think about it as individuals, we have to think about it as a people.

For you see, we rise and fall together as a people. If I were using a New Testament Scripture to go with the Old Testament one, I would use a simple line, and that simple line would be the one Jesus had. He went, and what he was looking at from that mountaintop was his people suffering over Jerusalem. You're suffering under the oppression of the Romans, and you are being ripped off—if I can use the term—by those tax collectors. Oh, I don't want to say you're being ripped off. Of course, I wouldn't say that. But what he's saying is your energies are being used for somebody else. What he's saying is that everything you seem to get and desire and want goes into the coffers of other people and does not come to you. Oh, Jerusalem, you are suffering, and we, too, suffer. You see, it's easy to talk about what we ought to do. It seems, however, how to get it done becomes the important thing, and this is what we've come to talk about. It's interesting that 95 percent of our preaching—of course, not this preacher's preaching—is talking about how bad things are, and 5 percent [is] talking about how to get rid of [the badness], while 3 percent of that is simplistic. What we really need is some hard answers to some difficult problems.

Our use of what was left over, and our use of simply what we had in spite of the difficulties around us is what has saved us. We had what was left over after everything else had been taken by somebody else, and we added soul to it and made it the best stuff that anybody had, ever. [applause] We took what was left over—the little that we had. My grandmother—I lived in a five-generation family, so I talked with my great-grandfather for years, as well as my grandmother, and mother, and all the rest. I remember they told me how they used to take the juice off of the cabbage and the meat in somebody else's kitchen because they told them to pour it off. They poured it off and brought it home, and now, the scientists tell us the juice has got "more good" in it than the meat. [laughter, applause] It's a matter of taking what you got and using it. It's a matter of taking what God has given you, even though other people think there's nothing to it. See, when David came out, the giant said, "You insult me by coming with a staff. Who do you think I am?" David showed him who he was, because he knew who his God was.

We're in the middle of the Olympics. Who was on the field yesterday in track? We were. We took it all from all over the world. First, second, third, and, if you look, we took fourth and fifth.[1] There just weren't enough prizes for that. [laughter] We not only did it for men's track, we did it for women's track. Now, why is that? It's because we used the only thing they left us with, and that was the ground. See, you didn't see us in swimming because we haven't got the swimming pools. [laughter, applause] But we use what we got and make the most of it, and the world knows who we are! Eighty-five thousand people came to watch us, while there were five thousand watching the swimming. [applause] I'm talking about using what you got.

See, why is it that we are so religious? Why is it that our churches are so great? Why is it that we teach them so much? Why is it that the only American music has been created by us? It was church music, and it came out of us because you can't take our souls away. [applause] We use what we got. What I want to talk about is how we've always done that, not only on a local level but on a national level. We've done it as a people because not to see it is not to understand where we are and that God has been giving us the victory all the time. We just live in a world where we turn on electric lights, and we expect them to beam all at once. But, you see, in the real world, there's no light switches you turn on. Your answers don't come all at once. God is working with millions of people toward our end. It's not so easy. We live in a world where we want it all to come to us individually. But, you see, God isn't concerned so much about individuals as He's concerned about whole people[s], and [people] that, in fact, He so created that we rise together. That's what creates a kingdom of God on Earth. I might be good, whatever that is. But I, by myself, can't take the kingdom of God. God's concern is thy kingdom come on Earth, even as it is in Heaven.

When one of our first great leaders—Frederick Douglass—looked at the scene, he had to see what he had; what he had was a people in slavery. What he had was a few people that were free in the North. What he had was a people with great faith and willing to struggle and fight for what they want. Don't you ever get the idea that we liked slavery and that we didn't mind, and we were just good ol' boys grinning. What we were always doing, and the one thing that Black people have been about, is how do you free a race? How do you save a race? How do you save a whole race of people from difficulty? How do you save them, not simply from sin, as we know it, but how do you save the nation from sin so a people can be free?

The great sin of this nation has not been on Black people. The great sin of this nation has been slavery and everything that followed it, everything that caused other people to be enslaved. Do you understand what sin really is? We begin to think about the great sins of gamblin' and cussin' and smokin' and drinkin' and dancin'. You remember when they told you that? You see, the great sin was putting you in the position [where] that was all you could do. Do you understand the difference? The difference is what it's all about. Frederick Douglass took what he had and went to Lincoln and said to him, "You can't control a nation half free and half slave. You are about to lose the Civil War, and I've got 169,000 Black troops that are willing to fight for freedom. You can win, and we can win. It'll be a win-win, and when it comes out, God will be praised, and evil will be taken from the land." Lincoln didn't want to do it. Don't you ever think that Lincoln was crazy about freeing Black folk. In fact, one of the things that he said was that he'd like to send us all back to Africa to get rid of the problem, but we weren't going anywhere. God didn't want us to go anywhere, plus the fact that America can't be saved without [us]. [applause]

Ultimately, God isn't simply about saving us; he's about saving all his people. You have to understand what God's about, not what you want at a given moment. What God is doing in history is what's important. Where do you fit, as an individual, in that? Where do we fit, as a people, in that, and how does this nation fit in a world that God's trying to save? That's what's important. So, Frederick Douglass went, and the Civil War was on. 169,000 Black troops marched across the South behind Sherman and did what White folk could not do until we got on the scene. We ran through the South like castor oil. [applause] It was the Black troops that brought the Confederate generals back into Richmond, Virginia, with their heads bowed. They don't show you those pictures, but they're there. They don't want you to get too arrogant and too proud. The truth is that it was not because of white troops, but it was because of Black troops, we came to be free.

We had God on our side, and we knew it. For the end of the great evil in American life, He took what he had, and all He had was an enslaved people. What He had were a few Northerners who were free, and they came down to fight, and a nation was free. Do you understand this? Because we gave up the slave handle and took on [the role of soldier] and picked up the guns. We picked up the guns when we weren't even allowed to be soldiers. We followed the troops. We ate what was left over. Our whole families came. And in the battles, we picked up the guns and did what they could not do. That's why they made us soldiers. They made us soldiers because we took what we had and did so well by it that they had to make us soldiers in order to win the battle. Do you understand?

When the war was over, what was left was a lot of free people, but they didn't have jobs, and no one wanted to give them jobs. They didn't have anything quite to do. Were they going to go back into a similar slavery? That's what was attempted. Then Booker T. Washington came on the scene, who, many of you need to know, was a preacher and an ordained minister. You see, we ordained ministers have many tasks to do because God's kingdom is more than [the] inside of a church. Booker T. Washington had the idea of using your hands because that's what you got, and we used our hands so well that if you wanted a wall built, you had to come to a Black America. If you want that beautiful steelwork that you still see, you have to come to Black America. If you wanted a house built, you had to come to us—we had the skills to do it. We had the know-how—we used the skills that we had and made the difference. We created the economy of this nation. We're talking about salvation and economic development. We're talking about how do you gain the wherewithal that you need [so] that you live above poverty, so that, in fact, you're not tempted? Why, in fact, pray that you not be tempted when, in fact, you live a life that says you don't want to get rid of the things that tempt you? Do you hear me? [applause]

One of the reasons that I got out of the pulpit, per se, and hit the street in Nashville was because at every Sunday morning and Wednesday prayer meeting, I was telling my folk that they're supposed to stand up and take it all and love thy neighbor. Love everybody in spite of. But I found that I wasn't doing too much loving because I was sending them out to do it, and I was living too easy. If I loved them, I was gonna get rid of what was kicking them. You understand? If you love your neighbor, then you do something to get rid of the problems that the neighbor is facing, or, in fact, you are kind of playing with God about loving your neighbor as yourself. We only get there because we obey Him, and we obey Him by loving one another. Not simply saying *I love you*, but by, in fact, helping them fulfill their goals and dreams and desires. It's that fulfilling that's important. Booker T. Washington did that.

Finally, W. E. B. Du Bois gave us an educated populace so that we had an education, we had skills, and we had the stuff to work with. God was working. All the way through slavery, remember, God put Israel, his chosen people, in a wilderness for forty years without land, without nothin'. Because He had to prepare them for the next step He was gonna put them in. It wasn't gonna happen overnight. Our freedom will not come overnight. It'll come because we use what we have in order to get where we're going. But Douglass knew instinctively what Walt Whitman said in one of his greatest poems—every struggle makes a greater struggle necessary.[2] Every struggle makes a greater struggle necessary. Now, of course, what Douglass had to deal with, coming out of slavery, you don't have to deal with, but the complexity of the problems that come after that are so complex that it makes a greater struggle necessary. It's always, *Are we ready for that greater struggle*?

Let's look at it again because, you see, Martin King knew that you use what you got. By the time you get to a Martin King and get our evolution into full freedom under God's guidance, and by the time you get to Martin, what we had was a great number of people, but the one thing we had was soul. The next thing we had was faith. The one thing we knew we had was God in our churches. The only thing we had was numbers and our churches. But what Martin also knew is that what had happened, we now had twenty million *potential* voters in a democratic society. And I say potential because, if you were in the South, you could not vote. Yeah, I know about fifteen of us could. But I'm talking about if you were in a town, and you were the college president, they might let you vote. But it didn't make any difference; it didn't change nothin'. That was set up to divide us. *I'm gonna let you vote because I know you, and you work for so-and-so. You understand. But the rest of you?* So, what Martin did was to make sure we had a voting rights bill. And how did we use it? We got it because we had enough soul not to fight back but to fight back with our spirit.

If you look at the text in David, it said they tried to put the armor on David, they tried to give him a big sword. In other words, imitate the way we do war now. And David said, "It doesn't fit me because I do war out of another understanding." [applause] You understand what I'm saying? So he threw away their armor, threw away their sword; they wanted us to pick up the gun. How many young people wanted us to pick up the gun? David said, "I don't need guns. I'm not delivered by violence. I'm delivered in another way." Do you hear me? So we used our soul, and we began to be delivered. Now we have politics that bring us to now. We have more mayors than we ever thought we would have. We control more cities than any other place. We are now ready for the next move. We have more congressmen than I thought we were gonna have, and I was in the midst of the movement. We have more power than ever I would have thought.

John Lewis is now the most powerful congressman there, and he's our congressman. Do you understand what I'm saying? God is allowing us to be used, and I want you to know something else. John Lewis and I were in seminary together, but I'm telling you he was trained as a minister. God uses His people on every level. God uses church people. God is using us, who are called by God to do His work. And every one of us is called of God to fulfill and bring His kingdom on us. Do you understand what I'm saying? As a result of that, we have to see that now we have political power, more so in this city than in any other. Strangely enough, we've had three straight [Black] mayors. No other place has had that. We not only have had three great mayors, but each one of them has added to this city more so than we think anybody else would have done, and they think it too. That's why when they had to get the Olympics, they went through Andrew Young. Billy [Payne][3] could not get what he wanted without Andy. [applause] When we look at that, what that means is that the world is being turned over by our influence. The world would not have come here had it not been for an Andy Young, and Andy wouldn't have been here had it not been for Martin King, and a Martin King wouldn't have had meaning unless millions of us moved under the influence.

Look at it again. Because you know they just got that Mercedes plant in Alabama. Now, that means that hundreds of thousands of people—Black, white, yellow, pink, and polka dot—are going to eat, are going to send their children to college, and are going to be able to have a house that they wouldn't have had before. You know how they got that plant? When they handed out the material to Mercedes-Benz, they had one of those beautiful etchings of Martin King. And it had one of those pretty little pieces of thin paper over it, and what they were saying was that we used to be what you think we are, but now we honor Martin King, who taught us so much, and aren't we glad? What I'm saying is, people are eating because of you! We don't talk about economic development for Black people alone without talking about it for the nation. We are the force to save a nation and bring them up, and you can't get where you want to be unless you help other people get where they want to be. [applause]

Now, what have we got after thirty years? What we have now is what we got; the raw materials that we can use. We now, for the first time, have over a million and a half Black people who make over fifty thousand dollars a year. You see, you don't have to have all the people. You just need enough people to get it done. If you're working together, you always have enough. Look at it again. We control 365 billion dollars a year, meaning that basically—it's really about 400 billion. I said 365 only because what I wanted you to see is that billion a day. A billion a day flows into the Black community. We have something in our hands. We have raw materials we can use. This is what we've got, this is who we've become.

The next step is no longer political. The next step is economic. Every struggle makes a greater struggle necessary. We use it. How do we turn it into the saving of a people? How do we find out how to help those that don't have? How do we make it so that all of us come up together? A few of us can't make it without all of us making it, and to the extent you allow some to. Let me put it another way for you. In World War II, the French doctors [founded] something they call *triage*. Triage is important to us now, not because of medicine but because of economics. What the movement has given us is that about one-third of us are gonna be all right, no matter what happens. About one-third of Black people have a ride to a situation where they can't hurt us too much—we gon' be here and we gon' make it—ut there's about a third of us that are going to fall off the edge if things remain as they are. Then there's about a third in between that, if we don't save [them], a good part of those [people] is going over the edge. The issue is, Can we bring them this way instead of that way? And do we have enough political clout to force America to save this third down here? America is not gonna save the third in the middle. We've got to do that.

So, our problem is how do we do that, because what really makes the difference is right there, and that's the most important thing that we've got to face. How do we do it? There are some things that we must believe. Remember, everything that David did was based on what David believed. There are some things we have to believe if we're gonna make it, and one thing we have to believe is that things can change. There are a lot of people going around in every one of those groups who don't believe that change can come. There's a lot of people that come to church every Sunday but don't have enough faith that things can change. There are a number of people who are giving up and turning to dope because they don't believe that things can change. There are a number of people that don't want to help nobody because they don't believe that things will change, and they just want to help themselves. The truth is that we've got to believe that things can change for all of us.

When I first came to this town—oh, Rev, you were talking about it today—I couldn't be picked up by a taxi at the airport. I had to have a Black cab in the city. Got to call them and had to find out who they were. Got them from a red cab and then wait for them to come get me. They say the dollar is the most important thing. Not in a racist society. The cab driver didn't want my money. He didn't want me in his cab. He didn't want to drive me to a Black neighborhood because he knew that's where I was going. We have to consider, and remember, if you've lived in this town, we have to teach our children, so that they know that what now is once was not. [applause] Change comes when you decide that it can happen. When we decided that we weren't going to put up with the old stuff anymore, the leadership was there and things changed. You understand what I'm saying? When you decide to use what you got, things can change.

Now there's another thing we've got to think about. The change you want does not come just when you want it. The change you want does not necessarily come when you want it. It is not an artificial work. The world is a real place we live in. It does not come immediately. It doesn't come because you think it. It becomes [real] because you make it happen. Your business wouldn't work just because you wanted a business. Your business is still working because you're making it work. Am I right? This church doesn't work simply because God's here. It's because you made it work. You have to make things happen, and it takes time for it to happen. You have to be allowed to be able to play, or you can't get on the Olympic team. You have to work in spite of, and in order to, overcome the obstacles that stand in your way.

Another way to think about it is: How did we change things? How did we make it happen? We made it happen because we had a means and a method and [a] man that represented us. In every one of those areas, God gave us a person so that the change could happen. Now, we have known for the last twenty-five years, at least, that the change we needed was economic. We've known that. We've known that we've come to the point that we've got to be able to have money to go with our political power. We have learned that you can have all the Black political power you want, but if you don't have the green to go with it, you don't have any power. In this town, we control it politically but we don't control it economically. And as a result, the real control is going out in Buckhead, where they're creating another town, another city, and living so the money flows out there. And we get worse and worse in the inner city, so that until we can figure out how to create the economic power, things do not change.

You see, we've got to use what we got. We got a million-and-a-half people with fifty thousand dollars. We've got over a billion dollars a day coming into the community, and we are one of the richer communities in Black America. There's more hope for it to happen here than any other place, and Sister just looked at me, frowned at me, and said, "Goodness, the rest of them must be in real trouble."

[laughter] Well, the sister wasn't too wrong. When we look at it, now we've been given a leader. That man's name is not one that you know. He is not a minister. His name is Ernie Lindo, who has come forth with economic development, which means that it isn't just good for one man becoming a millionaire. It's not enough for one millionaire. I'd rather have a million people with just a few dollars than one man who has a million because the level of life is not decided by a millionaire or two. The level of life is decided by what the average person has. And if the average doesn't have nothin', no matter if you have a million or not, you're still in America. [laughter] I didn't say that. [laughter]

We've known that we needed an economic program. When Martin came on the scene, he was the man with the means and the method that was able to deliver us politically. Now we have a man with the means and the method. Who is the person with a program that can do it? Come on the scene not to make himself a millionaire but to help us? What the program consists of is 336 people coming together, and we learn together. Oh, it's not enough to want money. You've got to know something about money. It's not enough to even know about money, you gotta know about the conditions under which you live, or you will use it foolishly anyway. And you won't make the decisions. Business is not easy! You got to pick out everything that makes the difference in order to make it work. We have too long not known what it takes, but it's not just us. Poor white people don't know what it takes, either—that's why they're poor. Had every opportunity but never learned what it takes. That's why they never had that course in capitalism; they don't want you to know, whether you're Black or white or yellow or pink. You have to find out on your own. The truth is, nobody can save us but us, and we have a means and a method for doing that now, where 336 of us get together.

We started our first restaurant in Atlanta.[4] Now we have 336 customers, and every one of us has a friend, so we opened the restaurant with over seven hundred customers. And you can't lose that way. You got enough people right in this room to do the same thing here, in this town alone. When you organize, it's not just 336 people throwing money in a basket, saying, Look what we got. Not only do you learn, but look at what it means. It means that 336 will set up twenty-one businesses. I'm talking about the practical aspects of economic development and how God really delivers people. Ask yourself: How did it happen that Jews made it? How did it happen that the Irish made it, and the Italians? When the Irish first came to this land, the Irishman wasn't worth as much as Black people are. We were slaves. Nobody was going to send a slave out to the West and get shot by an arrow. We were valuable, so who did they send? They sent the Irish. They hated the Irish so much, mostly because they were Catholic and because they were poor. They had signs in Virginia: "IRISHMEN AND DOGS KEEP OFF THE GROUNDS." How were they saved?

They were saved because the church—the Catholic Church—created a strategy under God that allowed them to work together in such a way that they were saved.

Look at the Italians. They came here and were hated. No southern European has been white in America. Understand that? That's why the Spanish aren't light. The difference is that the Spanish never got their own priests concerned about them. I'm telling you, it's all religious. But you see the Italians only had Italian priests because Italians were head of the Catholic Church in Rome. Those priests were concerned about delivering their people, so they created a strategy to allow—if you were in a Chicago—[white people] to be either Italian or Irish. You understand what I'm saying? The jobs were given to those that belonged to that church. Why do you think we have Black Catholics in Chicago? Because they like it? Because they learned [that] if they could send their kid to a Catholic school, that kid was gonna get a job.

The strategy that lifted a people came up out of their religion, and they did it through creating small businesses. Most of us want to start out with a Cadillac. As soon as we turn the key in the door, we want to go down to the Cadillac place and buy a Cadillac. Don't have enough money to eat yet, but I want a Cadillac. The point being is, get down on your knees and pray to God to deliver you! To allow you to serve somebody, become a part of your church. Every Black business that I've ever known of started in the Christian church. The Black church made the difference for all of us. When the preacher got into the pulpit and said there's a new man in town, he set up this barbecue stand, and I want you to go eat some barbecue. I know where you eat barbecue now. But, right now, I want you to go eat with him. That's how they did it in the Jewish church. As soon as a Jewish person comes to this country, if he has any skills or ability, he goes to the synagogue, and when he sets up his business, everyone in the synagogue knows that if you want something done, you go to him. Isn't it interesting that we're going to all the Asian restaurants to eat, but you don't see the Asians eating with us? [applause] They eat with Asians, and it's not just because that's the food that they like, [but] because they gotta make certain where the money goes. My daughter—who's sitting here at the end of the row, pretty thing in her red dress, just one of my seven beautiful children—she's living in Miami now, and she's just coming to visit us and take in the Olympics.[5] I haven't gotten a ticket. [laughter] When she went to Miami, she said Kmart is sending me to be a manager in Miami, what should I do? And I said, "Learn Spanish, baby." [laughter]

We make it together. And if we organize it together, we win it together. If your own business is in your community, then you control your community. If you don't own nothin', you don't control nothin'. [applause] Read the Scriptures.

The first thing that every one of them did was to claim the land. Think about it. Joshua came to take over the land because if you don't control where you live, somebody else will control it. And they don't control it for you, they control it for them. And you don't count. If you own the businesses where the money is, then you control the land and make certain you can grow and develop. The reason we're so poor is because we can't give jobs to each other. Everybody else gives jobs to their own. We don't have any jobs to give because we don't own nothin,' And if you don't own nothin', you don't control nothin'. [applause]

God's trying to deliver us. We've come a mighty long way to where there's enough of us with enough money to invest. Now we have a plan [so] that you don't have to be rich—sixty-nine dollars a month—and you can get involved in saving yourself and saving your neighbor and creating jobs for all of us. That's what makes the difference, and you know how you get big businesses? By having little businesses. Now, I heard a young man say the other day that he wants to be president of NationsBank. I said, "Brother, that's all right. I'm glad you want to be, but the only thing you're going to be president of is a Black bank." You might as well get that now, but the point being is that we now have a Black bank. If we didn't have a Black president who learned it inside NationsBank, we wouldn't have a bank out here. If all you wanted to be was president of somebody else's bank, you not only never will be, but will never serve the people that need you. What we're talking about is, Do you have a means and a method for deliverance, or is it just a rap? Anybody can rap! "We ought to save our people." Yeah, that's right. We need money—agreed. How you gonna get it? And then they start talking something else. That's right, because you have to have a means and a method. Now, when there is a means and a method, do you really move on it?

Within three years, everyone in this room could be having a second salary. That is probably more than 90 percent of us are making right now. Don't even have to give up the job you got—and also be involved in a unity that allows for everything to happen for everybody else and to claim the ground on which we move. This allows us to learn as we grow. One of the many things we have to really do is realize that millionaires come together and put a million in the pot. But you don't have to have a million in order to move. If you just put a little in from everybody, then you can move and have the things you need. What that really means for us is that there are some things that we have to remember, and some things that we have to hold very, very clear. Hundreds of Black families would be able to dream again and be able to have the jobs they need. But there are some other things we have to think about or we will be defeated in the attempt. We must learn to do business—not Black business, but business. Black men may own it, but poor business practices will run you out of business. I don't care whether you Black, white, yellow, pink, or polka dot. A poor businessman is going to be a non-businessman.

The greatest Black millionaire that we've had, he died—he owned Beatrice Foods.[6] No sooner than he owned Beatrice Foods, he started living in France. He got away from here. [laughter] They make it nice. They say he became a Francophile. That means he loved to live in France. He also died there. [laughter] I think he would've lived here longer on greens and grits, but he wrote a book,[7] and he said, "White boys shouldn't have all the fun." The real fun of this culture is being able to work with your brothers and sisters, to have the fun, to have a good family, to not have to worry to see your children being taken care of in this period, and to be able to just know that they're going to have jobs and a real future. That's the real fun in life. The real fun in life is not playing a piano. But I'll tell you what, [that] goes along with it. The real fun in life is to be able to dream and fulfill your dreams. The real fun in life is to have the wherewithal to change life around you. The real fun in life is to make it what you really want it to be and to create the kind of world around you that you really want. That's what we dream for, that's what we pray for, and we can have it by working together.

One thing that will destroy us is that we must trust each other. I remember they used to say Black people think that white people's ice is colder. Now, science says ice is ice. We gotta trust each other. We didn't trust each other. If we're willing to trust each other, we can change the world in which we live, and we can give God the victory He really deserves for bringing us a mighty long way. I don't want to just sing about God bringing us a mighty long way; I want to see it all around me. I don't want it just for me. I want it for everyone that I know, for everyone that's growing up. I want it for every child that goes to school. I want to be able to look at an audience and say that God gives you the possibilities to fulfill your dreams and your potential. [It's] said I need to relax. Well, maybe so. But you see the hereafter that I'm thinking about is right here as well as over there. And I think I'm going over there with a great more rejoicing if I can do it.

Delivered: July 28, 1996
The Greater Piney Grove Baptist Church
Atlanta, Georgia

COMMENTARY

Vince Thomas Jr.

In my personal interactions with C. T. Vivian, I came to know him as a man of action. One particular story, which I often share with anyone willing to listen, always moves me. Even in his nineties, Vivian continued to help others by opening doors and offering words of admonishment and encouragement. One evening, after finishing a delightful dinner and as we awaited our cars at the restaurant's entrance, I couldn't help but notice Vivian holding doors and warmly greeting people as they entered and exited the establishment. That was who he was—always serving and using whatever he had to assist others. The question we all must answer is, How can we use what we possess?

We can learn a model of using what we have by observing how God used what He had to shape the world we see today. From the very beginning, when God created man, He formed us from the dust of the ground. And when it was time to create woman, He took a rib from the man's side. Fast forward to the abolition of slavery, where God used enslaved and freed individuals in the North to take up arms and fight against the Confederacy.

The story of David provides another example of not conforming to ineffective methods but rather using what he had—a slingshot and smooth stones—to defeat the giant oppressing his people. Against all odds, he used what he had, even when his challenge seemed impossible. The ability to use our resources is not solely acquired through knowledge acquisition but also through putting that knowledge into action.

When churches and pastors use what they have—the Word of God and their influence over the community—they can realize political and economic power. This power can be discovered only by using what we have. A connection exists between the Black experience within the church and society. We express our passion and pain through singing, dancing, shouting, and preaching. It is a constant contradiction to live in a nation supposedly built on biblical principles while witnessing the hypocrisy of systematic disenfranchisement of minority groups. Yet our focus remains on claiming the prize. Pastors and spiritual leaders have a significant responsibility to connect their communities with the broader context they live in. Vivian believed that "the purpose of the preacher is to take what is ancient and interpret it for what is modern, to take what is old and make it contemporary, and to find the wisdom of yesterday and make it the wisdom of today."[8] If we fail to understand history, we will not pass it on to the next generation. Without passing on history, the struggles, victories, tragedies, and triumphs will remain hidden. Attaining a blueprint for success will become even more challenging.

Today, as there has been in the past, there is a deliberate effort to erase American history from educational curricula. Recent reports have exposed the source of intense attempts to ban literature that highlights the Black experience in America. Restricting literature is not a new phenomenon in the American experience. What sets post-2020 book bans apart from previous instances?

Published reports have revealed an intriguing shift: Historically, parents have been responsible for most book removal efforts. However, researchers found that between the 2021 to 2022 and 2022 to 2023 school years, more bans were initiated by legislators.[9] Many of the targeted books focus on the history of racism and human and civil rights issues. As long as income inequality, housing discrimination, underfunded educational systems in minority-dominated areas, and attacks on the right to vote persist in our democratic society, we must, against all odds, use what we have to achieve seemingly impossible goals.

Before passing judgment or showing disdain toward someone facing difficulties, let us consider that they may be playing the cards they have been dealt. They might have experienced nothing but death, degradation, and destruction throughout their lives. How can we expect the church to use what we have? How will we address the income inequality in our community? How will we use our resources to combat food insecurity and food deserts? How will we reduce recidivism rates?

Change occurs when we decide that it can happen, but it doesn't happen simply because we want it to. We must be the ones to initiate the change we desire in the world.

Vivian highlighted the fact that the Black community possessed a billion dollars a day in spending power. He believed that if we truly love our neighbors, we must take action to address the problems they face. We have the power to uplift and save our nation, but we cannot achieve our own goals without helping others reach theirs. Spending power represents the untapped potential of a community to bring about change. Just imagine the impact we could make if we all united our means, influence, and resources to work toward a common mission of uplifting the disenfranchised. What could we accomplish?

Dillon Burroughs, in his book *Activist Faith: From Him and For Him*, writes, "We cannot do everything, but we can all do something."[10] I encourage you to make the most of what you have. Your contribution will go toward a greater society and the pursuit of a more perfect union.

CONTRIBUTORS

Donald Edward Bermudez is a multifaceted artist, designer, and creative strategist whose work brings to life visual stories about the human and civil rights struggle. Bermudez has worked with Coretta Scott King, Congressman John Lewis, C. T. Vivian, Ambassador Andrew J. Young, Xernona Clayton, and others. In 2008, Lewis selected Bermudez to design the annual White House Christmas Ornament for Georgia's 5th Congressional District. Bermudez's "I Have a Dream" poster of Martin Luther King Jr. received an award of merit in the HOW International Design Awards competition. Bermudez helped develop an initial prototype for *Your Soul Is Required*. A native of New Orleans, he lives in the Atlanta area with his wife and three children.

Gary Dorrien is the Reinhold Niebuhr Professor of social ethics at Union Theological Seminary and a professor of religion at Columbia University. He was previously the Parfet Distinguished Professor at Kalamazoo College, where he also served as dean of Stetson Chapel and director of the Liberal Arts Colloquium. Dorrien is the author of 24 books and more than 300 articles. He received a bachelor of arts degree from Alma College, a master of divinity from Union Theological Seminary, a master of arts and master of theology from Princeton Theological Seminary, and a PhD from Union Graduate School. He also has received an honorary doctor of letters from MacMurray College; doctors of divinity from Trinity College, Virginia Theological Seminary, and Wake Forest University; and a doctor of humane letters from Meadville Lombard Theological School.

Gerald L. Durley is pastor emeritus of Providence Missionary Baptist Church in Atlanta, Georgia. Durley was the pastor of C. T. and Octavia Vivian. He served as a past president of the Concerned Black Clergy of Atlanta, cochair of the Regional Council of Churches of Metropolitan Atlanta, and executive director of Head Start. He also has served on the boards of the March of Dimes, Civil and Human Rights Global Advisory, Communities in Schools of Atlanta, Georgia Power Diversity Council, Georgia Interfaith Connections, Interfaith Power and Light, and the NAACP of Atlanta. He earned a bachelor of arts degree in psychology from Tennessee State University, a master of science degree in community mental health and psychology at Northern Illinois University, a master of divinity from Howard University, and a doctorate degree in urban education and psychology from the University of Massachusetts. He is the author of the autobiography *I Am Amazed: Reflections on an Awe-Inspired Life*.

Earle J. Fisher is the senior pastor of Abyssinian Baptist Church in Memphis, Tennessee, and founder of #UPTheVote901, a nonpartisan voter empowerment initiative committed to producing political power and increasing voter turnout in Memphis and Shelby County. Fisher holds a bachelor of science degree in computer science from LeMoyne-Owen College, a master of divinity degree from Memphis Theological Seminary, and a PhD in communications from the University of Memphis. Fisher is the author of *The Reverend Albert Cleage Jr. and the Black Prophetic Tradition: A Reintroduction of The Black Messiah* and two provocative essays, "Brother Malcolm, Dr. King and Black Power: A Close and Complementary Reading" (*Black Theology*, Fall 2020) and the groundbreaking "Introducing Sermonic Militancy—A Call Toward More Revolutionary Homiletics and Hermeneutics" (*Journal of Communication and Religion*, Fall 2021).

Eddie S. Glaude Jr. is the James S. McDonnell Distinguished University Professor of African American studies at Princeton University. Glaude is a passionate educator, author, political commentator, and public intellectual who examines the complex dynamics of the American experience. His books include *Democracy in Black: How Race Still Enslaves the American Soul*, *In a Shade of Blue: Pragmatism and the Politics of Black America*, and the *New York Times* bestseller *Begin Again: James Baldwin's America and Its Urgent Lessons for Our Own*. Glaude is a former president of the American Academy of Religion. Glaude is also on the Morehouse College Board of Trustees. He frequently appears as a columnist for *Time* magazine and as an *MSNBC* contributor.

Edward Austin Hall considers himself as an Alabama escapee and lifelong Southerner. Hall writes and edits poetry, fiction, journalism, and games. He is an anthologist and a bricoleur. Hall served as the book's first editor, reviewing and editing the transcriptions of C. T. Vivian's sermons from audiotapes.

Forrest E. Harris is president of American Baptist College as well as professor of the practice of ministry and director of the Kelly Miller Smith Institute on Black Church Studies at Vanderbilt University Divinity School. Harris holds a bachelor of arts degree from Knoxville College, a bachelor of theology degree from American Baptist College, and a master of divinity and doctor of ministry degrees from Vanderbilt University Divinity School. Harris has published three books: *What Does It Mean to Be Black and Christian: The Pulpit, Pew, and the Academy in Dialogue*, *Ministry for Social Crisis: Theology and Praxis in the Black Church Tradition*, and *What Does It Mean to Be Black and Christian: The Meaning of the African American Church*.

Otis Moss III built his ministry on community advancement and social justice activism. As senior pastor of Trinity United Church of Christ in Chicago, Illinois, Moss practices a Black theology that unapologetically calls attention to the problems of mass incarceration, environmental justice, and economic inequality. Moss is committed to preaching a prophetic message of love and justice, which he believes are inseparable companions that form the foundation of the Gospel of Jesus Christ. He earned a bachelor of arts degree in religion and philosophy from Morehouse College, master of divinity degree from Yale Divinity School, and a doctor of ministry degree from Chicago Theological Seminary.

Kevin R. Murriel is the senior pastor of Cascade United Methodist Church in Atlanta, Georgia. He received a bachelor's degree in business administration from Jackson State University, a master of divinity from Emory University's Chandler School of Theology, and doctor of ministry from Duke University. Murriel's research focuses on translating the methods of the civil rights movement into a modern strategy for social justice. Murriel is as assistant professor in the Practice of Practical Theology and director of the Black Methodist Seminarians Program at Emory University's Candler School of Theology. Murriel is the author of *Breaking the Color Barrier: A Vision for Church Growth Through Racial Reconciliation*.

Gary Percesepe is the senior pastor of the Congregational Church in the Highlands in White Plains, New York, and teaches in the philosophy department of Fordham University. Percesepe was coordinating director of the Baptist Peace Fellowship of North America, where he worked with C. T. Vivian on Churches Supporting Churches, a program designed to assist Black churches in New Orleans following Hurricane Katrina. Percesepe also is vice president of the Metropolitan Association of the New York Conference of the United Church of Christ. He holds a PhD from Saint Louis University, and master degrees in philosophy and theology from the University of Denver and Denver Seminary. Percesepe is the author of eleven books, including *Future(s) of Philosophy: The Marginal Thinking of Jacques Derrida*, *Introduction to Ethics: Personal and Social Responsibility in a Diverse World*, and *Moratorium: Short Story Collection*.

Michael Louis Pfleger is senior pastor of the Faith Community of Saint Sabina in Chicago, Illinois. Pfleger received his bachelor of arts in theology from Loyola University, master of divinity from the University of Saint Mary of the Lake, and an honorary doctor of divinity from North Park Theological Seminary. He has also completed post-graduate studies at Mundelein College and the Catholic Theological Union. Pfleger has been recognized for his fight against drugs, racism, and injustice and for his commitment to equality.

Susan K. Smith is the director of clergy and resource development at the Samuel DeWitt Proctor Conference and a consultant with People for the American Way's African American Ministers' Leadership Council. Smith has served as a cochair of the minority vote subcommittee of the Nonpartisan Ohio Voter Outreach Committee. She also served as a tri-chair of the Ohio Poor People's Campaign. She is a member of the board of directors for the League of Women Voters Ohio and the founder of Crazy Faith Ministries in Columbus, Ohio. She is the author of several books, including *Rest for the Justice-Seeking Soul* and *With Liberty and Justice for Some: The Bible, the Constitution and Racism in America*. Smith is a graduate of Occidental College with a bachelor of arts in English degree and Yale Divinity School with a master of divinity degree. She earned a doctorate of ministry degree from United Theological Seminary.

John K. Stoner has been a pastor, teacher, writer, and administrator with the Mennonite Central Committee's Peace Section. He coauthored *If Not Empire, What?: A Survey of the Bible*. He helped establish Every Church a Peace Church, an organization that advocates that churches hold the key to turning the world toward peace through the teachings of Jesus Christ. A war tax resister, Stoner practices symbolic war tax refusal as part of his affiliation with the organization 1040 For Peace. Stoner earned Bible and theology degrees at Messiah College and the Associated Mennonite Biblical Seminary. Married with children and great-grandchildren, Stoner believes that empires tremble in the face of nonviolent power and ultimately will fail to overcome life by their way of death.

Vince Thomas Jr. is the founder and lead pastor of the Outlet Community Church in Atlanta, Georgia. He is an advisor to high-profile leaders and organizations locally, nationally, and globally. Thomas travels extensively, speaking and conducting leadership training for schools, churches, nonprofit organizations, for-profit entities, and conferences. He earned a bachelor of arts in religious studies and master of arts in leadership studies from Beulah Heights University. Thomas is an adjunct instructor of urban leadership at Oglethorpe University.

Emilie M. Townes is the Martin Luther King Jr. Professor of religion and Black studies at the School of Theology of Boston University. She is dean emerita, the former E. Rhodes and Leona B. Carpenter chair, and the former University Distinguished Professor of womanist ethics and society at Vanderbilt University Divinity School.

Townes was the first African American to serve as dean of the Vanderbilt's Divinity School. She also is the former Andrew W. Mellon Professor of African American religion and theology at Yale University's Divinity School and was the first African American woman elected to the presidential line of the American Academy of Religion. An American Baptist clergywoman, Townes holds a doctor of ministry degree from the University of Chicago Divinity School and a PhD in religion in society and personality from Northwestern University.

Jonathan Lee Walton is president of Princeton Theological Seminary. He is a social ethicist, religious educator, and influential scholar known for engaging American evangelical traditions. He is the author of *Watch This!: The Ethics and Aesthetics of Black Televangelism* and *A Lens of Love: Reading the Bible in Its World for Our World*. Walton also served as the Plummer Professor of Christian morals and Pusey Minister in the Memorial Church of Harvard University. Additionally, he is a past dean of the School of Divinity and past presidential chair in religion and society at Wake Forest University. Walton earned a PhD and master of divinity from Princeton Theological Seminary and a bachelor of arts from Morehouse College. He also received an honorary doctor of divinity degree from Wake Forest University.

René Whitaker is pastor at First Presbyterian Church in Macomb, Illinois. She has also worked with congregations in transition in Pennsylvania, Michigan, Ohio, Virginia, Kentucky, and Texas. She earned a master of divinity degree from Austin Presbyterian Theological Seminary and a doctor of ministry degree focusing on science and theology from Pittsburgh Theological Seminary. She has written five books of poetry and continues to find beauty, hope, and possibilities for change in our extraordinary world.

Robert Christopher Wright is bishop of the Episcopal Diocese of Atlanta. He is the first African American to become diocese's bishop. He is the past rector of St. Paul's Episcopal Church in Atlanta, Georgia. Wright graduated from Howard

University with bachelor of arts degree in history and political science. He holds a master of divinity degree from the Virginia Theological Seminary and certificates from Ridley Hall Cambridge University, Oxford University, and the Harvard Kennedy School of Public Policy. Wright is an adjunct teacher at the Candler School of Theology and the chair of the board of the General Theological Seminary. He serves on the boards of Habitat for Humanity International and the Rabun Gap-Nacoochee School.

Andrew J. Young is a politician, former diplomat, and activist. Beginning his career as a pastor, Young was an early leader in the civil rights movement, serving as executive director of the Southern Christian Leadership Conference and a close confidant to Martin Luther King Jr. Young served as a US congressman from Georgia, US ambassador to the United Nations, and mayor of Atlanta. Young has founded or served in many organizations, working on issues of public policy and political lobbying. He earned a bachelor of science degree in biology from Howard University and bachelor of divinity degree from Hartford Theological Seminary. He has received honorary degrees from more than 60 institutions, including Morehouse College, Emory University, Swarthmore College, Duke University, Clark Atlanta University, and the University of Georgia.

NOTES

PREFACE

1. C. T. Vivian, "God Is with You," in *Your Soul Is Required*, ed. Jo Anna Walker, Mark E. Vivian, Al Vivian, Anita Charisse Thornton, Kira E. Vivian, and Denise Vivian Morse (Fortress, 2025), 25.
2. Vivian, "God Is with You," 25.
3. C. T. Vivian, "America: A Christian Nation," in *Your Soul Is Required*, ed. Jo Anna Walker, Mark E. Vivian, Al Vivian, Anita Charisse Thornton, Kira E. Vivian, and Denise Vivian Morse (Fortress, 2025), 173.
4. Vivian, "America: A Christian Nation," 168–169.

INTRODUCTION

1. *Eyes on the Prize: America's Civil Rights Movement,* episode 6, "Bridge to Freedom (1965)," directed by Henry Hampton, aired March 3, 1987, on PBS.
2. *Eyes on the Prize,* episode 6, "Bridge to Freedom (1965)," directed by Henry Hampton, aired March 3, 1987, on PBS.
3. *Eyes on the Prize*, episode 4, "No Easy Walk (1961–1963)," directed by Henry Hampton, aired February 10, 1987, on PBS.
4. C. T. Vivian, "Law of the Spiritual Life," in *Your Soul Is Required*, eds. Jo Anna Walker, Mark E. Vivian, Al Vivian, Anita Charisse Thornton, Kira E. Vivian, and Denise Vivian Morse (Fortress Press, 2025), 152.
5. Vivian, "What Does It Mean to Be a Christian," in Walker et al., *Your Soul Is Required*, 138.
6. Vivian, "God of History: Five Stones," in *Your Soul Is Required*, in Walker et al., *Your Soul Is Required*, 98.
7. Vivian, "This God of History and Racism," in *Your Soul Is Required*, in Walker et al., *Your Soul Is Required*, 37.
8. Gary Percesepe, "This God of History and Racism," in *Your Soul Is Required*, in Walker et al., *Your Soul Is Required*, 174.
9. Percesepe, "This God of History and Racism," 174.
10. Vivian, "This God of History and Racism," 37.
11. Vivian, "America: A Christian Nation," in Walker et al., *Your Soul Is Required*, 169.

12. Vivian, "Peter: The Profound Nigger," 88.
13. Vivian, "Your Soul Is Required," in Walker et al., *Your Soul Is Required*, 51.
14. James Baldwin, *The Price of the Ticket: Collected Nonfiction, 1948–1985* (New York: St. Martin's Press, 1985).
15. Vivian, "America: A Christian Nation," 168.

CHAPTER 1: IT DOES NOT YET APPEAR

1. Nell Irvin Painter, *Sojourner Truth: A Life, A Symbol* (New York: W. W. Norton, 1996), 51.
2. Rev. Henry Highland Garnett.
3. C. T. Vivian, "It Does Not Yet Appear," in *Your Soul Is Required*, eds. Jo Anna Walker, Mark E. Vivian, Al Vivian, Anita Charisse Thornton, Kira E. Vivian, and Denise Vivian Morse (Fortress Press, 2025), 10.
4. Vivian, "It Does Not Yet Appear," 10.
5. Vivian, "It Does Not Yet Appear," 10.
6. Vivian, "It Does Not Yet Appear," 10.
7. Vivian, "It Does Not Yet Appear," 10.
8. Vivian, "It Does Not Yet Appear," 10.
9. Vivian, "It Does Not Yet Appear," 16.
10. Vivian, "It Does Not Yet Appear," 17.

CHAPTER 2: GOD IS WITH YOU

1. Likely referring to one or more pieces of civils rights legislation.
2. Likely referring to one or more of the Black intellectuals who lived in Harlem, New York, during this period.
3. The Weathermen, which later changed its name to Weather Underground, was a group of white militants in the 1960s and early 1970s that launched violent campaigns to protest the Vietnam War.
4. Condoleezza Rice's father, John Wesley Rice, was a Presbyterian minister.
5. Sean McBride, one of the founders of Amnesty International. He was awarded the Nobel Peace Prize in 1974.
6. The anti-apartheid movement in the US is often credited for helping end apartheid in South Africa.
7. The 42 Laws of Maat, often referred to as the "negative confessions," found in *The Egyptian Book of the Dead*.
8. C. T. Vivian, "God Is with You," in *Your Soul Is Required*, eds. Jo Anna Walker, Mark E. Vivian, Al Vivian, Anita Charisse Thornton, Kira E. Vivian, and Denise Vivian Morse (Fortress Press, 2025), 21.
9. Vivian, "God Is with You," 22.

10. Vivian, "God Is with You," 24.
11. Vivian, "God Is with You," 24.

CHAPTER 3: THIS GOD OF HISTORY AND RACISM

1. Paraphrase of Philippians 2:5.
2. C. T. Vivian, "This God of History and Racism," in *Your Soul Is Required*, eds. Jo Anna Walker, Mark E. Vivian, Al Vivian, Anita Charisse Thornton, Kira E. Vivian, and Denise Vivian Morse (Fortress Press, 2025), 35.
3. Vivian, "This God of History and Racism," 36.

CHAPTER 4: YOUR SOUL IS REQUIRED

1. St. John of the Cross, *The Dark Night of the Soul*, translated by David Lewis (Thomas Baker, 1908).

CHAPTER 5: THEY DON'T KNOW HOW TO DO RIGHT

1. Benjamin Rush, a signer of the US Declaration of Independence, wrote a 1793 essay in *Banneker's Almanac* supporting the creation of US Department of Peace. *Banneker's Almanac* was published by Benjamin Banneker, an African American mathematician and astronomer.

CHAPTER 6: THE EVIL OF RACISM

1. It's unclear to whom C. T. Vivian is referring.
2. Pope John Paul II.
3. C. T. Vivian, "The Evil of Racism," in *Your Soul Is Required*, eds. Jo Anna Walker, Mark E. Vivian, Al Vivian, Anita Charisse Thornton, Kira E. Vivian, and Denise Vivian Morse (Fortress Press, 2025), 73.
4. Albert B. Cleage Jr., *Black Christian Nationalism: New Directions for the Black Church* (William Morrow, 1972).
5. Wilderson, Frank B, *Afropessimism* (Liveright Publishing Corporation, 2020).

CHAPTER 7: PETER: THE PROFOUND NIGGER

1. James Baldwin, "Debate with William F. Buckley," in *The Fire Is Upon Us: James Baldwin, William F. Buckley Jr., and the Debate over Race in America*, ed. Nicholas Buccola (Princeton University Press, 2019), 373–400.
2. C. T. Vivian, "Peter: The Profound Nigger," in *Your Soul Is Required*, eds. Jo Anna Walker, Mark E. Vivian, Al Vivian, Anita Charisse Thornton, Kira E. Vivian, and Denise Vivian Morse (Fortress Press, 2025), 83.
3. Vivian, "Peter: The Profound Nigger," 84.

CHAPTER 8: GOD OF HISTORY: FIVE STONES

1. C. T. Vivian, "God of History: Five Stones," in *Your Soul Is Required*, eds. Jo Anna Walker, Mark E. Vivian, Al Vivian, Anita Charisse Thornton, Kira E. Vivian, and Denise Vivian Morse (Fortress Press, 2025), 93.
2. Vivian, "God of History: Five Stones," 93.
3. Walter Brueggemann, *First and Second Samuel: Interpretation: A Bible Commentary for Teaching and Preaching* (Westminster John Knox Press, 1990).
4. Vivian, "God of History: Five Stones," 100.

CHAPTER 9: MLK: THE PROPHET

1. World Conference against Racism, Racial Discrimination, Xenophobia and Related Intolerance, sponsored by the United Nations in 1997 in Durban, South Africa.
2. C. T. Vivian, "MLK: The Prophet," in *Your Soul Is Required*, eds. Jo Anna Walker, Mark E. Vivian, Al Vivian, Anita Charisse Thornton, Kira E. Vivian, and Denise Vivian Morse (Fortress Press, 2025), 105.
3. Vivian, "MLK: The Prophet," 106.
4. Vivian, "MLK: The Prophet," 110.
5. Vivian, "MLK: The Prophet," 110.
6. C. T. Vivian, *Black Power and the American Myth* (Fortress Press, 1970 and 2020), 6.

CHAPTER 10: AMERICA'S JOSEPH

1. Michael Harrington, *The Other America: Poverty in the United States* (New York: Simon & Schuster Inc, 1962).
2. The Kenwood Oakland Community Organization was founded in the Kenwood and Oakland communities of Chicago, Illinois, in 1965. The organization's focus includes equity and educational opportunities.
3. Lerone Bennett Jr, *The Negro Mood and Other Essays* (New York: Ballantine, 1965). A second edition of the book later was published as *The Black Mood* by Barnes & Noble in 1970.
4. On February 18, 1965, C. T. Vivian led a protest of the arrest of civil rights activist James Orange in Marion, Alabama. Alabama State Trooper James Fowler shot and killed protester Jimmie Lee Jackson.
5. Albert Murray, *The Hero and the Blues* (Vintage Books, 1973), 61.
6. An adapted phrase from Langston Hughes's poem "I, Too," published in *The Collected Works of Langston Hughes* (University of Missouri Press, 2002).
7. United States National Advisory Commission on Civil Disorders, *Report of the National Advisory Commission on Civil Disorders* (United States Kerner Commission, 1968), 1.
8. C. T. Vivian, "America's Joseph," in *Your Soul Is Required,* eds. Jo Anna Walker, Mark E. Vivian, Al Vivian, Anita Charisse Thornton, Kira E. Vivian, and Denise Vivian Morse (Fortress Press, 2025), 123.

9. Vivian, "America's Joseph," 122.
10. Vivian, "America's Joseph," 126.
11. Vivian, "America's Joseph," 125.
12. Vivian, "America's Joseph," 129.
13. Vivian, "America's Joseph," 123.
14. M. Shawn Copeland, "Wading Through Many Sorrows: Toward a Theology of Suffering in a Womanist Perspective," in *A Troubling in My Soul: Womanist Perspectives on Evil and Suffering*, ed. Emilie M. Townes (Orbis Books, 1993), 29–42.
15. Murray, *The Hero and the Blues*, 51.

CHAPTER 11: WHAT DOES IT MEAN TO BE A CHRISTIAN?

1. Ephesians 6:12, Contemporary English Version.
2. In 2005, televangelist Pat Robertson suggested that the US government should assassinate Venezuelan president Hugo Chávez, who became highly critical of the George W. Bush administration.
3. 2005 earthquake and tsunami in South Asia.
4. The Iraq War was led by the United States from 2003 to 2011.
5. C. T. Vivian, "What Does It Mean to Be a Christian?" in *Your Soul Is Required,* eds. Jo Anna Walker, Mark E. Vivian, Al Vivian, Anita Charisse Thornton, Kira E. Vivian, and Denise Vivian Morse (Fortress Press, 2025), 135.
6. Vivian, "What Does It Mean to Be a Christian?" 138.
7. Vivian, "What Does It Mean to Be a Christian?" 139.

CHAPTER 12: LAW OF THE SPIRITUAL LIFE

1. Habakkuk 2:4, King James Version.
2. Vivian, "Law of the Spiritual Life," 147.
3. Vivian, "Law of the Spiritual Life," 148.
4. Vivian, "Law of the Spiritual Life," 148.
5. Vivian, "Law of the Spiritual Life," 148.
6. Vivian, "Law of the Spiritual Life," 151.
7. Vivian, "Law of the Spiritual Life," 148.
8. Vivian, "Law of the Spiritual Life," 148.
9. Vivian, "Law of the Spiritual Life," 149.
10. Vivian, "Law of the Spiritual Life," 149.
11. Vivian, "Law of the Spiritual Life," 150.
12. Vivian, "Law of the Spiritual Life," 150.
13. Vivian, "Law of the Spiritual Life," 149.
14. Vivian, "Law of the Spiritual Life," 150.
15. Vivian, "Law of the Spiritual Life," 152.

CHAPTER 13: CREATING THE PROMISED LAND

1. Joshua 1:1–9.
2. This refers to the practice and impact of white flight among churches.
3. C. T. Vivian, "Creating the Promisd Land," in *Your Soul Is Required*, eds. Jo Anna Walker, Mark E. Vivian, Al Vivian, Anita Charisse Thornton, Kira E. Vivian, and Denise Vivian Morse (Fortress Press, 2025), 157–158.
4. Vivian, "Creating the Promisd Land," 158.
5. Vivian, "Creating the Promisd Land," 159.

CHAPTER 14: AMERICA: A CHRISTIAN NATION

1. UN Secretary General Kofi Annan called for the Millennium World Peace Summit of Religious and Spiritual Leaders, which was held August 28–31, 2000 at the UN headquarters in New York.
2. US Chairman of the Joint Chiefs of Staff Colin Powell consulting President George W. Bush about a possible invasion of Iraq in 2004.
3. Pope John Paul II.
4. C. T. Vivian, "America: A Christian Nation," in *Your Soul Is Required*, eds. Jo Anna Walker, Mark E. Vivian, Al Vivian, Anita Charisse Thornton, Kira E. Vivian, and Denise Vivian Morse (Fortress Press, 2025), 169.
5. Vivian, "America: A Christian Nation," 169.
6. Vivian, "America: A Christian Nation," 169.
7. Vivian, "America: A Christian Nation," 171.
8. Vivian, "America: A Christian Nation," 171.
9. Vivian, "America: A Christian Nation," 172.
10. Vivian, "America: A Christian Nation," 172.
11. Vivian, "America: A Christian Nation," 173.
12. Vivian, "America: A Christian Nation," 174.
13. "C. T. Vivian Stopped on Courthouse Steps, Alabama, 1965," YouTube video, posted by Huntley Film Archives, published July 31, 2021, https://www.youtube.com/watch?v=dV20DIY3ynk.

CHAPTER 15: USING WHAT YOU HAVE

1. The 1996 Olympic Summer Games held in Atlanta, Georgia.
2. Walt Whitman, "Song of the Open Road," *Poetry Foundation*, accessed April 28, 2025, https://www.poetryfoundation.org/poems/48859/song-of-the-open-road.
3. Billy Payne was CEO and president of the Atlanta Committee for the Olympic Games.
4. Referring to a community development project that C. T. Vivian supported.
5. Anita Charisse Thornton.
6. Reginald Lewis.
7. Reginald Lewis and Blair S. Walker, *Why Should White Guys Have All the Fun: How Reginald Lewis Created a Billion-Dollar Business Empire* (John Wiley & Sons, 1995).

8. C. T. Vivian, "Using What You Have," in *Your Soul Is Required,* eds. Jo Anna Walker, Mark E. Vivian, Al Vivian, Anita Charisse Thornton, Kira E. Vivian, and Denise Vivian Morse (Fortress Press, 2025), 179.
9. PEN America, *Banned in the USA: The Mounting Pressure to Censor* (PEN America, 2023), https://pen.org/report/book-bans-pressure-to-censor/.
10. Dillon Burroughs, Daniel Darling, and Dan King, *Activist Faith: From Him and For Him* (NavPress, 2013), 15.